D1564993

UNRECOGNIZED PATRIOTS

Dedication of Monument, Chicago, December 15, 1941, to "This Great Triumvirate of Patriots" (George Washington, Robert Morris, and Haym Salomon). From This Great Triumvirate of Patriots *by Harry Barnard. Copyright 1971 by the Patriotic Foundation of Chicago. Used by permission of Follett Publishing Company.*

Unrecognized Patriots

The Jews in the

American Revolution

Samuel Rezneck

With a Foreword by Jacob R. Marcus

GREENWOOD PRESS
Westport, Connecticut ● *London, England*

Library of Congress Cataloging in Publication Data

Rezneck, Samuel.
    Unrecognized patriots.

    Bibliography: p.
    Includes index.
    1. United States—History—Revolution, 1775-1783—
Jewish participation.   I.   Title.
E269.J5R49   973.3'15'03924   74-15160
ISBN 0-8371-7803-7

Copyright © 1975 by Samuel Rezneck

Library of Congress Catalog Card Number: 74-15160
ISBN: 0-8371-7803-7

First published in 1975
Second Printing 1976

Greenwood Press, a division of Williamhouse-Regency Inc.
51 Riverside Avenue, Westport, Connecticut 06880

Manufactured in the United States of America

But here at length the Truce of God prevailed;
The oppression and the contumely ceased.
No more were they molested, nor assailed
By royal tax or malison of priest.

From an early version of the poem "The Jewish Cemetery at Newport," by Henry Wadsworth Longfellow, written after the poet's visit to the cemetery in 1852. (As quoted in an article by Longfellow's grandson, Henry Wadsworth Longfellow Dana, and published in the Dedication Memorial of the Touro Synagogue as a National Historic Site. Newport, 1948).

Contents

vii

Illustrations

ix

Foreword

In some respects the American Revolution was the most important event in world Jewish history since the third century. In the year 212 the Emperor Caracalla granted Roman citizenship —whatever it meant then—to all free inhabitants of the empire. After that day the Jewish people lived through a dozen holocausts nursed by social and legal disabilities that reduced them to the status of second-class citizens or, worse, outcasts.

Then came the American Revolution with its Great Promise in the Declaration of Independence, that inasmuch as all men are created equal they are endowed with certain inalienable rights. The Jews interpreted "life, liberty and the pursuit of happiness" to mean political, social, and economic opportunity, as well as religious equality. There is ample evidence that most Jews in the land, even the merchant elite, threw in their lot with the Whigs. Liberty and freedom are contagious. Immigrants and natives alike, they had chafed under the disabilities that persisted, for they were determined to be completely free.

They gave money, ran the British blockade, fought as regulars and militiamen, and died or bled on the battlefields to win rights and immunities for themselves and their children. It is a tribute to their ability and to their persistence that men who as Jews could not have hoped during the colonial period ever to become commissioned officers now rose to relatively high rank when the opportunity was afforded them.

The courage that prompted them to leave their homes and the cities and to go into exile inspired them also to fight doggedly to make the Great Promise come true. New York was the only state to emancipate the Jews during the war; the federal government gave them equality in 1789 under the Constitution; but it was not until 1876—just one hundred years after the new republic was born—that New Hampshire, the last of the thirteen original states, put the final seal on the Revolutionary pledge. It was only then that Jews were granted all rights in that commonwealth.

The Revolutionary Period is a period of romance, of new hope for all men in all lands. This book, on the role of the Jews in the American Revolution, attempts to depict in detail what happened in those decades when the world was young with expectation. As this bicentennial of our freedom draws nigh, we are grateful for the meticulous research and labor embodied in this work. The knowledge of what has happened will give many the courage in the future to build solidly, confidently, liberally, on a proud past.

> Dr. Jacob R. Marcus
> Distinguished Service Professor
>   of American Jewish History,
>   and Director of the
>   American Jewish Archives,
>   Hebrew Union College,
>   Cincinnati.

Preface

The author of any work in history of necessity acquires obligations to many who have preceded him and prepared the ground for him.

In the first place, and on the most basic level, are those whose actions and ideas constitute the very subject of his endeavor. To these individuals belongs the credit for what they did to merit recognition, and they deserve even more thenauthor's gratitude for such records of their activities as they have left behind. These are the ultimate and foremost source of information.

Following them are those who have, like the author, been concerned with collecting, interpreting, and presenting the events in question. The history of the Jews in America, from the colonial and Revolutionary era on, is now a well-established field, which many have cultivated with varied results. To all who have preceded me, I must acknowledge my indebtedness and extend my grateful thanks.

Finally, there are those who have most recently and directly provided me with help, advice, and encouragement in my labors to collect and utilize the vast volume of knowledge in existence on this subject. First are to be mentioned the libraries and other research facilities, together with their many, often invisible and anonymous custodians. Among them are the Library of Congress, the National Archives, the library of the Daughters of the American Revolution, but also the more specialized resources of the American Jewish Historical Society, the American Jewish Archives, the Newport Historical Society, B'nai B'rith, and the Washington Hebrew Congregation.

A number of individuals deserve special mention and recognition as contributors of counsel as well as their expertise. I extend my thanks to Robert Shosteck, curator of the B'nai B'rith Museum, whose advice and assistance have been constantly at hand. I am also indebted to Drs. Jacob R. Marcus, Malcolm H. Stern, and Stanley F. Chyet, of the American Jewish Archives. To my wife, Betty, I owe more than can be expressed for her help in every aspect, from typing to encouragement and sound counsel. The editorial staff of Greenwood Press has earned my gratitude for their expert guidance.

To all that these have supplied, I can claim only to have added my own understanding and insight, as well as the long and arduous labor required to bring it to an orderly fruition. For this, and for such errors as may have been committed, I alone assume responsibility. It has been my intent, and, hopefully, my accomplishment, to have established that the Jews of early America, however few, made a subtle and notable contribution to the American Revolution in its several aspects. In consequence, they and their descendants have earned the benefits resulting from it in terms of their recognition as an equal and honorable part of American society.

Washington, D.C.   SAMUEL REZNECK

UNRECOGNIZED PATRIOTS

1

Introduction

The Jews had become a small but integral part of the American scene well before the Revolution. They had first arrived in New York in 1654, when it was still Dutch New Amsterdam. Along with other immigrants, more Jews arrived from Europe all through the colonial period and settled in the principal towns along the Atlantic seaboard.[1] At the outbreak of the Revolution, they were to be found mainly in five communities: Newport, New York, and Philadelphia in the north and Charleston and Savannah in the south. Their number is estimated at between 1,500 and 2,500, in a total population of 2 to 2.5 million.[2].

A small number of Jews were distributed individually or in small groups in the interior of the country, particularly in central Pennsylvania in places like Lancaster or Easton; in Connecticut towns; and up the Hudson Valley above New York. They were able to maintain a Jewish way of life only when they were plentiful enough to constitute religious and social communities. In Newport by 1763, despite their small number, they had achieved the distinction of erecting a handsome synagogue, designed by Peter Harrison, America's leading architect. It was an architectural ornament of colonial America. In all the principal coastal settlements, moreover, an established cemetery gave evidence of the existence of a Jewish community, which thus made provision for its dead. Religious services were usually held in private homes or in rented quarters.

Although the Jews made up scarcely one-tenth of 1 percent of the American population, their relative concentration in a few towns probably gave them greater visibility if not importance. Their urban occupations, in trade and crafts, made their role in the colonial economy especially prominent. However different they were, religiously, socially, and culturally, the Jews were not totally isolated, as was so often the case in Europe with its homogeneous national and religious divisions. America was already in the eighteenth century a composite aggregate of peoples from many different lands. While the predominant population was of English origin and character, especially in New England and in the South, in the center of the country there were substantial German settlements, as well as Scottish, Dutch, and Irish, and even a scattering of Swedes. Nor should one omit the French population in Britain's recently acquired province of Canada, which the Americans attempted to conquer and incorporate early in the Revolution. In addition, approximately one-fifth of the colonial population was then black and predominantly slave. Although the Indians were outside of American society, they nevertheless figured prominently in colonial affairs and greatly influenced their course in war and peace.

Altogether, here was a complex, composite social pattern, into which the Jews fitted. Moreover, the Jews were themselves of diverse origin and character. The oldest element, dating back to the 1650s, were of Sephardic background, having come from Spain and Portugal by way of Holland, Brazil, and the West Indies. In the course of the eighteenth century, many more came from Ashkenazi sources in northern Europe, and even some from Poland and Eastern Europe. Despite the Sephardic tradition, the northern European Jews were probably in the majority by the time of the Revolution. Many of them were now native-born and were thus an integral part of the population. The Revolution affected the Jews' role and future in America, as will become evident in due course. It literally revolutionized and altered their special and peculiar place in a Christian society of European origin.[3]

Hitherto, in America nearly as much as in Europe, the Jews had lived within but essentially apart from the larger community of which they were a part. They did not expect, and were not permitted, to share in any significant way in the political and social concerns and controversies of the dominant society, even though they had won certain rights of denization or naturalization, chiefly for the conduct of their business. A surprising exception was, however, the active role of Jews in the contemporary growth of Masonry in America, which provided a transitional bridge and a bond between them and the general community. Superficially and at first sight, the American Revolution would appear to have been a local, internal squabble in the British Empire, on its outer edge at the westernmost frontier of the European world. It was, however, more than an ordinary political and military conflict. It was as well a complex process of radical, intellectual, and social change. It preceded by a dozen years, and pointed the way to, the French Revolution, which would stand at the very center of European life and thought. In both cases, the Jews had a particular interest in the outcome, in which they saw the prospect of emancipation. Hence they were attracted to and took an active part in the American Revolution, both on its military and economic side and in its intellectual implications. It was, moreover, a people's conflict rather than one between kings as was then usual, and there was, therefore, room for all people who desired to participate in it. Like other Americans, the Jews were caught up in the Revolution, whose full scope and context they perhaps scarcely comprehended. They responded and participated in it in many different ways, according to their situation and capacity.

The key idea of natural law and rights, as expressed by Jefferson in the Declaration of Independence, stemmed from a process of rationalism and enlightenment that embraced the whole Western world. It was the same intellectual enlightenment that transformed the thought of Moses Mendelssohn in Germany, of Voltaire in France, Hume in England, and of Jefferson and Franklin in America. Here was generated a broad concept of equal rights for all men under a law of nature, a concept that emerged from the more immediate issues of the respective rights and powers of Englishmen on both sides of the Atlantic. For the Jews the Revolution carried a special meaning. It promised to incorporate and integrate them into American society on an equal basis politically and intellectually, and thus to end the long, parochial age of their segregation in a Christian world. As Dr. Benjamin Rush, a friend of Franklin and Jefferson, put it, the Jews chose for the most part to be Whigs, even though they had no particular grievances against the British, who had treated them, on the whole, liberally and not ungenerously, both at home and in the colonies. Rush perhaps exaggerated, since the Jews, like the rest of the population, split, and some were loyal to the British cause, as will be noted later.[4]

The American Revolution was thus more complex than the many other conflicts of the age. Although as a war it was of small scale and scope by modern standards, in issues and effects it was of transcendent importance. This was especially true as applied to the Jews, whose role in it is, therefore, of particular consequence. It was the first war since antiquity anywhere in which Jews participated actively in its several aspects; it was, in fact, their war in every sense, as had not been true of any earlier conflict, and as many persons were then fully aware. The Revolution was a composite event, to be viewed on several levels. It was, in the first place, a colonial war between Britain and her American colonies, excluding Canada and the West Indies. In a larger sense, it was a civil conflict, dividing both England and the colonies. There were Whigs and Tories in both lands, embroiled in verbal polemic, and one need only mention Tom Paine, Edmund Burke, and the Earl of Chatham, to appreciate how deep was the division in England proper.

In America, too, the Tories, now known as Loyalists, including some Jews, constituted a substantial part of the population and many fought actively on the British side. The civil war was fought locally and bitterly in many parts of colonial America between neighbors, former friends, and even relatives. The American Revolution also became part of an international conflict of large proportions. Ultimately Britain confronted the hostility and military forces of France and Spain, which it had humbled in defeat only a dozen years earlier. Holland and even Russia were scarcely neutral and indeed welcomed Britain's impending reduction in power and influence. In this larger sense, the Revolution was another stage in a century of wars, which, since the seventeenth century, had embroiled the imperial powers of Europe, particularly Britain and France. A new dimension now entered this long series of conflicts, setting all the colonies of America against the empires of Europe; the dispute was to last into the nineteenth century. The ultimate outcome was the secession of the American colonies from European domination and the creation of a political world composed of two hemispheres, as expressed subsequently and eloquently in the Monroe Doctrine of 1823. The American Revolution had great and significant consequences, far transcending its scope as a war. In the first place, its successful conclusion by 1783 resulted in the creation of a new nation as well as a new government, the first of the federal type in America, if not in the world. Thus was enlarged and extended the world system of powers, no longer confined to the states of Europe. Moreover, a model form of republican government was established, which embodied the ideas and ideals of the Enlightenment. Slowly and painfully, it pointed to the gradual emergence and evolution of democratic government. This proved to be more durable than the similar efforts undertaken in Europe and elsewhere in this age of revolutions. Out of the American Revolution and its sequel came a great series of documents, among them the Declaration of Independence and subsequently the state and federal constitutions, with their accompanying Bills of Rights. In American Federalism was embodied a model form of social and political organization. It consolidated but also federated and preserved the diversity of elements deriving from different geographical and cultural sources.

All this was inherent and implicit in the American Revolution, both as ideal and as actuality. It brought into being an age of growth, both externally and internally, lasting some two centuries. Despite many successive crises and problems, including a civil war, the new American nation has endured and prospered. This may be the ultimate value and import of the bicentennial celebration of Independence in 1976. It may, one hopes, usher in a time of rethinking of and rededication to the ideals and goals of the Revolution, reborn and reshaped to the future needs and conditions of American society.

In all of this the Jews of America have had a great interest and role to play. The concept of a pluralist society, so basically American in reflecting and promoting its diversity, was particularly congenial to Jewish needs and circumstances. Contrariwise, as a consequence of the Revolution, the Jews were able to break out of their historic isolation and alienation from the encompassing society. Despite their small numbers and modest situation, they participated notably in the actions of the Revolution in many different ways, as will be shown subsequently. Following its successful conclusion, they continued their public activity with increasing scope and intensity, as opportunity afforded and their numbers permitted. Thus was initiated the distinctively American character and pattern of Jewish life and activity. There was created a kind of tension but also a compromise between the traditional values and forms of Jewish institutional structure and the demands of modern secular life as they existed in America. A balance had to be struck, if the Jews were to succeed in developing and enlarging their opportunities in the New World, while maintaining the historic framework of Judaism. Many were tempted to wander away and were lost, as secularization and assimilation gained ground. As Dr. Jacob R. Marcus put it, the colonial Jews had already achieved considerable adjustment to a new frontier society. The American Revolution gave a great impetus to further secularization, which threatened to weaken the Jewish bonds, but it also expanded the horizons of Jewish life in America.[5]

In addition to secularization, Americanization and assimilation proceeded apace in the generation following the Revolution, as the Jews remained relatively few, counted only in the thousands and acquiring a largely native-born character. Immigration was minimal during this period and did not expand greatly until after 1840, with an influx of new arrivals from Germany. M. M. Noah had hoped to promote Jewish immigration earlier but failed. Thereafter the tension of American society resumed, but perhaps more slowly. The essential elasticity of American social pluralism was balanced by the tenacity of Judaism, especially as manifested in the growing Jewish communities, fed by continuing immigration. This equipoise was reinforced even further by the expanded flow of immigrants after the 1880s, particularly from Eastern Europe. Thus the heritage of the American Revolution renewed itself in every generation, as the Jews were progressively integrated into American society, winning a place for themselves by virtue of their own efforts and contributions. Herein lies the significance of the Revolution in relation to the role of the Jews. It initiated and accelerated the process of the incorporation of the Jews as an integral component of American society on a philosophically and constitutionally equal basis, which continued even as their numbers increased.

To return to the Revolution, one may begin to define its relation to and impact on the Jews then in the country. It was a multiple relationship, at once disruptive and constructive, and derived from certain conditions that characterized the distribution and basic activities of the Jews. They lived, as already indicated, in a few principal towns on the eastern seaboard, from Newport to Savannah. Because they were engaged chiefly in local and maritime trade, they were a mobile group, related often by kinship as well as by business association, reaching even into Europe, Canada, and the West Indies. The records of intermarriages, family correspondence, and the remarkable mobility of the few official functionaries among the Jewish communities point to a great interdependence of the Jews in America, which even transcended the historic division between Sephardic and Ashkenazi Jews. The Ashkenazi Jews were somewhat more numerous, but all belonged to the same synagogues, which had a Sephardic orientation because of their chronological or historic priority. Their very small numbers in a few communities reinforced their collective closeness and dependence on one another.

The first impact of the Revolution was thus disruptive. As British occupation and the effects of the blockade were felt across the country, the Jews were faced with the dilemma: should they stay or leave? This also raised the issue of loyalty. In any event, there was the further question of how the Jews would earn their livelihood amid the unsettling conditions of war. Altogether this condition produced much displacement of the Jewish population and required an adjustment to different circumstances and new possibilities of trade. Added to this was the financial instability of monetary values. In all these problems and predicaments of wartime trade, the Jews as a business group were particularly involved and affected. That they survived at all is evidence of their considerable adaptability and acceptance of the Revolution.

There were other relationships as well between the Jews and the Revolution. The Jews were not merely the passive victims of a revolutionary situation; they also made positive decisions affecting their attitudes and actions. What did the Jews do for and during the Revolution? This depended on many factors, as defined by the requirements of the war and by the capacities and inclinations of the Jews themselves. There was also the expectation of the general community and its readiness and willingness to accept the services of Jews on equal terms with all others. In this respect the Revolution established novel precedents, perhaps from the necessities of an internal war as much as from principle. As never before, Jews were active in the war on many fronts. First there were the military services, in which numerous Jews participated, some with distinction. Many were enrolled in the local militia, as was then customary and required of all citizens. The Jews were thus admitted to equal standing. Others, however, engaged in the more active staff and line services of the state and continental forces. This may well have been the first war in the Western world in which the Jews were permitted to serve on an equal basis. It was a precedent followed in all subsequent American wars. The military recognition and service of the Jews represented a basic admission to a full and equal national participation.

No less important, and in a special sense more comprehensive, was the economic role of the Jews during the Revolution. Because of their experience in trade and their established position in American business society, they were able to contribute significantly to the financial and economic aspects of the war. It was with them, as with all others, both a means of livelihood and survival under trying conditions and also a demonstration of patriotic zeal. To illustrate briefly, Isaac Moses, like others, was engaged in privateering for personal gain but also as a public contribution. Aaron Lopez, on the other hand, carried on an extensive trade in the supply of a great variety of available commodities to the general market. Was his contribution to the war less noteworthy? Simon Nathan, however, was busy supplying funds and war commodities to the state of Virginia, and there is no evidence that he found this trade remunerative, judging by his difficulties in securing payment. There was finally the case of Haym Salomon, who ably served the nation (and Robert Morris, Superintendent of Finance between 1781 and 1784) in the disposition of foreign bills of exchange, and thus provided public funds in a trying time. Public service and private profit were here blended together, and the Jewish role cannot be separated from that of the more numerous non-Jewish merchants who acted similarly. The opportunities for profit-making, let alone prof-iteering, were probably restricted in a war of this character, marked as it was by a great deficiency and instability of money and goods. Speculative activity became more rampant in the years after the Revolution, when the prospects of stabilization and redemption of credit increased considerably.

A third kind of significant relationship between the Jews and the American Revolution may be suggested at this point: What did the Revolution do for the Jews? This is more than a question of how the Jews fared, whether they prospered or not in the war. It is rather a matter of how they emerged from the Revolution in relation to their status and position in the general society. This has intellectual, political, and social connotations rather than merely economic significance. The Revolution was an emancipa-ting event, which conferred equal rights on the total population, and in which the Jews were peculiarly the beneficiaries. They affirmed and asserted their freedom from political and especially religious discrimination. They participated in political activity on both the state and federal levels. They sought appointment to public positions, and they responded to subsequent calls for military duty. There appeared even the beginnings of a military professionalism among some Jews, hitherto unknown and un-characteristic of the Jewish tradition.

The test of this ultimate achievement came in the generation following the Revolution. It constitutes in a sense a sequel to the Revolution and affected not only the original veterans and survivors of the war, but also their children and successors. This post-Revolutionary generation was largely native-born. It was brought up within the memory and with a strong patriotic sense of the Revolution. Subsequently it almost disappeared in the wave of immigration that began in the 1840s. The original small generation was composed of both Sephardic and Ashkenazi elements, the latter becoming predominant. This group first tested and experienced the full promise and implications of the Revolution. While retaining a Jewish character, it was shaped into an American pattern, and it acquired a strong sense of

Americanism. Even the fact that some of the veteran survivors of the Revolution later made claim to pensions as their due reflected their awareness of their American identity and a rightful share in the responsibilities and returns of full citizenship.

Almost a century later, the numerous offspring of these veterans were admitted to membership in the honor societies such as the Sons and Daughters of the American Revolution. Such recognition of their claim to a place in the honor rolls of the Revolution was part of the process of Americanization. This movement reached a climax after 1900 in a strong, concerted effort to win recognition and tribute for the Jewish role in the Revolution in the person of one of the leading participants, Haym Salomon. Because of his Polish background he was acclaimed by the Jews of east European origin, organized as the Federation of Polish Hebrews, who agitated actively for a statue in New York in his memory at the time of the sesquicentennial of Independence after 1926. Somewhat sentimentally, these Jews, many recent immigrants, exalted Haym Salomon and elevated him to the role of "financier of the Revolution." They succeeded in making him the best-publicized and best-known Jewish figure in the Revolution, as will be elucidated subsequently.

Thus the role of the Jews in the American Revolution began with a variety of military, economic, and social activities performed by a substantial number out of the approximately 2,500 Jews in the country. There followed a sequel in which the Jews reaped the fruits of their participation in terms of rights, honors, and other rewards of citizenship in the new country.

2

Distribution and Dispersion of the Jews During the Revolution

The Jews were not significantly involved in the events tharevolution, since they were neither numerous nor important in colonial America. Neither politically nor intellectually were they actively aware of or articulate about the underlying causes and controversies of the Revolution. Scarcely any Jews were involved in the policy-making activities that preceded or accompanied the Revolution. In the ten years of debate preceding the war, a few Jewish businessmen in New York and Philadelphia signed the nonimportation agreements by which the American merchants hoped to exert pressure on the British government. This was the first Jewish participation, although it is not clear whether such action was either wholly voluntary or greatly solicited by the business community. Thus, in Philadelphia, out of 375 signers of the nonimportation agreement of 1765, following the Stamp Act, 10 were Jews. They included the patriarchal Mathias Bush, the brothers Barnard and Michael Gratz (who were relative newcomers to America), Joseph Jacobs, Benjamin Heyman, Samson Levy, Moses Mordecai, and Abraham Mitchel, of doubtful Jewish identity, but a partner of Joseph Simon, the Indian trader of Lancaster.

The descendants of some of these signers subsequently acquired membership in the Daughters of the American Revolution on the basis of this first patriotic service. David Franks was also a signer, although he later turned Loyalist, and his whole family had close personal and business associations with the British. A similar nonimportation agreement of 1770 in New York included the names of some dozen Jewish merchants. Among these were such subsequently prominent patriots as Manuel Josephson, Jonas Phillips, Hayman Levy, and Isaac Seixas, but also Uriah Hendricks, who remained in New York all through the British occupation and was the founder of a prominent and wealthy Jewish family in post-Revolutionary America. Other signers were Abraham and Daniel Jacobs, Samuel Judah, and Jacob Myers, who were less conspicuous figures.[1]

New York was also the first community to present the Jews with the dilemma of whether they should stay or leave. An answer either way would constitute an apparent commitment to one side or the other. When Boston was evacuated by the British in mid-1776, the conflict shifted to New York, which was the site of a succession of bitter battles, accompanied by the maneuverings of the rival forces. Washington retreated across the Hudson, and New York became the principal headquarters of the British army during the remainder of the war. Normal trade was disrupted, and the Jews had to face problems of how they would fare and earn their livelihood.

There was the additional resulting question of loyalty, whether to the American or British side. New York thus early set the pattern for the Jewish response to the Revolution. Under the leadership of the young and patriotic spiritual leader of Shearith Israel, Rev. Gershom Mendes Seixas, the Jewish community split on the issue. Seixas, of a Sephardic family and first American-born minister of a Jewish congregation, preached a last sermon, and according to the report, tears were shed by all. He urged his people to leave New York, and he set an example by departing and settling for a time in Stratford, Connecticut, where he joined his father, a refugee from Newport. He carried with him the scrolls and other sacred objects of Shearith Israel, which was thus closed officially for the duration of the war. The building was occupied by the British, but was subsequently reopened and used by the Jews who remained in New York. As the Minute Book of the congregation noted in 1783: "During the interval [since 1776] most of the Yehadim had left the city in consequence of the Revolutionary War and the city having been taken possession of by the British troops, it was not until peace took place that the members returned to the city, when Mr. Hayman Levy called the meeting."[2]

Later in the Revolutionary War, in 1780, Seixas left Connecticut for Philadelphia, to join many of his followers who had gone there earlier. He became the minister of Mikveh Israel, which included the refugees from New York and other places. Philadelphia was, in fact, the American headquarters of the war, and it attracted many of the prominent Jewish merchants, such as Isaac Moses, Jonas Phillips, and Haym Salomon. The much enlarged congregation even undertook to erect a permanent building in 1782. Ironically, the war ended shortly thereafter, many of the temporary residents returned to their original home towns, and Mikveh Israel became financially embarrassed. Rev. Gershom Seixas arranged for his return to the New York congregation in 1784, and Jacob Raphael Cohen, who had come from Canada during the war and served in New York, replaced Seixas in Philadelphia, where he remained until his death in 1811. Seixas achieved distinction as the first Jewish trustee of Columbia College and as a Regent of the New York State Educational Board after the Revolution. He was minister in New York until his death in 1816.[3]

About thirty families, however, remained in New York under British occupation. Some did so because of their Loyalist convictions (a subject that will be treated elsewhere more fully). Others may have stayed because of convenience and because it was not easy for all to make such a drastic move. Some sixteen New York Jews signed an address of loyalty to the British crown, among almost a thousand signers. These included such notable names as Abraham and Moses Gomez, although their kin, the patriarchal Daniel Gomez, and his grandson and namesake, were among those who left for Philadelphia and served in the Revolution. Other notable signers were Uriah Hendricks, David and Barrack Hays, George Simpson, and Isaac Solomons. The most outspoken Loyalist, Abraham Wagg, who later went back to England, did not, however, sign the document, perhaps because he was not considered important enough.[4]

Significantly, among those who remained in New York during the early years was young Haym Salomon, who had come to New York from Europe only in 1772. Until 1778 he played a somewhat anomalous and ambivalent role in New York, where he was even married at this time to Rachel Franks, only sixteen years old, and had his first son. On the one hand, he carried on business with the

Hessian forces, whose officers and men welcomed his command of the German language. On the other hand, he was distrusted by the British and was twice arrested and imprisoned by them as a suspected spy and troublemaker for the Americans. In 1778 he managed to escape and to reach Philadelphia, where he began a new career as a successful broker and a financial aid to Robert Morris in the Finance Office during the later years of the war. In a petition in 1778 to the Continental Congress, pleading for assistance, he claimed to have left behind in New York several thousand pounds in accumulated funds, which would indicate a successful business career in British-occupied New York.[5]

An interesting addition to the Jewish community of New York during the British occupation was Alexander Zunz, who came to this country as a provisioner or sutler to the Hessian forces. He became the active head of the Shearith Israel synagogue during the war and remained in New York thereafter, establishing a business and his family there.[6] New York thus had the first and most important Jewish community to experience a disruption and division of its activities and loyalties during the Revolution. However troublesome this may have been during the war, re-union and reconciliation were not difficult afterward, perhaps because some of the most outspoken Loyalists left the city with the British and went either to Canada or to England. The rest, among them Uriah Hendricks, founder of a prominent family and an important metal industry, made their peace and stayed on in the country and city.

Other Jewish communities experienced similar although less severe disruption for the duration of the war. Philadelphia had a considerable accretion of Jews, as already indicated, and Baltimore, Richmond, and Boston received small numbers of Jews who thus founded new Jewish communities by the end of the Revolution. There was also a certain migration of Jews to the small towns of Connecticut as part of the evacuation of New York. Aaron Lopez and his sizable clan, including the Rivera and Mendes families related to him, settled in Leicester, Massachusetts, where they remained until the end of the war. Here they built houses and maintained a store. Lopez also carried on an extensive nationwide trade during the Revolution, but was drowned in 1782 on the way back to Newport. This was part of the dispersion from Newport, which was second only to that of the New York Jews.

In Newport, as early as 1776, a Committe of Safety made up a list of some seventy-seven persons described as "inimical to the United Colonies in America." Four prominent Jews, including the *hazzan*, Rev. Isaac Touro, were among them. They were required to take an oath of loyalty, which they refused. Moreover, they challenged the propriety of this action, which will be elaborated more fully elsewhere. Significantly, Rev. Ezra Stiles, Newport divine and self-styled friend of the Jews, recorded in his *Literary Diary* in 1777 that "the Jews were very officious as informing against the inhabitants" to the British. When the British occupied Newport in the early years of the war, the Jews divided sharply, as did the rest of the population, and many left.[7]

As Stiles reported it, however, some Jews remained in Newport during the occupation. Rev. Isaac Touro, Isaac Hart, and Myer Polock affirmed their loyalty to the crown. Hart later paid with his life in a battle on Long Island, while defending a Tory fortification. Touro and his family made their way to New York, and from there to Jamaica, where he died prematurely. Moses Michael Hays, alone of the four who refused to take the oath of loyalty in 1776, opted for the American side and settled in Boston. Here he was later joined by Touro's widow (his sister) and her two sons, Abraham and Judah, who were to have distinguished careers in Boston and New Orleans as merchants and philanthropists. Judah Touro, like some other sons of Loyalists who resumed their American loyalty in the War of 1812, even fought with Andrew Jackson in the Battle of New Orleans in 1815 and was severely wounded there.[8]

Newport's Jewish community, so prosperous in the colonial era, was dispersed and diminished still further after the Revolution. Its trade never recovered, and the Jews drifted away from Newport. Two decades later, almost the last Jew remaining there was Moses Seixas, brother of Rev. Gershom Seixas. Moses Seixas had written the famous letter of welcome from the Newport Jewish community to President Washington in 1790. He was the cashier of a bank located in his house. Thereafter the famous

Newport synagogue remained closed and was not reopened permanently until after 1886, when an influx of Jewish immigrants from Eastern Europe occurred.

Southern cities and their Jewish inhabitants too experienced drastic changes of fortune as British and American forces contended for their control. Charleston and Savannah in particular were captured and occupied by the British in the later years of the war. In both cities there were old, well-established Jewish communities. Many of their prominent citizens participated actively in their defense, and some were taken prisoner by the British. This aspect of Jewish military activity was of particular significance and will be treated more fully elsewhere. Here too the Jewish population divided sharply. Such prominent figures as the Sheftalls, Philip Minis, and Cushman Polock either became British prisoners or fled to Philadelphia. Others, however, remained and accepted the British regime at least tacitly. After the war some Jews in Savannah were accused and convicted of defection. Levi Sheftall, brother of Mordecai, an important Revolutionary patriot, was one of these, although his punishment was considerably alleviated by his brother's intercession. Others were acquitted on the testimony of witnesses as innocent victims of a wartime situation.

Only after the war ended did patriotic Jews return to Charleston and Savannah and resume their normal life and business, as was the case also in New York. Charleston, unlike Newport, experienced a postwar trade expansion in which the Jewish community shared and grew. It became the largest and most active Jewish community in America in the generation following 1800. The South, indeed, proved to be hospitable and attractive to the Jews after the Revolution as many migrated and settled in communities from Baltimore southward, among them Richmond, Petersburg, and Alexandria in Virginia, and Georgetown in South Carolina. They played a prominent role, politically and culturally as well as economically, in the South after the Revolution, and their importance climaxed in the generation of the Civil War.[9]

Whether because of the dispersion induced by the Revolution or because of new opportunities afforded by national growth after the Revolution, the Jews were scattered even more widely.

ıdy migrated northward into Canada, and others
Hudson Valley and even into northern New Eng-
cipally westward to new frontier settlements in
Kentucky, Illinois, and Michigan. Such diffusion
perhaps weakened the community ties of the principal seaboard
settlements and even fostered a degree of intermixture and loss
of Jewish identity. This was both a cause and an effect of a
considerable degree of Americanization and assimilation that
occurred among Jews in the post-Revolutionary generation,
before a renewal of immigration after 1840 brought fresh Jewish
elements and with them a renewed sense of Jewish community in
the country. Significantly, the Sephardic element displayed a
particular tendency toward assimilation and even loss of Jewish
identity, perhaps because of their historic background and
experience.

It is clear, therefore, that the Revolution had a profound and
ambivalent impact on the Jews living in America. On the one
hand, the immediate effect was to disrupt and divide the Jewish
communities, as loyalties were required, rejected, or assumed
either willingly or passively. A kind of American patriotism
emerged that stimulated an active participation in military or
other forms of social activity. A migration ensued, either
enforced or voluntary, as some left the country and many others
shifted from one community to another, in line with the fortunes
or misfortunes of war. Business activity changed in scope and
character as a result of the war, which created its own demands
but also introduced new handicaps, particularly as a result of the
blockade. For many, even the matter of a livelihood became more
pressing as it became more uncertain. Only the more prominent
and energetic merchants such as Isaac Moses, Aaron Lopez, the
Gratzes, and Simon Nathan accepted and adapted themselves to
the possibilities and opportunities provided by the war, as will be
shown subsequently. For others the struggle for economic survival must have increased. This was not the kind of war to produce
the familiar type of business prosperity based on expanded
demand. The demand may have been there, but the supply was
greatly curtailed by the interruption and closing of the normal
maritime and land routes. In addition, the inflation and depreciation of money enhanced the risks and handicaps of trade.

Following the Revolution, the revival of overseas trade was increasingly hampered by the events and effects of the French Revolution after 1789, and the resulting world wars and the disruption of world trade. This affected in particular the struggling effort of a small, new power such as the United States to maintain its neutrality in a world at war. Only the shift westward and the growth of frontier trade somewhat compensated for the other losses. The Jews too, like the rest of the population, began to migrate inland and to disperse widely over an expanding interior. Such movement strengthened and confirmed the influence of the American Revolution in integrating and incorporating the Jews into the general community, of which they remained a small and inconspicuous part. But westward expansion may also have weakened the integrity and identity of the Jewish community. The great migration of the nineteenth century slowed this process and revived the forces that strengthened the Jewish community in America. Their combined effect was to preserve and balance the centrifugal and centripetal forces in American Jewish life: Jewish community and identity on the one hand, and assimilation and integration on the other hand. We must now, however, return to the Revolution in order to examine more fully the complex part that the Jews played in it and the consequences that flowed from it as outlined generally here.

3

Major Military Contributions

It is scarcely to be expected that the relatively few Jews, probably not more than 2,500 altogether, would figure prominently in the military operations of a country with more than 2 million people. This was especially so since the Jews were not historically or culturally accustomed to military service in the Western world. Moreover, whereas the Jews lived primarily in the five principal seaboard towns, the military activities of the Revolution took place over the whole countryside. Often they were conducted on a local, dispersed basis, by local militia, from the southern border adjoining Florida to the extensive northern Canadian frontier and westward into the Ohio Valley and beyond. Nevertheless, the Jews were not insulated from the conflict, since their home towns were strategically located and were directly involved in the struggle for power. They were subject to the successive shocks of occupation and evacuation, and hence they were at the center of the conflict. The Jews were thus affected by their mere presence as well as by the necessity or opportunity of participation.

The contributions of the Jews, whether military or any other kind, were mainly operational and had little to do with basic policy-making. Despite their probable Whig inclinations, the Jewish role in military operations was a matter of local chance or special circumstances and did not greatly affect their course or outcome. It would be an exaggeration to state otherwise. As is often the case with great events, the actual succession of happenings and individual contributions arises out of a great mixture of motivations and activities, in which exalted or heroic elements are not always visible or even present. This is the real nature of any war, even one of a revolutionary character such as this one, in which ideals were presumably important.

Despite these pragmatic observations and reservations, the Jews figured with surprising prominence in the military aspects of the Revolution. This was true both numerically and also in regard to the level and character of their service. Their role varied from place to place, since they were involved in many zones of the war from north to south. Their participation, moreover, ranged from the lowest level of foot soldier to relatively high officer rank, and from supply service to actual combat. With such diversity, it is difficult to generalize, and it becomes necessary to specify individual cases. The total number of Jewish soldiers and the degree of their participation cannot be determined precisely for lack of accurate statistics or even of positive identification as Jews in all cases. The prevalence of Hebraic and Biblical names in the general population creates the temptation to include some that are of dubious origin or identity. On the other hand, there were undoubtedly others who had drifted away from the few Jewish communities and subsequently appeared in remote places, serving as individuals without clear-cut Jewish identification.

The frequent occurrence of intermarriage and conversion of Jews during this period might also tend either to an overcount or an undercount of Jews in service, depending on their inclusion or exclusion. Perhaps it might be more practical to err on the liberal side, since this would permit one to more nearly gauge the total Jewish population in the country rather than merely the faithful or affiliated parts of the Jewish community, which were substantially smaller. It is also useful to appreciate, if not to measure accurately, the extent and degree of separation or disaffiliation among Jews in this period, which was not inconsiderable.

Moreover, there is no single standard or common denominator of patriotic service in a Revolution. As the records of membership applications for both the Daughters and Sons of the American Revolution a century later indicate, participation ranged widely from actual military service to some other civic or patriotic duty. Even military engagement might consist merely of a brief enrollment in a local militia unit, or a more prolonged and active enlistment in a state or continental contingent. There were thus many kinds and degrees of Jewish roles in the war proper. Nor was age itself a limiting factor. Jared Sparks, the nineteenth-century chronicler of the Revolution, records an anecdote, perhaps apocryphal, relating to Daniel Gomez, the son of Lewis Moses Gomez, who had established an Indian trading post in the mid-Hudson Valley early in the eighteenth century. The son was already eighty years old at the time of the Revolution. Although others of the family were Loyalists and remained in New York under British occupation, Daniel patriotically left New York for Philadelphia in 1776, accompanied by his grandson of the same name. There he volunteered for service and offered to raise a company. When a delegate to Congress told him he was too old, he retorted, according to Sparks, that he could stop a bullet as well as a younger man. The younger Daniel served in the Philadelphia militia and died in 1784 at the youthful age of twenty-five. In 1779 Daniel Gomez senior, then eighty-four, and a year before his death, petitioned Congress to allow his grandson to go to New York to collect the rents on some property he had left behind, pleading that he "has always had a real affection and zeal for the welfare of this country."[1]

A special case of Jewish military service ran its full course early in the Revolution and is unusual in its political respects as well, illustrating the remarkable circumstances in which individual Jews might find themselves. It is that of Francis Salvador, whose very name, signifying "savior," is scarcely recognizable as Jewish, although he had a synagogue name of Daniel Jezurun Rodrigues. Yet his is one of the best-known recorded examples of a Jew who served the Revolution to the ultimate degree of losing his life in it. Born in 1747 in London, of a prominent Sephardic family, Salvador migrated to America in 1773, when only twenty-six years old. He came to South Carolina, where his uncle and father-in-law, Joseph Salvador, had acquired large landholdings in District 96 on the South Carolina frontier. The family was in reduced circumstances, and young Salvador hoped to restore its fortunes. He established an indigo plantation and joined a group that played an important political role in the early years of confrontation with both the British and their Indian allies. Despite his English origin, Salvador shared in the strong anti-British sentiment characteristic of the frontier. He was a member of both the First and Second Provincial Congresses between 1773-1776, and he was actively involved in the preparation of the first state constitution for South Carolina. He also served in the first General Assembly established under it.

Salvador was thus the first and only Jew to be a member of a state legislature and to play a quasi-policy-making role in the Revolution. He was on intimate terms with several of South Carolina's Revolutionary leaders. He sat on several committees, including the one responsible for the enforcement of the Continental Association. This was Salvador's political role, but he also was drawn into military activity as a volunteer. He joined a local militia force raised under Major Andrew Williamson, which was to engage a band of Cherokee Indians incited by local Tories. On 1 August 1776 the Williamson contingent was caught in an ambush, and Salvador was shot and scalped by the Indians. Salvador's superior, Major Williamson, witnessed and reported the death in vivid detail. Salvador asked "whether I had beat the enemy. I told him yes. He said he was very glad of it and shook me by the hand, and bade me farewell, and said he would die in a few minutes." As John Drayton, Salvador's friend and later Chief Justice and historian of South Carolina, who worked with him in the first legislature, described him: "His manners were those of a polished gentleman and as such he was intimately known and esteemed by the first revolutionary characters of South Carolina."[2]

Many years later, South Carolina Jews dedicated a memorial plaque to Salvador in a Charleston park, and he became the only Jewish soldier of the Revolution to be individually commemorated in the United States. Interestingly, Salvador's father-in-law came to South Carolina in 1784 to claim his lands in District 96, now Abbeville County. He died here two years later and is buried in Charleston's Jewish cemetery. Francis Salvador, the first Jewish casualty of the Revolution, lies in an unknown grave on South Carolina's frontier.

Salvador served as a volunteer in the South Carolina militia rather than as a regular officer. There were, however, a number of Jewish officers in the Revolutionary armies. Some fifteen may be identified in Francis B. Heitman's *Historical Register of Officers of the Continental Army*, which records about fourteen thousand officers who served in the American forces. A few more may be added who are not included in Heitman's *Register* or who cannot be clearly identified as Jews. This is a small number, but surprisingly, it constitutes about the same proportion of the total listed (about one-tenth of 1 percent) as the Jews represented in the whole population. When one considers the novelty of the military experience for Jews in the period, the record is significant. A few even acquired a kind of military professionalism, since they served through the several years of the Revolution in what was virtually a professional capacity. The summary review of Jewish military officers, however few, may provide a telling and significant introduction to the whole subject of military service. Their record is more complete and more identifiable than is that of obscure, ordinary Jewish soldiers, who often served briefly and without special mark. This record offers a small but revealing insight into the opportunities and accomplishments available to Jewish participants in the Revolution.

The highest rank attained by Jewish officers was that of lieutenant-colonel. In the light of their lack of military background or experience, this was a significant achievement, even if only by a few. Probably the Jewish officer with the most extensive war record was Solomon Bush. In a petition to Congress on 8 December 1780, he wrote that he entered "the service of our country in the earliest period of our most glorious contest, that animated with zeal he pushed forward to meet the foe, and received a considerable wound which has deprived him of serving his country in the field." Solomon was the son of Mathias Bush, who came to America from Bohemia in the 1740s. The father was a prominent merchant of Philadelphia and he was an army purveyor in the French and Indian War. He was also an important leader in the Mikveh Israel synagogue in Philadelphia. In 1765 he signed the nonimportation agreement against Britain, as already indicated.

With such a family background and his native birth, young Solomon enrolled as a captain and adjutant early in 1776 in the famed "Flying Camp of Associators of Pennsylvania." He saw action in the Battle of Long Island, which led to a retreat and the loss of New York by Washington's army. Many of this unit were taken prisoner. It was mobilized again in 1777 for the defense of Philadelphia against an expected attack. It came in the fall, and Bush, now a major, had his thigh broken shortly after the Battle of Brandywine. In the meantime Bush had been promoted to lieutenant-colonel and was made deputy adjutant-general of the Pennsylvania militia.

The injured Bush hid out in his father's house during the British occupation, but was discovered, taken prisoner, and placed on parole. He was incapacitated for further service, although he wrote to a friend, Henry Lazarus, in Virginia: "My wishes are to be able to get satisfaction and revenge the rongs [sic] of my injured country." Bush appealed for public help. The Supreme Executive Council of Pennsylvania commended him for his earlier military exploits, "when the service was critical and hazardous." He was voted rations and pay as lieutenant-colonel. In 1781 Bush applied for the Corps of Invalids, since he was now sufficiently recovered to be "able to perform duty in said corps." He was denied admission, but in 1785 Pennsylvania allowed him a pension.[3]

Bush became a chronic applicant for public office, probably the first Jew to do so, although without success. In 1780 he petitioned Congress, on the strength of his service and injury, for the "post of Secretary to the Honorable Board of the Treasury now vacant." He supported his request with the recommendations of a dozen persons, none apparently Jewish, and including high-ranking officers of Pennsylvania regiments. He pleaded that "due to your petitioner's long services and sufferings, his prayer will be granted." It was not, nor were other applications for public office he made in subsequent years. In 1784 Bush wished to become Health Officer of Philadelphia. In 1789 Bush was in London, where he might have acquired some medical training. He apparently knew Washington, and he wrote him a letter congratulating him on his inauguration as President of the United States. He sent him a book, presented by an English admirer, and he asked for an appointment to represent the United States in London. Washington, unlike his usual austere and remote manner, replied and thanked him warmly for the gift and good wishes. Somewhat cryptically, he also acknowledged gratefully Bush's part in the liberation of an American ship "by a proper and spirited conduct." But there was no mention of a post.

In 1793 Bush again applied to Washington for an appointment as naval officer for Philadelphia. He named Robert Morris as his backer, and he detailed at length the sad state of his affairs. He had been compelled to leave London and to return home where he had a family to support. He made reference to an unfortunate brother, otherwise unidentified, who was "deprived of his reason in a campaign to the southward under General Nathaniel Greene." Bush himself had just undergone an operation for the removal of half a thigh, the result of his war injuries. In 1795 Bush boldly applied to President Washington for an appointment to succeed Timothy Pickering as Postmaster-General.

One may only wonder, at this late date, whether Bush's free and frequent approach to Washington stemmed from a new self-assurance on the part of Jews or was a manifestation of a kind of eccentricity perhaps related in some way to his brother's condition. One final and equally unusual action by Bush needs to be mentioned in this connection. Like many other Jews in this period, Bush was a Mason and was once designated Deputy Inspector-General of Masonry in Pennsylvania. In this capacity he addressed a letter on Masonry to King Frederick II of Prussia, the titular head of all Masonry. There is no record of an answer from one who was scarcely sympathetic to Jews.

It is noteworthy, however, that the prominent role played by Jews in American Masonry established a significant bond between Jews and non-Jews in the Revolutionary era. It connoted a liberal association, which was both intellectual and social. Ironically, however, Solomon Bush drifted away from Judaism in later life, for he intermarried, and was buried in the Friends' Cemetery of Philadelphia on his death in 1795. Altogether here is an unusually full and involved record of a Jewish life and career during the Revolution.[4] It is evident that, where the information is available in such cases, the entire career of such Jewish officers, both military and civil, must be dealt with, since it reveals the ambitions, aspirations, as well as achievements of these men. Many lived, as it were, on the margins of the Jewish and non-Jewish worlds in what was a transitional period.

Another instance of a Jewish officer during the Revolution presents equally dramatic and unusual aspects. David S. Franks enjoyed an even more colorful diversity of activities, military, political, and diplomatic, filling a total of eleven years of public service. His life, too, ended unhappily with premature death in

1793. Franks' revolutionary career began, surprisingly, in Canada. He was born in 1743 in Philadelphia, the son of Abraham Franks and member of the large and important Franks clan. He may have attended there the academy that later became the University of Pennsylvania, along with Moses (a son of David Franks) and Moses Levy. Both father and son were in Montreal by 1767, among the first Jews to start business there after the British conquest of 1763. Young David Franks became the head of Congregation Shearith Israel, founded in Montreal at this time and bearing, interestingly, the same name as New York's synagogue.

Significantly, David's rebelliousness started as early as 1775, and he split with his father over the issues arising then. David's first revolutionary assertion grew out of a minor episode, which is indicative of an intellectual attitude on his part. A statue of George III in Montreal was daubed with an inscription: "This is the pope of Canada and the fool of England." A reward was offered for the apprehension of the perpetrator. Although not involved, Franks was arrested and detained for a week when he was overheard making a remark that "in England men are not hanged for such small offenses." He was released but became a marked man thereafter. The governor, Sir Guy Carleton, included him in a "list of the principal leaders of sedition. We have too many remaining amongst us that have the same indication." Franks had the opportunity to join up with the enemy when an American army captured Montreal in 1775. As he himself put it: "My good offices and purse were ever open to them, at a time when they had neither friend nor money." He was apparently even paymaster to the army there. Congress subsequently acknowledged an indebtedness of $3,748.84 to cover his advances, of which $2,148.84 was still due him many years later.

When the American army retreated from Canada, Franks followed it south, receiving permission to enter at Albany 29 June 1776. His pass certified that he "is a friend to the American cause."[5] Franks attached himself to Benedict Arnold, whom he had met in Montreal, and was possibly with him as a volunteer at the Battle of Saratoga in 1777. He was perhaps with him, too, in the Albany hospital where Arnold recovered from serious wounds. Because of his knowledge of French, he was later a liaison officer to Count D'Estaing, the commander of the French forces in America, and he was perhaps also for a time an aide to General Benjamin Lincoln in South Carolina. His early movements are vague and even mysterious.

In 1778, Franks, named a major in the American army, was appointed an aide to General Arnold, who took command of Philadelphia following the British evacuation. Arnold's questionable conduct in assuming control of all supplies in the city as a possible source of personal profit stirred the mistrust and antagonism of the Pennsylvania civil authorities, headed by Joseph Reed, president of the Supreme Executive Council. Arnold was tried and found guilty in a court-martial, and Franks was involved in it, at least as a witness. Enjoying Washington's favor, despite his censure, Arnold was transferred to the command of West Point in 1780, and Franks accompanied him there. He served as his aide in various capacities, from personal attendant to Mrs. Arnold to the issuance of instructions for the supply and disposition of the forces there. They concerned such prosaic matters as the shipment of flour to Albany, the procurement of milk cows, and the removal of the sick from a crowded hospital.

The character of the war is well indicated by these and such other matters as the delivery of two horse thieves to Colonel Lamb with the injunction that "one of the rogues, Akely, is a notorious villain, and will escape if not properly secured." In one message to Colonel Lamb, Franks expressed concern that "no more men can be by any means taken from the garrison," but a draft of two hundred men was, nevertheless, authorized to go up the river to cut wood for the garrison. Here are revealed the normally prosaic but yet necessary activities of an army at war, and Franks' modest part in them, as representing Arnold's command.

Then came the explosive affair of Arnold's treason and the attempted surrender of West Point to the enemy. Arnold fled precipitously and left behind his wife and staff. Colonel Varick and Major Franks, his aides, were in Arnold's household at the time and had to bear the brunt of an investigation. They naturally came under suspicion, but Washington, who was visiting the Arnold ménage at the time, expressed faith in both men. Arnold took the trouble to write to Washington on 25 September 1780: "I think myself in honor bound to declare that they . . . are totally ignorant of any transactions of mine that they had reason to believe were injurious to the Public." It would appear, in fact, that Franks had become somewhat estranged from Arnold, perhaps because of his strange behavior and questionable company, and contemplated leaving his service. Franks and Varick requested a public court of inquiry to clear them. Washington complied with their request, After public hearings, the court exonerated them completely, concluding that "every part of Major D. S. Franks' conduct was not only unexceptionable but reflects the highest honor on him as an officer, distinguishes him as a zealous friend to the independence of America, and justly entitles him to the attention and confidence of his countrymen."[6]

In the meantime, Franks performed one final service for his former superior by escorting Mrs. Arnold, who was in an understandably hysterical state, back to her family, the Shippens of Philadelphia. He also bore a message at this time from Washington to Lafayette, then on the way south, and he may have been briefly a courier for Washington. This was, in fact, to become Franks's major function, in the diplomatic as in the military sphere. The discreditable close of Arnold's military career apparently left Franks without a patron. In 1781 he acquired a new one in Robert Morris, who had just become Superintendent of Finance and subsequently the frequent employer of Haym Salomon as a broker of foreign exchange. Morris found employment for Franks, who was released from the army, in which he had apparently attained the rank of lieutenant-colonel, although it is not clear how this happened. Washington and Jefferson referred to him as Colonel Franks, as did others. At a later date Franks complained that unknowingly and unwillingly he had been "deranged from the army." He was restored and received compensation until the general demobilization occurred in 1783, when he chose a five-year commutation instead of half-pay for life. Franks was thus, at least nominally, an officer in the American army virtually during the entire Revolutionary War.

Actually, however, between 1781 and 1787, Franks was assigned to various diplomatic missions. He shuttled back and forth between Europe and America. He set great hopes on this assignment, which he owed first to Robert Morris. As he wrote to

General Knox on 17 July 1781, on board ship at the Capes of Delaware: This "will be a means of introducing me to further employment in this way. . . . If I find encouragement, I may very probably settle as a merchant in France." In fact, Franks later acquired higher aspirations—for example, to serve as an American consul in France. He thanked Knox for his helpfulness in the Arnold affair, and he offered to bring back something from France for Mrs. Knox. His visits abroad brought him into association with Jefferson, Franklin, John Adams, John Jay, and lesser American diplomats in Europe. He complained of inadequate compensation and means to pay his way, and was frequently forced to appeal to the American diplomats, particularly Franklin and Jefferson, for loans. They too, however, protested their financial stringency and distress, partly to discourage his requests, partly also because the United States Congress did not have the funds to supply either them or Franks more generously. Members of Congress too, such as James Madison and others, paid by their states, were often in financial distress and received assistance from Haym Salomon, as will be related later. Whether in business, politics, war, or diplomacy, the Revolution did not provide an occasion for lavish profits or compensation.

Franks' first mission in Europe kept him there for more than a year, shuttling between Paris and Madrid and the American ministers there. He was the first Jew to function, as it were, in both a civilian and a military role during the Revolution. Moreover, on his return to America in 1783, he applied for a consular appointment in France. Thirteen prominent men supported his petition and attested to his "regular education in the Mercantile Line, his knowledge of the language of that Kingdom, and his acquaintance with the manners and customs of the people, acquired by his residence in Canada and France." All this, they concluded, "added to his general character, renders it highly probable that he will make a useful and valuable officer of the United States in that Department." Among the signers were William Bingham, Samuel Meredith, James Wadsworth, C. A. D. and Jacob Morris.[7]

Early in 1784 Franks was on his way to Europe again, this time as the bearer of one of the three copies of the treaty of peace that had just been ratified by Congress. This was to assure the delivery of the treaty in a time of uncertain and insecure travel. He stayed three years on this mission, carrying messages and papers to and from Jefferson, John Adams, and John Jay. Jefferson, whom Franks served briefly as an amanuensis, and who came to know Franks well, wrote a characterization to Madison as early as 1783:

> He appears to have a good eno' heart and understanding, somewhat better than common but too little guard on his lips. I have marked him particularly in the company of women where he loses all power over himself and becomes almost a fright. His temperature would not be proof against their allurements, were such to be used as engines against him. This is in some measure the vice of his age but it seems to be increased also by his peculiar constitution.

Apparently the wiles of women of the Mata Hari type have been feared in diplomacy in all ages. In Franks' case this judgment is somewhat surprising, since he never married and was thus presumably proof against the attractions of women. Madison agreed and was even more distrustful: "Your portrait of your amanuensis is I conceive drawn to life. For all unconfidential services he is a convenient instrument. For anything farther . . . I am afraid." Interestingly, in none of these rather harsh criticisms is there any suggestion of an anti-Jewish bias. The distrust was purely personal.[8]

For a time, during his second and longer stay in Europe, Franks was United States vice-consul at Marseilles, by appointment of Thomas Barclay, consul-general, but he received no compensation. His principal contribution to American diplomacy at this time was when he accompanied Barclay as his secretary to Morocco in 1785 and participated in the negotiation of a trade treaty with Morocco's ruler, which he then brought back with him to America in 1787. Notably, Franks preceded by more than a quarter of a century the appointment as consul to Tunis of another prominent Jew, Mordecai M. Noah, the versatile son of a Revolutionary veteran. Jefferson, writing to John Adams, approved the appointment of Franks, since he knew French perfectly and "a little Spanish." Later, Jefferson wrote to Franks, still in Europe, urging him to return to America, even without his baggage, and to deliver the Moroccan treaty to Congress for speedy ratification. He regretted the long delay and urged that "in the meantime, our whole commerce is paying a heavy tax for its insurance till publication." Interestingly, Franks carried along a translation of the original Moroccan treaty, made by an interpreter, named Isaac Cardozo Nunez, who was a Moroccan Jew prominent at court. This name appears also among contemporary American Jews.

During this period Franks maintained friendly exchanges with Jefferson. He had the usual fiscal troubles, reporting to Jefferson once that he had a letter of credit from Lafayette, which was not in proper form. He needed money, and Jefferson advanced him two hundred florins, even though he complained of his own fiscal troubles. Before leaving France, Franks sent Jefferson a gift of some fourteen Moorish coins "as a very small mark of attachment which I have always had for you. . . . Besides, I owe you 200 livres which you kindly lent me when I very much wanted it, and for which tho' I cannot repay you I shall not think myself quit of the obligation." Jefferson wished him "health, happiness, and good passage" on his departure for America. To Madison Jefferson wrote at the same time: "You will see Franks, doubtless he will be asking some appointment. I wish there may be one for which he is fit." His recommendation was somewhat mixed: "He is light, indiscreet, active, honest, affectionate."[9]

In April 1787, Franks reported to Jefferson on his arrival home after a long and disagreeable passage of fifty days' duration. He had delivered his papers, and he concluded with an illuminating comment on the political situation at home: "Everybody here seems much displeased with it, and not much expected from the Convention which is to meet next month." This pessimistic prediction regarding the Constitutional Convention was fortunately not borne out by its successful outcome.

No other Jewish person played such a diverse role in the Revolution in close proximity to some of its principal figures. Franks continued his quest for public employment after the war, apparently without success. As early as 1785 he had written to Jefferson, "opening myself to you in this manner, as I know of no one in whose indulgence I can so fully confide." He preferred to serve in the United States, but with the prospect of war "would

consider serving in the French army." He knew one of the French
generals, in whose "military family . . . I should be happy to
serve." He protested that he did not wish to "follow the profession
of a Soldier of Fortune, but I do assure you that my circumstances
are such as to induce me to accept of anything that would be
honorable and profitable. I should certainly prefer being employed in the service of my country to all others, but I do not see
any immediate prospect of so pleasing a circumstance."[10]

Despite Jefferson's somewhat equivocal recommendation,
Franks, whose public life had begun in war and revolution, was
unable to pursue it further in peacetime. In 1789 he addressed a
memorial to the new federal Congress seeking office. He
reviewed his activities, both military and diplomatic, concluding:
"Thus I have devoted eleven years to the service of my country, in
all which time I am bold to say that I have been actuated by a
disinterested zeal for her honor and prosperity." He was granted
a warrant for four hundred acres of land as part of a congressional program for veterans of the Revolution, but received no other
individual recognition.

In 1790 Franks again addressed his friend Jefferson, who had
just returned from France in order to become Secretary of State.
He welcomed him home and offered to join "your family as
Private Secretary, till some further provison can be made for me."
He would accept the salary of a "common clerk. . . . That salary,
with the pay of the Interpreter of the French language (if you
thought proper to give me the office) would enable me to live and
to do honor to some debts which I owe abroad." This, too, did not
materialize. Franks appears only once more in the public records
as the secretary of a Commission on Indian Affairs named to
negotiate a treaty with the Creeks in 1789. The mission failed, but
the commission, including Franks, had dinner with President
Washington on its return.[11]

Franks concluded his career with something of an anticlimax
when he became an assistant cashier of the Bank of North
America in 1791. This was headed by Robert Morris, who had
once before befriended Franks a decade earlier. Franks remained in this humdrum post until his premature death in 1793,
during the great yellow fever epidemic of that year. Only fifty
years old, he had been estranged from the Jewish community and

was buried without formality in a Christian cemetery. He had never married, and he left a modest estate of two thousand pounds.[12]

In a sad sort of way, Franks' public career ended like that of another Jewish veteran of the Revolution, Solomon Bush, also a lieutenant-colonel. They were the first Jews to seek public office, but neither succeeded in securing it, and both died obscurely, estranged from Judaism. There is no evidence to attribute their failure to their Jewishness, since this had been greatly diluted in both cases. The primary factors may have been the limited scope of government and the shortage of public positions available in the early republic, as compared with the great competiton for them. The political quest for public office, long characteristic of American government, had begun early and was to flourish all through its history. Jewish contenders were to have a modest place in it and enjoyed relatively moderate success, more under Democratic than under Federalist auspices in the first years after the Revolution.

A third Jewish soldier of the Revolution, who attained the rank of colonel, although not until more than a decade later, was Isaac Franks. Like David S. Franks, he belonged to the large and important Franks clan, divided between New York and Philadelphia, and he was distantly related to him. Isaac was born in New York in 1759, the son of Moses B. Franks, who was also the father of Rachel Franks, the wife of Haym Salomon. He was scarcely seventeen when he enlisted in Colonel Lasher's Volunteers of New York. He served in the Long Island campaign in 1776, when he was wounded and taken prisoner. He escaped to New Jersey in a leaky skiff with one paddle and rejoined Washington's army, with which he remained through all its many changes of fortune. He became a forage master and performed its routine functions conscientiously. There are letters extant to General Arnold, commander at West Point in 1780, in which Franks complained of the poor quality of hay and the short weights received, and he asked for a scale. In 1781 he was commissioned an ensign in the Seventh Massachusetts Regiment, also stationed at West Point, and he remained with it until he was discharged in the following year for a complaint of kidney gravel.[13]

After the war, Franks settled in Philadelphia, opened a broker's office, and engaged in land speculation with Dr. Benjamin Rush, among others. For a time he prospered. He acquired a large house in Germantown, through which he won a measure of fame in history. In 1793, the year of the deadly yellow fever epidemic in Philadelphia, President Washington was hesitant about returning to the city after a summer at Mount Vernon. He negotiated for a suitable house in the country, and he thought "unquestionably Col. Franks' (if to be had) would suit me best, because more commodious for myself and the entertainment of company." Ironically, in his letter of inquiry, Washington alluded to four thousand reported deaths from the fever, among them, as he heard, "Col. Isaac Franks and many others of our acquaintances [who] have fallen victims to the prevailing malignant fever." Isaac Franks was, however, alive enough to rent his house to Washington for two months, and it was Colonel David S. Franks who had died then. The total cost amounted to $131.56, which included, aside from $66.66 as rent, such interesting items as $2.50 for cleaning up the house after Washington gave it up, as well as the losses of one flatiron worth 1 shilling, 1 large fork and 4 plates, and the consumption of 3 ducks, 4 fowls, 1 bushel of potatoes, and 100 pounds of hay.[14]

Franks' rank of colonel, as used by Washington, was actually acquired in the Pennsylvania militia after the Revolution, when he was named to the command of the Second Regiment, largely from Germantown, in 1794, during the Whiskey Rebellion in western Pennsylvania. Franks had married a Mary Davidson in 1782, and his family drifted away from Judaism. One of his children, Samuel D. Franks, became a judge of common pleas in Pennsylvania. His fortunes declined in later life, and in 1818 he was able to meet the requirement of indigence in order to qualify for a veteran's pension of twenty dollars a month as an officer. In the last three years of his life, he was a prothonotary, or chief clerk, of the Pennsylvania Supreme Court.

The Jewish officers during the Revolution, while few, often had some special distinction of unusual origin or assignment of responsibility. This was especially the case of Benjamin Nones, who was of French origin, born in Bordeaux in 1757, and who came to America in 1777 at twenty. He was a volunteer at first. In an autobiographical note, written in 1800, to Thomas Jefferson, he boasted that "as an American throughout the whole of the Revolutionary War, in the militia of Charleston, and in Polaskey's [Pulaski's] legion *[sic]*, I fought in almost every action which took place in Carolina, and in the disastrous affair of Savannah, shared the hardships of that sanguinary day, and for twenty-three years I have felt no disposition to change my politics, any more than my religious principles."

Legend, not always a reliable guide, had Nones carry the mortally wounded Baron DeKalb from the battlefield, with the help of two other Jewish officers, Captains Jacob de Leon and Jacob de la Motta. A French Captain Verdier, attached to Pulaski's corps, wrote in December 1779,

> to certify that Benjamin Nones has served as a volunteer in my company during the campaign of this year and at the seige of Savannah in Georgia, and his behavior under fire in all the bloody battles we fought has been marked by the bravery and courage which a military man is expected to show for the liberties of his country and which acts of said Nones gained in his favor the esteem of General Pulaski as well as that of the officers who witnessed his daring conduct.

Another Jew of French origin was David Lewis, who served in Colonel Bland's First Regiment of Light Dragoons, in the Continental Army. He later married Rachel Solomon, and one applicant for membership in the DAR in his name, more than a century later, was named Mrs. Milly Einstein Falk.[15]

Interestingly, the Jews of Bordeaux, Nones's home town, subscribed to a fund for the purchase of a warship that they presented to the American cause. It was apparently in memory of Abraham Gradis, also of Bordeaux, who had financed the French defense of Canada in an earlier war. By his own later assertion, Nones acquired a major's rank in the Pennsylvania militia after the Revolution. In 1781 Colonel Balfour, the British commandant of Charleston, banished him for refusal to accept British protection. He settled in Philadelphia, married Miriam Marks, and raised a large family that played a loyal and prominent role in American affairs during war and peace. Both he and his sons sought public office, as will be explained in another context. He was in and out of business and was insolvent for a time in the postwar period because of the troubled relations with revolutionary France. He was active in Democratic politics and was a loyal member and leader of the Jewish community in Philadelphia. Even more extraordinary was the case of Colonel David Maysor, a non-Jew. Maysor, also a Frenchman, came to this country as an aide to Lafayette. Here he married Sarah da Costa, daughter of Isaac, *hazzan* of Beth Elohim synagogue in Charleston, and an active patriot in the Revolution. They had one daughter, named Rebecca, who was raised in the Jewish faith by her mother, after her father died prematurely in 1780. She married David Hyams and thus helped to perpetuate a prominent Jewish family in South Carolina. More than a century later, her Jewish descendants were accepted as members in the Daughters of the American Revolution on the basis of her father, Colonel Maysor's service.[16]

Intermarriage was not uncommon during the colonial period, and the Revolution may have even accelerated the process by dislocating and scattering Jews. One such was was that of James Pettigrew, Scottish-born, who became a lieutenant in a Continental regiment. He eloped with and married Judith, daughter of Myer Hart, a founder and leading merchant of Easton, Pennsylvania. They were married, first by a Christian chaplain and then, on the insistence of Judith's mother, by a Jewish functionary of Philadelphia's synagogue. By mutual consent, it was agreed that the sons of the union would be Christian and the daughters Jewish. As a result, three daughters out of five children married Jews. The widow, too, remarried after her first husband, Pettigrew, died in 1793. As Mrs. Judith Hart de Shara she received a Revolutionary War pension in 1837 in Pettigrew's name. There was also Shinah, one of the five daughters of Joseph Simon, an early settler, trader, and central figure in the small Jewish community of Lancaster, Pennsylvania. During the war she married Dr. Nicholas Schuyler, an army surgeon and member of the prominent Schuyler family of upstate New York. Her father supposedly remained unreconciled with Shinah until just before his death, but she corresponded with her family, especially with her niece, the celebrated Rebecca Gratz. The Schuylers were childless. Thus did the Revolution promote, in some cases, the assimilation and even absorption of Jews into the general population.[17]

Both in terms of relative numbers and degree of involvement in the Revolution, the Jews of the South particularly distinguished themselves. The reasons are not easy to find and formulate. Perhaps it was chiefly because they had deep roots in two communities, Charleston and Savannah. Both towns were greatly affected by the war after 1778; they were captured and long occupied by the British. Thus many Jews enrolled in the military forces of both places, fought in their defense, and were taken prisoners. Other Jews faced the dilemma of leaving, or submitting to the British occupation, and were subsequently forced to clear themselves of the charge of collaboration or defection. Thus the wartime exploits and experiences of a number of the Jewish participants were unusually adventurous as well as painful, and are recorded fully. Such military and even political activity became part of the Southern tradition, and Jews figured prominently in its long and troubled history, even down to the Civil War.

One may begin with Savannah, in which the role of Jews was peculiarly prominent during the Revolution. Here lived Philip Minis, son of Abraham, and reputed to have been the first white child born in Savannah in 1733. He was thus a native Georgian whose deep loyalty could not be disputed. Ironically, he was married to Judith Polock of Newport, whose family remained strongly Loyalist. As early as 1776 Minis was acting paymaster and a commissary of Georgia's forces, and he is reported to have advanced eleven thousand dollars for the troops. After the British capture of Savannah in 1778, Minis, together with his mother, Abigail, and a number of other Jews, left and established themselves in Charleston. A year later, at the British seizure of Charleston, some of these had to move again, this time to Philadelphia. In 1779 Minis and another Savannah Jew, Levi Sheftall, whose family record during the war was especially noteworthy and will be related subsequently, performed an unusual feat. The French under Count D'Estaing were planning a combined naval and land expedition for the recapture of

Savannah, in conjunction with the Americans under General Benjamin Lincoln.

In their accustomed fashion, the French prepared the campaign carefully, collecting information about the best approaches to Savannah by land and water. The French military archives contain a long document in French covering the detailed itineraries supplied by Levi Sheftall and Philip Minis. Minis was described as being "thoroughly acquainted with the neighborhood of Savannah. . . . He is able to guide any party, even through the woods," and he volunteered to do so. Sheftall confirmed Minis' report and proposed another landing at Thunder Bolt, where a battery might be set up. In addition to such advice, "the two guides . . . will conduct the forces when ordered to do so." Unhappily, the Savannah expedition proved to be a disastrous failure, and General Lincoln's force barely extricated itself, while the French escaped by sea. Savannah remained in British hands until the end of the war, as did much of the South. The next significant venture by the combined American and French land and naval contingents was not until 1781, at Yorktown in Virginia, where a number of Jewish soldiers were present. This was successful and ended in the surrender of Lord Cornwallis and his army. Peace was, however, not concluded until 1783.[18]

Among the greatest feats and the most dramatic contributions by Jews to the Revolution were those of the Sheftalls. One of the first families to settle in Savannah in 1733, it was founded by Benjamin Sheftall, who came from Germany by way of London. Benjamin began a diary, which was continued through the eighteenth century by his descendants and provides a record of the family and Jewish life in Savannah. It is almost eloquent on the Revolution, which, it reported in labored English, "did ocation [sic] many Jews to be continually coming and going that there was no possibility to keep a register . . . , as there was nothing but war talked of etc. Everybody has there [sic] hands and herts [sic] full." At the time of the Revolution, the Sheftalls were represented by two half-brothers, Mordecai and Levi, sons of Benjamin. One aspect of Levi's role in the Revolution has already been recounted. Mordecai was, however, the more prominent figure both in the general and in the Jewish community. He owned a warehouse and wharf in town, and he also had a ranch and a registered cattle brand. He had given land for a Jewish cemetery as early as 1762, and the congregation met in his house. The epitaph on his grave in Savannah describes him as a "Colonel in the Revolutionary War, a patriot of note. . . ."[19]

Mordecai Sheftall was a prime mover in the early confrontation that led to revolution in Georgia. He was a chairman of a district or parish Committee of Safety in Savannah. Its role was to rally the patriots and to discredit the Loyalists. He organized and led a group that boarded a vessel in the harbor and removed the gunpowder from its stores by a show of force. It was then shipped to Boston to supply Washington's army there in 1776. The royalist governor of Georgia, Wright, complained to the government in London that the Jews "were found to a man to have been violent rebels and persecutors of the King's loyal subjects. They must not be allowed to return to Georgia." In the Disqualifying Act of 1780, the British listed Mordecai Sheftall as "chairman of the Rebel Parochial Committee," who had ordered ships out of the harbor and interfered with the King's business. They had invaded the Collector's office and removed papers from it. This act, which disqualified many Georgians from future political activity in the state, also excluded by name Mordecai, Levi, and Sheftall Sheftall, Philip Minis, Cushman Polock, and Philip Jacob Cohen, all shopkeepers.[20]

In the early conflict that opened the Revolution in Georgia, Mordecai Sheftall was named to the general staff of the Georgia Brigade with the rank of colonel. In 1777 he was appointed Deputy Commissary General of Issues for the Georgia troops, and in the following year he became Commissary General for Purchases and Issues of the Continental forces in South Carolina and Georgia. He in turn named his son Sheftall, barely seventeen years old, an Assistant Commissary of Issues, and he recommended him "as a young man of probity and well attached to the American cause." During this crucial year in Savannah's fate, the records indicate how busy the Sheftalls were with the acquisition, storage, and issue of supplies to the military. Both father and son were taken prisoner on the capture of Savannah by the British on 29 December 1778. They were treated harshly on a prison ship, and Mordecai was labeled by the British "a very great rebel," to be especially watched. In 1779, when the British withdrew from Sunbury, where the prisoners were kept, in order to defend Savannah, the paroled prisoners, including the Sheftalls, embarked on a brig for Charleston. They were captured by a British frigate and taken to Antigua in the West Indies. Another prisoner on this ship was Moses Volloton, later known as Valentine, a member of a prominent Jewish family of Savannah. They were again paroled and allowed to leave for Philadelphia. This dramatic tale of adventure was recounted by Mordecai Sheftall, and his son, Sheftall, retold it vividly in his application for a pension in 1832.[21]

Young Sheftall had still another wartime experience following his arrival at Philadelphia. In 1780 General Washington requested a passport from Sir Henry Clinton, the British commander, to permit the sloop *Carolina Packet* to proceed under a truce flag to Charleston, bearing provisions and clothing, as well as $1,600 in specie, for the supply of General Moultrie and the American prisoners there. Young Sheftall Sheftall was named flag master of the vessel, in charge of the mission, which he executed successfully.[22] Mordecai Sheftall was now settled in Philadelphia, where his family finally joined him. Undaunted, he engaged in a privateering enterprise and directed the operations of the schooner *Hetty*. He became an active member of Mikveh Israel, which experienced a considerable expansion, thanks to the refugees from other places. He also began a long process of petitioning Congress for compensation, to cover his services and substantial losses as Commissary General and as a prisoner of the British. To the Georgia delegation in Congress he complained of his treatment by the Board of War, which denied him pay and rations when "I considered myself as a continental officer whose duty it was to render his country what services he could." He claimed extra compensation for his losses due to depreciation, and he pleaded for consideration for one who had sacrificed everything in the cause of his country.[23] The account of Sheftall's prolonged financial controversy with the government will be developed more fully in another context, since it was only one of a number of such claims for compensation, by Jews and others, growing out of the Revolution.

After the war the Sheftall family returned to Savannah, where it resumed its business operations. Many other Jews came back too, as related in the Sheftall diary. On 13 April 1783, Mordecai wrote to his son Sheftall, who was still in Philadelphia, that peace was at last declared: "Every real well wisher to his country must feel himself happy to have lived to see this long and bloody contest brot *[sic]* to so happy an issue. Now we have independence. . . . An entier *[sic]* new scene will open itself. . . . Come home after Passover."[24] Levi Sheftall, who, like his brother Mordecai, had been active as a patriot in the early part of the Revolution, was caught between the two sides at the end. He had apparently stayed on in Savannah under British occupation and was subject, with many others, to subsequent punishment as a defector. Thanks to his brother's intercession, he was, however, relieved of the severe penalties of confiscation and banishment by the state legislature in 1785. With Isaac de Lyon, another convicted Jew, he was returned to citizenship but was denied a vote or the right to hold office for fourteen years, and his property was made liable to a fine of 12 percent.[25]

Mordecai Sheftall, who had remained loyal through the Revolution, was able to acquire several hundred acres of confiscated Loyalist land in Georgia. He regained a prominent place in both the general and the Jewish community. His role as a merchant is indicated by one substantial transaction. He obtained permission from the governor and council to ship to Charleston a number of commodities, since there was no market for them in Savannah. These included sixty-two whole and twenty-nine half-barrels of Philadelphia flour, eight firkins of butter, four barrels of bread, thirty kegs of biscuit, four barrels of pork, and "some loose onions." This provides something of a measure of the scale and character of Jewish business after the war.[26]

Two sons of Mordecai became professional men in post-Revolutionary Savannah. Sheftall Sheftall, his father's able assistant during the war, was a lawyer, and Moses, who trained with Dr. Benjamin Rush of Philadelphia, became a physician. Interestingly, Abraham de Lyon, who married their sister, Sarah, had been a surgeon during the Revolution. It is noteworthy that the Jews of Savannah had attained a professional level in the community by the end of the Revolution. Sheftall, who never married, did not prosper in his old age. In 1832, then seventy and indigent, he applied for a pension, reciting his adventurous war career in great detail. He was allowed $320 per year as an officer, which was raised to $460 in 1846. He died in 1847. In his last years he became something of a town character in Savannah. Attired in quaint and ancient garb, he was known as "Cocked Hat Sheftall," who was ready to tell his tale to whoever would stop and listen.[27]

There were other Jews who achieved some prominence in Revolutionary Georgia. Cushman Polock was commended by the Georgia delegation to the Continental Congress in 1780 for his conduct "for many years past; that he gave early demonstrations of his attachment to the American cause . . . has been in several engagements against the enemy." He was now a refugee from his state and "is entitled to every indulgence usually given by sister states to persons of his description." Polock settled in Philadelphia and was active in Mikveh Israel there at the end of the war.[28]

A Jew of more doubtful origin was Abraham Simons. His place of birth was unknown, and he settled in the Georgia upland on the frontier. During the Revolution he was a captain in a Georgia regiment and fought in the peculiarly vicious conflicts with Tories and their Indian allies. After the war he settled near Augusta and prospered in trade. He was known locally as a Jew of strong, plain sense, although uneducated. He was a member of the Georgia legislature in 1804. He was married twice, and his surviving widow married a Reverend Jesse Mercer, founder of what is now Mercer University, which was endowed in part with Simons' fortune.[29]

Another even more distinguished Georgian was David Emanuel, whose Jewish origin and character are also questionable. Originally probably from Virginia, Emanuel settled on the Georgia frontier, in Burke County. He was active in frontier warfare during the Revolution. On one occasion he was captured by some Tories and was due to be shot on the spot. Two of his companions were killed, but Emanuel escaped into a swamp. He lived to become active in Georgia politics and was elected governor in 1801. His Jewishness is vouched for indirectly in the account of a great-grandson of his sister Ruth, Judge H. D. D. Twiggs, who asserted on the basis of family tradition that "I only know that, beyond a doubt, he was a Jew." David Emanuel also had a brother named Levi, who was a lieutenant in the Georgia forces.[30]

Such persons as Abraham Simons and David Emanuel are among many who belong to a kind of twilight zone, in which their Jewish origin is doubtful and a Jewish identity appears to be lacking. There is perhaps little to be gained by including them in the record, since there are enough others who are undoubtedly Jewish. Nevertheless, they may serve to illustrate the complex and not uncommon process of migration, dispersion, and assimilation among the Jews of early America. The country was large, and the Jews were few. The scattering of individual Jews was thereby facilitated, and the process of assimilation was accelerated, since there were few barriers to intermarriage. A remarkable example was that of Daniel Nunez, who turned up in Lewes, Delaware, intermarried, and founded a prominent family there during the eighteenth century. Its many members are buried in the church-yard of St. Peter's Episcopal Church. A son, Daniel Nunez, Jr., was sheriff of Sussex County and member of the county's Committee of Thirteen in 1774, even before the Revolution started. Its object was to rally local support for Boston's early resistance to England.[31]

Only where the Jews were clustered together in a few central communities such as Philadelphia or New York were the conditions favorable to survival and the preservation of a Jewish community life and religion. Even here intermarriage was not infrequent, and prominent families such as the Frankses and the Levys were lost through intermarriage in the very midst of Revolutionary Philadelphia where the Jews were numerous and had a thriving community and synagogue. The recognition and mention of such doubtful Jews is appropriate chiefly because they illustrate this important aspect of Jewish life in early America. Here was a kind of continuous drain upon the Jewish population, which was renewed only by increased immigration more than a half-century after the Revolution.

4

Other Military Contributions

Thus far the Jews who attained relatively high rank and made individually notable contributions to the military record of the Revolution have been dealt with in some detail. The very abundance of documentation marks them as important figures in that war. There were, however, many others, some no more than names in military rosters. One may begin with the numerically impressive situation in Charleston. Here virtually all of the available Jewish men enlisted in military service. The principal factor was the sharp, sudden impact of the war in the form of the siege, capture, and occupation of the city by the British by 1780. No other city, except Savannah, experienced the war so violently, and nowhere else was the whole population summoned to the city's defense.

To introduce this episode we turn to a remarkable narrative by a participant, Jacob I. Cohen, who later became one of the founders and leaders of the Jewish community in Richmond. In 1822, when Cohen was eighty-seven years old, he related it to his nephew, Dr. Joshua Cohen, and it was preserved by Colonel Mendes Cohen, another member of the same distinguished family. Included with the narrative was a copy of Cohen's enlistment certification, as well as a commendation by Captain Lushington for Cohen's behavior, stating that he had "in every respect conducted himself as a good soldier and a man of courage" at the Battle of Beaufort. Cohen's account referred to a "Jew Company" under Captain Richard Lushington, which enrolled many of the Jews living on King Street in Charleston. There were between twenty-six and twenty-eight Jews in it, and Jacob Cohen himself recalled and listed some fifteen names. Among those given were Samuel Jones; Abraham Seixas, brother of Rev. Gershom M.

Seixas of New York; Nathan Phillips, Cohen's business partner; Isaiah Isaacs, who later helped to found Beth Shalome synagogue in Richmond; and Solomon the Chasan. Rev. Barnet Elzas, a century later the rabbi and historian of Charleston's Jews, recorded that thirty-four Jews served as soldiers in South Carolina beginning with Francis Salvador. He concluded that the Jews gave proportionately as many as their neighbors and contributed "as freely of their means to the cause. Is it not enough?" He rejected, however, as mythical the "Jews' Company" of Charleston, although he listed some twenty odd Jews in it.[1]

Beaufort, scene of the first battle in which the Jews of Charleston participated in 1779, involved a strange and accidental confrontation of forces. It occurred in February 1779, when General Moultrie's force came upon the British, "this side of Half-Way House on Beaufort Island on February 3." Colonel Maitland, the British commander, sent a flag of truce to Major Huger. He said it "was not their wish to engage in battle with citizens, men unaccustomed to war, that their object was a meeting place for their soldiers, and that if the American commander would withdraw he will pass on." If the American did not consent to this, he should fire a gun "as a signal of his willingness to engage in battle." General Moultrie harangued his men and "begged of them not to lay down their arms like cowards, but to consider the cause they were engaged in." Battle was then joined and was fought for an hour and forty-five minutes. Moultrie rallied his men, and at daylight the British left in their ships. Jacob Cohen reported that a Moses Cohen was killed and Ephraim Abrams was wounded in the battle. Moses Cohen is known, however, to have survived until 1789, and Elzas reported that Joseph Solomon was the one killed.[2]

Lushington's company, which fought in the Battle of Beaufort, was part of the Charleston Militia Regiment, known as the "Free Citizens." It was the only instance of a group mobilization of Jews in one city and into one company. This contingent was also part of General Benjamin Lincoln's force that attempted to recapture Savannah late in 1779, in conjunction with a combined French fleet and army, for which Philip Minis and Levi Sheftall provided guidance. Lushington's company was finally involved in the British siege of Charleston in 1780, which lasted two months and which ended with the surrender of Charleston and General Lincoln's entire army. It was one of the most disastrous events for the American side in the whole war. In this siege Rachel Moses, youngest daughter of Myer Moses, was killed by a cannonball; she was apparently the only Jewish female casualty of the Revolution. Many Jews were among the prisoners taken at Charleston, some originally refugees from Savannah. They included the Sheftalls, father and son; Philip Minis; David Sarzedas, a lieutenant in the Light Dragoons of Georgia; and Abraham Seixas, also a lieutenant in the Georgia Brigade. Those from Charleston were David Nunez Cardozo, a first sergeant in the Grenadier Corps; Jacob I. Cohen; and many others. Some of them had been in the assault of the "Forlorn Hope" on the British lines at Savannah the year before. Cardozo had been severely wounded in the leg there. He was one of three brothers who served in the Revolution; the others were Isaac and Daniel W. Cardozo.[3]

Another Jew in Charleston's military mobilization was Abraham Alexander, English-born, who was *hazzan* of the congregation there for many years. He was a lieutenant in Colonel Wade Hampton's Regiment of Light Dragoons. A Captain Jacob de Leon, also from Charleston, took part in the battle of Camden, South Carolina, and was reputed to be on General DeKalb's staff when the latter was killed there. Samuel Mordecai was described by his son-in-law, the famous publicist Isaac Harby, as a brave grenadier of South Carolina who "fought and bled for the liberty he lived to enjoy." Joseph Israel of Charleston was engaged in the defense of the upper Savannah River line against British invasion. Samuel Mendes Marks served in a South Carolina unit and was described as "a Revolutionary patriot of great wealth," who came from the Danish West Indies and was married to a Charleston woman, Sarah Harris, of Portuguese Jewish origin. Another Jewish officer was Major Myer Myers, who served with General Sumter and was present at the surrender of Cornwallis at Yorktown. His house was burned and his plantation pillaged by Tories. Jacob Tobias was in the South Carolina militia but died prematurely in 1775. Jacob Phillips also served in the militia and was later paid nearly seven pounds by an indent of 1785. Altogether thirty-four Jews from both South Carolina and

Georgia served in the Revolutionary War, and some twenty of them were in Captain Lushington's company of Charleston.[4]

The surrender of Charleston in 1780, following the loss of Savannah the year before, marked a low point in the Revolution in the South and in the country generally. During the long siege of Charleston, many of its residents petitioned General Lincoln that further resistance was hopeless and urged surrender. Among the signers were a number of Jews, both civilians and soldiers. After the capture, the population was faced with the necessity of accommodating themselves to British occupation and accepting their role. Known as "addressers," these included Abraham Alexander and Levi Sheftall, who had escaped from Savannah the year before. Others who had served in the Revolutionary forces and now submitted to British authority in Charleston were Emanuel Abraham, Gershon Cohen, and Jacob Jacobs. After the war, some Jews who had remained in Charleston during the British occupation were examined by a committee of patriots and were acquitted of disloyalty or collaboration with the enemy. In his testimony, General Sumter lauded Myer Moses for his care of the wounded prisoners. Jacob Jacobs and Gershon Cohen seemingly commanded confidence and vouched for the conduct of a number of other Jews.[5]

On the other hand, other Jews were banished from Charleston as "disaffected to the British government." Such were Isaac da Costa and Abraham Seixas, a brother of Rev. Gershom Seixas. They found refuge in Philadelphia, the gathering place of many of these refugees. After the Revolution many returned to Charleston and resumed their business. The Jewish community of Charleston prospered and grew considerably after the Revolution. The congregation of Beth Elohim built and dedicated a new synagogue in 1794, and General, now Governor, Moultrie attended the dedication ceremony. *The South Carolina Gazette* boasted that the Jews "are here admitted to full privileges of citizenship, and bid fair to flourish and be happy."[6] By 1810 the Jewish population of South Carolina was approximately 1,000, of whom more than half (some 600 or 700) lived in Charleston, and the rest in other towns, such as Georgetown and Camden. For a time Charleston had the largest Jewish population in the country, and it produced such notable leaders in religious and social life as Isaac Harby, the publicist and founder of the Reformed Society of Israelites, and Penina Moïse, the religious poetess and educator, who ranks close to Rebecca Gratz, her contemporary in Philadelphia, as an outstanding Jewish woman.[7]

Virginia, which, unlike South Carolina, had few Jews before the Revolution, nevertheless recorded several Jewish soldiers. Mordecai Abrahams (or Abrams) commanded a company of militia of German origin in Virginia. He was married to a Sarah Levy, and both came from Europe. This was attested to by their descendants, Miss Lily Abrahams and Mrs. Ida Cobb, when they applied for membership in the Daughters of the American Revolution more than a century later.[8] More unusual was the case of Isaac Levy (Levi), who was born in Hungary and came to America at seventeen years of age, according to his pension application in 1832. He claimed to have enlisted in Lexington, Virginia, and served with the forces of General George Rogers Clark in the western campaign for the conquest of Vincennes. He subsequently lived in Kentucky, Ohio, and Indiana, where he died in 1850, over one hundred years old. He pleaded indigence in his application for a Revolutionary pension in his old age.[9] A Judas Levi was for two years a private in Captain Howard's company of Colonel Buford's Virginia Regiment and was wounded in the battle of Waxhaws, North Carolina. A marriage to Mary McGraw suggests a probable estrangement from Judaism, if indeed there had ever been any identification, but Mary bore a daughter named Rebecca.[10] An Ezekiel Levy may have been one or three separate soldiers. Three different men of this name lived in Philadelphia, Charleston, and Virginia, respectively, during the war period. In Charleston he was with Lushington's "Jew Company" at the Battle of Beaufort in 1779. He also served in Virginia and ended his career as a converted Episcopalian and vestryman at Williamsburg, Virginia.[11]

A more authentic case was that of Jacob Cohen, who was captain of a cavalry company in the continental line of Virginia and was at the Battle of Yorktown in 1781, as attested to by Lafayette. He was a silversmith who died at Alexandria, Virginia, in 1798. He, too, intermarried, and his four children, led by a son William, for many years pursued claims for compensation both in the Virginia legislature and in the United States Congress. The younger Cohen presented many affidavits in support of his father's military service, including a letter from General Lafayette in 1832, recalling that he had known a Captain Cohen in a Virginia unit when he commanded a division there. A congressional committee later reviewed and rejected the claim for want of evidence, suggesting that he may have served in the Virginia militia rather than the continental line. Virginia did allow a grant of four thousand acres of bounty land to his descendants in 1838.[12]

Moses Myers, born in New York in 1752, the son of Hyam Myers, became a major in the Virginia militia, the highest rank attained by a Jew in that state. He served with General Sumter and was present at Yorktown. Samuel Myers, the son of Myer Myers, the famous New York silversmith, also served in a Virginia unit during the Revolution. Both men became partners, with Isaac Moses of Philadelphia, in a large mercantile firm in Richmond after the Revolution. Moses recommended Samuel Myers to be consul in Amsterdam after the Revolution. Both lived in various places in Virginia thereafter; Moses Myers finally settled in Norfolk, where he was elected president of the city council, and Samuel resided in Richmond, where he served as an alderman.[13]

Michael Israel resided in Albemarle County, Virginia, where he fought the Indians as early as 1758 and enlisted in the militia during the Revolution. One son, Joseph Israel, married a Quaker and served in the Delaware militia; another son, Israel Israel, was captured by the British in Philadelphia. In later life, Israel Israel was a tavernkeeper in Philadelphia and high sheriff there. He was active in Democratic politics and had apparently become a Christian.[14]

The Historical Register of Virginians in the Revolution, moreover, lists several other Levys or Levis, named Abraham, Isaac, Jacob, Judah, and Solomon, but without further identification. It is unlikely that they were all Jews. Jews apparently migrated into Virginia during the Revolution, among them for a time Simon Nathan and Michael Gratz.[15] An unusual sidelight on the Revolution in Virginia is supplied by Dr. John de Sequeyra of Williamsburg. Born in London of a Portuguese Jewish family, he was trained as a doctor at Leyden in Holland and emigrated to Williamsburg in 1745. Here he practiced medicine for half a century, dying in 1795. He was too old to participate actively in the Revolution, but he kept a diary reporting diseases prevalent in Virginia for many years. It is interesting to note that for 1781, the year of the great victory of Yorktown, de Sequeyra recorded the serious spread of smallpox brought by the British army, from which many died.[16]

Other states, such as North Carolina, Delaware, Maryland, and New Jersey, as well as northern New England, had few Jews during the war period. Nevertheless, there is evidence of a number of them serving from those states, which may indicate the extent of their migration and mobility in this period. Such mobility eventually led to the creation of new Jewish communities at various points on the eastern seaboard. Thus a Jacob Franks is reported as a patrolman in North Carolina's Wake County, which must have had military significance, since he subsequently received a land grant as a reward for his services. Lazarus Solomon was also a private in the North Carolina militia. Aside from his name, there is no evidence that he was Jewish. An applicant for membership in the Daughters of the American Revolution in his name a century later, a Mrs. Wilmer Solomon Boswell, stated that she was a descendant of his marriage with Elizabeth Bedgood. Elijah Isaacs was authorized payment in 1782 for his services, which included a period of captivity, by the auditors of the District of Salisbury in North Carolina. There were others, with Jewish-sounding names but no evidence of Jewish origin or affiliation, who appear in the North Carolina records as soldiers. These were Abraham Moses, Isaac Sampson, and Moses Stern. They compound the serious problem of Jewish identification in the period, as already abundantly indicated.[17]

Maryland provided examples of more conspicuous and identifiable Jews who served in various military capacities. There was Reuben Etting, son of Asher Etting. He came from the interior of Pennsylvania and became a clerk in Baltimore. He was only nineteen years old at the start of the Revolution, when he enlisted in the Maryland militia. He was captured by the British at Charleston in 1780. According to tradition, he refused to eat pork, the only meat offered him in captivity. He suffered from malnutrition and was afflicted with tuberculosis, from which he died prematurely. Another Reuben Etting, from a different branch of the family, residing in the interior of Pennsylvania, also found his way to Maryland and enlisted in the militia there. He lived to become prominent in the affairs of the nation as well as Baltimore Jewry. His brother, Solomon, was a leader in the long political struggle in Maryland for the abolition of religious test oaths and the adoption of the so-called Jew Bill in 1826, which opened public office to Jews. Solomon Etting was promptly elected to the Baltimore City Council and became its president.[18]

Nathaniel Levy, also of Baltimore, served under Lafayette in the First Baltimore Cavalry Regiment. Four other Levys, David, Jacob, Nicholas, and Samuel, are listed in the muster rolls of Maryland troops as members of the First German Battalion of the Continental line. Whether they were Jewish is not known. Presumably they knew German, in order to serve in that unit.[19] The most unusual account of a Jewish soldier in Maryland is that of Elias Polock, who served under the alias of Joseph Smith for an unknown reason. The strange story was revealed many years later, when Polock (alias Smith) applied for a pension in 1818. He was then indigent, and his affidavit narrated his circumstances in detail. He signed it in Hebrew characters as Elias Polock. He told how he had enlisted early in the Revolution as Joseph Smith. In 1778 he was a private in Captain Joseph Marbury's company of the Third Maryland Regiment commanded by Colonel Mordecai Gist. A supporting affidavit by a former comrade, John Williams, related how they marched to Philadelphia and joined the Northern Army, with which they served until 1780. They then marched southward under General Smallwood, but were separated and did not meet again until 1786 in Baltimore. Polock's own account mentions several actions in which he took part on the Hudson River and the winter he spent at Morristown, New Jersey. In 1780 he went south, was wounded and taken prisoner at Camden, South Carolina. He was sent to St. Augustine, Florida, for internment, and from there to Halifax, Nova Scotia. Here he was liberated at the end of the war and returned to Baltimore. Altogether it was a notable war record, worthy of a veteran, who also happened to be a Jew, although one of modest and inconspicuous standing.[20]

The Delaware Military Lists record Moses Levy and Joseph Israel, both reported as delinquents who left their military units without permission. A Moses and Samson Levy took oaths of fidelity to Delaware in 1778, although there is no evidence of their actual service. Delaware was also the seat of an unusual case affecting two brothers, Israel and Joseph Israel. Both were the sons of Michael Israel, who fought in the Virginia militia during the Revolution but finally settled in Philadelphia. Children of a mixed marriage, they were brought up as Christians, and Joseph Israel married a Quaker woman from Wilmington. Joseph Israel was listed in the Delaware militia. During the British occupation of Philadelphia, the two brothers went there secretly to visit their mother and barely escaped being captured by the British, especially since Israel was in uniform. Joseph Israel returned to his Delaware farm, was taken prisoner, placed aboard a British frigate, and examined for his views. His heroic Quaker wife defended their home against marauders. Israel finally obtained his freedom when he gave a Masonic sign to the British officer questioning him. After the Revolution Israel Israel earned his livelihood as a tavernkeeper and later as high sheriff of Philadelphia. In episodes such as this one may discover the prosaic happenings that often have their own dramatic character. They reveal the inescapable involvement of simple, ordinary people, Jewish and other, in a war that was at once a Revolution and a civil conflict, and hence reached into every part of the country.[21]

New Jersey had few Jewish soldiers, but one was especially noteworthy. Asser Levy was an ensign in the First New Jersey Regiment of the Continental line. He was a namesake of the Asser Levy who was in the first group of Jews to arrive in 1654 at New York, then still the Dutch settlement of New Amsterdam. The younger Levy was probably a collateral descendant of the first one. Asser Levy, although only an ensign, was a witness in the court-martial set up by General Washington for his regimental commander, Colonel Ogden, who was accused of improper conduct. An Isaac Lopez, possibly a New Yorker, enlisted in 1777 in the Fifth Regiment of the New Jersey line. In 1818 Lopez, a pension applicant, submitted affidavits that vouched for his indigence as well as for his part in the battles of Brandywine and Germantown.[22]

Jewish military participation in the Revolution in the North was in sharp contrast with their role in the South. In the South the Jews lived primarily in Charleston and Savannah. Both of these cities were directly affected by war and were under British occupation during the later years of the Revolution. Here mobilization was virtually complete in the emergency and included many of the Jews as well. The Jews fought actively here, and many were taken prisoner by the British, as has been narrated elsewhere. In the North, however, the zone of war was more widely dispersed, and there was less activity during much of the time. Jews enlisted individually rather than collectively. Since they lived principally in Philadelphia, many enrolled in the local militia, which saw only occasional action. The ordinary Jewish foot soldiers were obscure participants in the conflict. Their total influence was neither as impressive nor as significant as that of the Southern Jews, and even their number may not have been as great.

Pennsylvania had the largest list of Jewish soldiers. Many came originally from other places and were in a sense refugees. An unusual case was that of Abram Mordecai, born in Pennsylvania of a Jewish father and German mother. He served for three years in the Revolutionary War and took part in many of the local engagements. After the war he migrated to the Georgia frontier and became a trader among the Creek Indians. He believed that the Indians were related to the Jews, a not uncommon concept, which linked them with the Lost Ten Tribes of Israel. He claimed to have discovered Hebrew words used in Indian rites. He even married an Indian woman. He is supposed to have introduced the cotton gin for use by Indian cotton growers in Alabama, where he later settled. He fought in the War of 1812 and lived into his nineties. In his old age he became something of a hermit. Known as "Old Mordecai," he lived his last years near Montgomery, Alabama. His life and work are more closely related to the American scene as it expanded after the Revolution than to his earlier Jewish background, which faded away perhaps as a result of the Revolution and the opportunities it created.[23]

In contrast to Mordecai was Moses Levy, born in Philadelphia and a graduate of the University of Pennsylvania in 1772. He was admitted to the bar in 1778, probably the first Jew to attain professional standing in America. Levy was in the Continental Army and served with Washington in the battles of Princeton and Trenton. After the war he became a lawyer, served as Recorder of Philadelphia for many years, and subsequently was appointed as a judge in the county court. Although a strong Federalist politically, he was considered by President Jefferson for appointment as Attorney-General. The scion of a mixed marriage, he married Maria Pearce and became an Episcopalian. He was buried in St. Peter's Cemetery beside his father and mother.[24]

A similar offspring of intermarriage was Jacob Mordecai, the son of Moses Mordecai and Elizabeth Whitlock, who, however, converted to Judaism under the name of Esther. Jacob was only twelve years old in 1774 and a student at the school of Captain Jacob Stiles when the First Continental Congress met in Philadelphia. In his reminiscences he recalled how the schoolboys were organized into companies, wearing uniforms, "distinguished by different colors, armed with guns, and trained to military exercises." Imbued with the new patriotism, they marched to Frankford, several miles from Philadelphia, in September 1774, "for the purpose of escorting the delegates to town. . . . The road was lined with people, and resounded with huzzas, drums, etc., and exhibited a lively scene. In the humble office of sergeant I had thus the honor of escorting into Philadelphia the first American Congress."

There is no record of Mordecai's further military service during the Revolution, but in 1784 he became briefly the partner of Haym Salomon in a business venture set up in New York, which ended abortively when Salomon died prematurely. Mordecai's later life and career were quite unusual. In Richmond he was a successful merchant and served as president of its congregation. He then established a female seminary at Warrenton in North Carolina, which he headed for a number of years. He married, successively, two daughters of Myer Myers, the famous silversmith, and fathered a remarkable family. His son, named Alfred Mordecai, was later a colonel, serving as a military engineer and noted expert in ordnance. He had a son, also named Alfred, who became a military engineer and equally expert in ordnance. He later reached the rank of general. Spanning almost a century, the Mordecais were the first professional military family of Jewish origin in the American army.[25]

In contrast to the patriotic schoolboy, Jacob Mordecai, there was Hayman Levy, who was already fifty-five when he left New York for Philadelphia in 1776. Despite his age, he enlisted as a private in Captain Adam Foulk's company of the Fourth Battalion of Pennsylvania militia. His son-in-law, Isaac Moses, also was in the same company. Both were actively engaged in wartime business enterprise, particularly Isaac Moses, who was busy with privateering ventures. After the war, both returned to New York and resumed their mercantile career there. They joined in an address of welcome to Governor George Clinton: "Though the society we belong to is but small . . . yet we flatter ourselves that none has manifested a more zealous attachment to the Sacred Cause of America, in the late war with Britain." They pledged their allegiance to the new Constitution of New York, "wisely framed to preserve the blessings of civil and religious liberty." They also urged the confiscation of Tory land, of which they acquired substantial amounts in New York.[26]

A similar story is that of Eleazer Levy, originally from New York, who, like many others, left that city for Philadelphia, "from Principles repugnant to British Hostilities." The son of Hayman Levy, who also served in the Philadelphia militia, as indicated, he was a private in Captain Samuel McLean's company, First Battalion of Pennsylvania militia. Levy's case has special interest because in 1779 he addressed a petition to the Continental Congress, in which he claimed to hold a mortgage on the West Point site, then occupied by the principal American forces in the North. The military use of the land, particularly its deforestation, had reduced its value and hence that of the mortgage of one thousand pounds he held on it. In 1783 he again petitioned Congress, complaining of the injustice of having been paid on his mortgage in currency at the rate of forty to one. In depreciated currency he had received the equivalent of thirty-seven pounds, although he had once valued the mortgage with interest at fifteen hundred pounds. After seven years in Philadelphia, Levy, now "in his eve of life" and back in New York, stated that he was "reduced from a comfortable subsistence to a state of poverty and wretchedness."

The Congressional Committee of the Week rejected the petition "as not expedient for Congress to take any other therein." Congress failed to recognize similar claims in other cases affecting Jews, as well as others. It appeared to corroborate the fact that this was not, on the whole, a profitable war, certainly as indicated by the number of such claims, as well as the distress and insolvency that accompanied the Revolution. To acknowledge such petitions favorably was beyond the economic capacity and legal liability of Congress. In Levy's case a long twilight of "poverty and wretchedness" followed in his last years. In 1803 he petitioned the Jewish community of New York for aid, and relief was granted to him and an infirm wife.[27]

Four others may be added to the roll of Jewish soldiers in Pennsylvania, although their service may not have been exclusively in this state. One was Joseph Nathan, whose wife, Jane, was a convert to Judaism. Benjamin Joel was another, but he also was living in New York by 1790. Solomon Isaacs was a private in Captain Lewis Bush's company of Colonel Irvine's Pennsylvania Regiment. Solomon Aaron was the proverbial wandering Jew, who served first in the Philadelphia militia and then found his way to Charleston, where he was in Captain Lushington's "Jew Company." Strangely, he took a Loyalist oath there in 1780, on the British capture of Charleston, but was back in Philadelphia by 1782, apparently restored to favor.[28]

Of special interest, among those clearly identified as Jews who made significant contributions to the war effort, was Philip Moses Russell. A Philadelphian by birth, he enlisted as a surgeon's mate in 1777, although there is no evidence of any medical training. He was present at the Battle of Brandywine and spent the winter of 1777-1778 at Valley Forge amid all its hardships. Exhaustion and an attack of camp fever affected his sight and hearing. Attached to the Second Virginia Regiment, he was forced to leave service in 1780, and he received a special commendation from General Washington "for his assiduous and faithful attention to the sick and wounded, as well as his cool and collected deportment in battle." For a time after the war Russell lived in Virginia, but he returned to Philadelphia and died there. He apparently sold drugs and practiced medicine, but did not prosper. Indigent in his old age, he applied for and received a pension under the first Pension Act of 1818. His case became almost a *cause célèbre*, because his widow and son, who was a lawyer, pursued the pension issue for many years, even to a successful appeal for congressional legislation. The documents in this case reveal Russell's record in full detail, and will be related elsewhere in another connection.[29]

Bearing a name subsequently made famous by his son, Mordecai Manuel Noah, Manuel Noah had an exceptional life of his own. German-born, he was a merchant in Philadelphia during the Revolution. He was also a private in Captain Thomas Willis' company of the First Battalion of Pennsylvania militia. After the war he married Zipporah, daughter of Jonas Phillips, who was a prominent merchant and member of the Jewish community both in New York and in Philadelphia. Tradition has it that General Washington attended the wedding. After the war Noah lived in Charleston, where his young wife died, and his son, Mordecai, was brought up by the grandfather, Jonas Phillips. The elder Noah did not prosper and, indeed, disappeared from the scene. According to family tradition, which has no factual basis, young Noah discovered his father many years later in Paris, dressed in an "old-style revolutionary uniform." He died in his son's house in New York in 1822. The son was by then launched on an exciting and diversified career of his own, which reached out into many directions and will be dealt with elsewhere. He was perhaps the most colorful and venturesome Jew of the time in America.[30]

Jonas Phillips, the grandfather of both M. M. Noah and Uriah P. Levy, was already a prominent figure in the Jewish community of New York at the outset of the Revolution. He moved to Philadelphia during the British occupation of New York and established himself as a merchant. He also enlisted as a private in the Philadelphia militia under Captain John Linton. After a brief return to New York following the Revolution, he had a dispute with the congregation there and came back to Philadelphia. Here he died in 1803 but was buried in the Chatham Street Cemetery in New York City.[31] His is one of eighteen graves in the New York cemetery that are marked as those of Revolutionary patriots. They are marked by the Daughters of the American Revolution and are decorated on every Memorial Day by the Asser Levy

Garrison of the Army and Navy Union. Shearith Israel congregation in New York has listed twenty-two of its members as Revolutionary soldiers, several of whom are buried in other cemeteries. Many of them actually served in Philadelphia, where they were refugees. It is not always clear what their military role was; probably it was primarily in the local militia. Its chief importance lies in the testimony it bears to an extensive Jewish participation in the Revolution in the North.[32]

Among the other patriots buried in New York (their home city, even though their military activity was in Pennsylvania or elsewhere) were Solomon Myers, Daniel Gomez, Ephraim Hart, Benjamin Jacobs, Abraham Judah, a private in the Philadelphia militia at sixty-one, Moses Judah, Eleazer and Hayman Levy, Isaac Moses, Simon Nathan, and Manuel Noah (some of them already named previously). These are some of the most distinguished names of Jews in Revolutionary America. They were perhaps more important for their business and community accomplishments than for their military achievements. Nevertheless, this military record was appreciable and noteworthy.

Several others are listed as associators, who rallied early to the military call of Pennsylvania. Joshua Isaacs, also of New York, turned up in Lancaster in 1781, where he took an oath of allegiance and fidelity and was enrolled in Captain Joseph Hubley's Third Company of the Eighth Lancaster Militia Battalion. Joseph Nathan, originally from New York, turned up as a private in the militia of Northampton County, in the interior of Pennsylvania. Michael Hart, known as "the stuttering Jew" at Easton, was a corporal in the same militia.[33] Included among the patriots' graves in New York was that of a third lieutenant in the Fusiliers' Company of the First Battalion of the New York militia. He was Benjamin Mendes Seixas, a brother of the Reverend Gershom Seixas, both of whom lived as refugees in Connecticut during part of the Revolution. A third brother was Abraham Seixas, who was an officer in South Carolina. Among the soldiers buried in New York an unusual case was that of David Nunez Cardozo, who served in Charleston but died in New York. He was one of three brothers who fought in Charleston during the Revolution.[34]

One of the most notable Jewish refugees from New York was Manuel Josephson, who played an important business role in wartime Philadelphia and had dealings with Robert Morris, Superintendent of Finance, in whose diary he appears. By his own account he fled across New York Bay in July 1776 in a leaky boat. He supplied information to the Americans about the enemy on Long Island, where he was a prisoner. There were some seven thousand British troops there, all from Boston, and "they appeared rather afraid that our people would set the town on fire." Josephson reported that a considerable number of Tories had joined them from the mainland, and he identified Messrs. Apthorp, DeLancey, Bayard, Barbarie, and Lawrence among them.[35]

New York as a whole was sharply divided in its loyalties, and the conflict on Long Island and in the Hudson Valley took on a violent character of civil war. This division affected even the Jews in New York, among whom were a substantial number of Loyalists (to be discussed in a later chapter). One of the most conspicuous examples was Barrack Hays, who had earlier been a second lieutenant in the New York militia, but then became an "officer of guides" in the Loyalist forces. He later claimed compensation from the British for his services. His kinsmen, the brothers David and Michael Hays, were patriots, living in Westchester County. Both were farmers, and David also had a store in Bedford. At one time David Hays was away driving cattle to the American army when a band of Tories, searching for him, attacked and burned his house. His wife, Esther Etting, barely escaped with a newborn baby, with the assistance of a Negro slave. Michael, David's brother, was also driven from his farm by Tories, but returned to it in 1782. The Hays family later played an important role in New York public affairs. One of David's sons, Jacob, was for many years High Constable of New York City, equivalent to the chief of police. He intermarried and founded a Christian branch of the family. Benjamin, the newborn baby saved from the burning home in 1779, followed in his father's footsteps as a farmer. At the time of his death in 1858, he was described as the "last Jewish farmer in the United States" and was known as "Uncle Ben the Jew, the best Christian in Westchester County."[36]

An interesting item is recorded in the minutes of the New York Committee of Safety early in 1776. Hart Jacobs was reported to be waiting "at the door." He wished to be excused from military patrol on Friday nights for religous reasons, "to be subject, nevertheless, to the performance of his full time tour of duty on other nights."[37] Isaac Marks was a private in the New York militia who later settled in Charleston. W. T. R. Saffel's *Records of the Revolutionary War* lists several Jews as members of New York military units. Isaac Samson was in the second company of a regiment commanded by Colonel Lewis Dubois, and Moses Samson was in Colonel John Lamb's Artillery Regiment of New York. Aaron Isaac, Sr. and Jr., father and son, living in East-hampton, on Long Island, were on the roll of associators and in the New York militia, but had ceased to be Jews. One of their descendants was John Howard Payne, the author and composer of "Home, Sweet Home." Jacob Levy, a weaver of Rhinebeck, was reported in 1780 to be improperly absent from the Second New York Regiment commanded by Colonel Philip Cortland.[38]

Nearby Connecticut had few Jews prior to the Revolution but acquired a substantial number of refugees from New York and Newport who were scattered in various towns. Their leader was Rev. Gershom Mendes Seixas, the *hazzan* of Shearith Israel in New York, who led an exodus to Connecticut. He carried the scrolls and other sacred objects with him to Stratford, where he lived until 1780, when he moved on to Philadelphia. Here he served as minister of Mikveh Israel during the period of its wartime growth, and he even presided over the construction of a new synagogue. He returned to New York in 1784, in an exchange with Rev. Jacob Raphael Cohen, formerly of Montreal and New York. As the first native-born minister, Seixas introduced English sermons into the service and was an outspoken advocate of the American cause. On one occasion he prayed for peace and victory for the American army: "May the supreme King of Kings through his infinite mercies save and prosper the men of these United States, who had gone forth to war. . . ."[39]

Among those whom the Revolution brought to Connecticut was the father of Rev. Gershom Seixas, Isaac Mendes, from Newport, who likewise settled in Stratford. There were also Joseph Simson and his sons, Solomon and Samson, in Wilton and

Norwalk. Samson Mears and his family lived in Norwalk. Two of his daughters married the brothers Myer and Asher Myers, noted silversmith and copper brazier, respectively. Myer Myers was considered for appointment as reducer of lead for bullets to supply Connecticut soldiers at two hundred pounds per year. Samson Mears carried on an extensive business as an agent for Aaron Lopez, then living in Leicester, Massachusetts. A British raid on Norwalk in 1779 did considerable damage. Seven or eight Jews were among those who received tax abatements in compensation for losses suffered. Samson Mears also expressed gratitude to Aaron Lopez for help he extended to those Jews. Solomon Mears, who may have been related to Samson, but apparently was not Jewish, was a lieutenant in a company of the Connecticut line. Together with David S. Franks and Solomon Pinto, both officers equally estranged from Judaism, he was a charter member of the Society of the Cincinnati, an association of veteran officers founded after the Revolution under Washington's leadership.[40]

Of established families in Connecticut, the best known and most active during the Revolution were the Pintos. There were Pintos in Stratford as early as 1725, and they later lived in New Haven. Other Pintos were prominent both in mercantile and Jewish affairs in New York. Jacob Pinto, who lived in New Haven and was a member of a patriotic committee, was the father of three sons, Abraham, William, and Solomon, all of whom served in the Revolution. All three attended Yale College, from which two, Solomon and William, were graduated. They were known to Rev. Ezra Stiles, later president of the college, who stated that they had "renounced Judaism and all religion," by which he probably meant that they were rationalists. William, while still at Yale, made neat copies of the Declaration of Independence for Governor Trumbull of Connecticut and President Daggett of Yale. All the brothers were enrolled in the force that resisted the British attack on New Haven in July 1779. Abraham was wounded in this encounter, and Solomon was taken prisoner but was released shortly thereafter. In 1780 Solomon became an ensign in the Seventh and later in the Second Regiment of the Connecticut line and served in the Hudson Highlands until the end of the war. Despite his college education and his charter membership in the prestigious Society of the Cincinnati, Solomon did not prosper. In his old age he pleaded indigence and insolvency, and he received a pension under the Pension Act of 1818.[41]

Another old established family in Connecticut was that of the Judahs, who lived in Norwalk. Michael Judah had intermarried with Martha Raymond, and one of their offspring was David, who was, however, circumcised as a Jew. During the Revolution he served in Captain Gregory's company of the Connecticut line. Somewhat surprisingly, the father returned to New York and died there in 1786. He left his entire estate to the Jews of New York, half to the synagogue and half to widows and orphans. A bequest of only five pounds went to his son, David. Other isolated Jewish families living in Connecticut were the Trubees of Fairfield and the Markses of Derby. Mordecai Marks became an Episcopalian. His sons were named Mordecai, Nehemiah, and Abraham; two served in the military forces of Connecticut during the Revolution, whereas Nehemiah was a Tory.[42] Still another Connecticut family, the Isaacs, were described as of "Jewish extraction." There were two brothers, both Episcopalian and graduates of Yale College. The older, Isaac Isaacs, was an officer during the French and Indian War. His brother, Ralph, a Tory, was a merchant and shipowner in New Haven, whose loyalty was suspect, and who was detained by the state's authority for a time.[43]

The *Record of Connecticut Men in the Military and Naval Service in the Revolution* lists Aaron and Levi Hart and an Isaac Isaacs as enlisted men. No other information is, however, available about these possible Jews. Few authenticated Jews are known to have lived in New England at the time of the Revolution, outside of Newport, Rhode Island, and several towns in Connecticut. A few questionable ones, however, appear in the record. In New Hampshire, one Benjamin Hart was reported to have been a rope manufacturer in Portsmouth. A Loyalist, he left for Newport, where he may have been related to other Jewish Loyalists of the same name. Asher Polock of Newport served for six years in a Rhode Island regiment, although others of his family were Loyalists. Samuel Benjamin, also of Newport, was a lieutenant in the Eighth Massachusetts Regiment, but there is no evidence that he was a Jew. It will be recalled that Isaac Franks of Philadelphia was an ensign in a Massachusetts regiment. Solomon Rophee and

Moses and Abraham Isaacs were also enlisted in Massachusetts military units, Rophee as an officer. An unusual case was that of Abraham Solomon, reported to be from Marblehead, near Boston. He was referred to as a Jew, although married to a Christian woman, and he signed the muster roll in Hebrew characters. He was in the army assembled at Cambridge as early as 1775 and may have taken part in the Battle of Bunker Hill. Out of the army by 1778, he acquired an unsavory reputation. He was arrested in Boston for speculation in paper currency and was subsequently found guilty of uttering "malicious, seditious expressions in favor of the present King of Great Britain and against all true friends of America."[44]

In summary, it may be estimated that the number of Jews engaged in some kind of military service during the Revolution approached one hundred persons, more or less. If the Jewish population at the time is estimated at 2,500 persons, something like 4 percent of this group served in a military force, or perhaps twice as much, if exception is made for women. The centers of greatest involvement were, as indicated, Pennsylvania, Georgia, and South Carolina, with smaller numbers outward from these areas. This corresponded fairly closely to the distribution of the Jewish population in colonial America, except for New York, which was under British occupation during most of the war and had lost much of its Jewish community. The Jewish military personnel were of all ranks, from private to colonel, and their activity ranged widely from active combat to little more than affiliation with the local militia. It corresponded closely with the general pattern of military activity during the war. The Jews in military service came from the various elements constituting the total population, from the wealthy and prominent to the humble and obscure, who left little more than their name in the record; some may not even have done that. The noteworthy fact is that, perhaps because this was an unusual war of Revolution, military service by Jews in America had become a general and even expected phenomenon and obligation for the first time in Western history.[45]

The Jewish soldiers differed in degree of Jewish identity, from native members of the several Jewish congregations to those who had intermarried or were the offspring of intermarriage and had lost all Jewish identification, to the point of being Christian. Whether the last should be included here is problematic, except to make the record complete. The sum total of Jewish military contributions to the Revolution is not easy to calculate, since it entailed qualitative as well as quantitative factors. No reduction to a common denominator is possible. A few Jews had staff roles of some importance, but the rest served in the ranks. Many of the Jews in the Revolutionary era were of foreign birth or origin. They came from a diversity of sources, among them Portuguese, Dutch, German, and Polish, although a large number came to America by way of England, often from Germany and Holland. Their background was thus varied. For example, Aaron Lopez was born in Portugal, Jonas Phillips was German-born, Francis Salvador was born in England of Portuguese origin, and Haym Salomon was of Polish birth, to mention only a few conspicuous examples. The offspring of this Revolutionary population made up the first predominantly native-born Jewish generation in America. To the military contributions outlined here must be added the business and financial activities in which the Jews figured prominently. This subject is to be developed in the following chapters.[46]

5

War-Related Economic Activities

From the time of their first arrival in America in 1654, the Jews had engaged primarily in trade. When the Revolution broke out, more than a century later, they had become well established commercially, especially in five centers of trade, from Newport, New York, and Philadelphia in the north to Charleston and Savannah in the south, but not yet in Boston and Baltimore. A few others were located in such smaller places as Lancaster, Easton, and York, Pennsylvania, and in some of the towns of Connecticut as well as up the Hudson Valley. Their business ranged from large-scale overseas trade that extended to Europe, America, and the West Indies, to local and retail trade. There were craftsmen among them as well, such as silversmiths and coppersmiths, and also chandlers, saddlers, and tailors. Jewish business was well integrated into the total pattern of American business. Economic activities, moreover, are essentially incapable of ethnic or group separation. They are all part of a total social system, in which the Jews had their place, even if at times marginally rather than centrally. They were subject to all the pressures and restrictions as well as to the opportunities that prevailed in the colonies.

The Revolution had a disruptive effect on American commerce. The English were able to intercept maritime routes of trade and communication by naval blockade at sea and equally so on land through a policy of occupation of all important towns. The wartime needs for goods were no less great, but supply was less certain since it depended on the success of blockade-running and privateering for the replacement of normal channels. The war also created new wants and opportunities for wares of all kinds, although the means and conditions of paying for them were not readily available and were aggravated by persistent inflation. The war created a problem of adjustment that tested the ingenuity of all merchants, including the Jews. Whether motivated by patriotism or profit or both, the merchants of the Revolution explored their capacity to survive and to develop new and substitute channels of trade. In respect to economics, the plight and problem of the Jews were similar to those of all other merchants. Their contributions were surprisingly many and diverse, and the rise and fall of their fortunes were, if anything, more precarious and uncertain than was common in this age of insecurity and increased risk. It is doubtful whether, patriotism aside, the Revolution provided great prospects of profitability, let alone the profiteering usually associated with war, except perhaps in cases of political favoritism.

The disruption of several of the Jewish communities, and their enforced migration and dispersion to various other places as a result of the early British invasion and occupation of New York and Newport, added to the plight of the Jewish merchants. There was a gravitation of trade and merchants toward Philadelphia, which, except for a few months of occupation in 1777, was least disturbed by the British threat. Philadelphia was also the political and hence the economic and financial capital of the Revolution. The Jews who settled here were, therefore, able to share in new opportunities for trade, and thus to compensate for other losses. These opportunities involved both ordinary business as well as war trades such as privateering and the supply of military forces. Even the monetary resources of trade, whether in the form of continental currency or foreign loans, were more available in Philadelphia than elsewhere, although their value was no more stable or certain.

The economic aspect of the Revolution is complex and composite, affecting the very life of a whole population. One may begin with the economic activities related directly to the war. First was the economic enterprise associated with privateering, a popular and on occasion a profitable form of maritime warfare in the eighteenth century. It allowed private persons to invest in armed vessels under letters of marque, granted by the national or state government for the seizure of "prizes," which had a double utility. In the first place, they provided profits for sharing among officers, crew, and investors in some established ratio. Equally important, successful privateering made possible a flow of goods lacking in a blockaded and besieged country that depended on the outside world for manufactures and other wares. That privateering was considered both patriotic and practical is suggested in an Address of Loyalty presented in Congress by many merchants of Philadelphia, among them such prominent Jews as Isaac Moses, Jonas Phillips, Isaac Franks, Isaac Levy, and Haym Salomon. They boasted of their services "not only in the Militia but also with their fortunes as citizens," and they offered to help all they could.[1]

Some Jews had acquired experience in this field in earlier wars. Thus Sampson Simson of New York applied to Governor James DeLancey during the preceding French and Indian War for commissions under which his captains would operate. Isaac Hart of Newport, later a Loyalist under the Revolution, fitted out the *Lord Howe* as a privateer in 1758, and Naphtali Hart operated the *Dolphin* and the *Diamond* in 1762 in partnership with others, including Governor Wanton of Rhode Island.[2] The Revolution offered great opportunities for such investments, as the number of American privateers grew steadily from 73 ships armed with 730 guns in 1776, to a peak of 449 vessels armed with 6,735 guns in 1781. Even in 1782, the last year of the war, there were 323 vessels carrying 4,895 guns and plying the seas in search of prizes. Privateers emphasized the real object of maritime war and substituted for an adequate American navy. The availability of merchant ships of all sizes, idled by war and easily converted to the purposes of privateering, supported and supplied a volume of prize goods in a badly depleted market.[3]

A number of Jewish merchants, especially in Philadelphia, engaged in privateering from a combination of patriotic and profit motives. Isaac Moses, a leading merchant of New York who lived in Philadelphia during the Revolution, was a major figure in this enterprise, as he was in a variety of other economic activities. His prominence is suggested in an entry in the diary of Judge John Fell, delegate to the Continental Congress from New Jersey, who recorded that he dined with Isaac Moses alone on 6 December 1778. No other information is given about the reasons for the event or what was discussed during dinner, but the importance of Moses, if not the occasion, must have rated a record for posterity.

On 27 July 1779, too, Isaac Moses addressed a memorial to Congress, asking for two or three hundred "weight of powder out of the public stores." Moses dwelled on his merits "as a true Whig and friend of the liberties of the country." He had outfitted a "schooner under a letter of marque with every necessary (but gunpowder) in a warlike manner, and has made all the search in his power for that article." He informed Congress: "It is needless to mention them here [his merits], or to remind your body of the assistance he has afforded these United States from time to time in the importation of divers articles which he spared them. But particularly when he and his partners spared these States upwards of twenty thousand dollars in specie, in exchange for Continental dollars at the time the Canada Expedition was on foot. . . ." Here is a contemporary and illuminating account of how helpful a patriotic Jewish merchant had been as early as 1775 in the Revolution.[4]

Isaac Moses was unquestionably the wealthiest Jew in Philadelphia, since his property was appraised at £115,000 for tax purposes in 1780, as compared with Michael Gratz, who was assessed at £92,200. Haym Salomon, by contrast, was listed as worth only £1200. Isaac Moses was useful to the Revolutionary government on other occasions and in other ways. He and Moses Mordecai were among those who agreed to accept paper money equally with gold and silver in 1780. In the same year, when public funds were short and a bank was proposed with a capital of £300,000 to facilitate financial operations, Isaac Moses became one of the stockholders. This was the Bank of North America, the first chartered bank, whose principal promoter was Robert Morris, Superintendent of Finance during the crucial later period of the war. Moses offered his credit for £3,000 to supply the army in 1781, and he bought bills of credit from Robert Morris to assist the Treasury, then in dire need of ready funds. On 27 August 1781 Robert Morris entered in his diary the various public services rendered by Isaac Moses. He offered to purchase bills, "with cash in hand . . . Isaac Moses is a large supplier of war goods." He had sold Osnaburgs (a coarse linen from Germany) "to make sandbags for the intended siege of New York," for which Morris authorized a payment to him of £704.

Interestingly, this transaction proved to be unnecessary, since the Yorktown campaign of 1781 replaced the proposed attack on New York and proved to be decisive in the war. Two years later, on 5 August 1783, Morris again noted a visit by Isaac Moses in his office: "I sold him a bill for 50,000 guilders on Holland and one for 10,000 livres on Paris, part in cash, part in notes." These contributions to the Revolution by Isaac Moses are not as well known as those of his contemporary, Haym Salomon, but indicate that others besides Salomon were helpful to the cause, including a number of Jewish merchants to be considered subsequently.[5]

Isaac Moses was, moreover, a partner of Robert Morris in some of his personal privateering ventures, as in the case of the *Black Prince,* a brig armed with twelve guns, bonded for £20,000. Isaac Moses and Company also owned the *Chance,* a schooner with six guns. With various partners, he operated the *Cornelia,* with four guns aboard; the *Fox,* a Pennsylvania brigantine with an armament of ten guns; the *Marbois* with sixteen guns; and the *Mayflower,* a schooner. Altogether Moses had interests in eight privateers, and his partners included Jews such as Benjamin Seixas, his brother-in-law, and Solomon Marache, as well as Robert Morris and Matthew Clarkson, the latter subsequently a mayor of Philadelphia. With such diverse business activity, one wonders how Isaac Moses also managed to serve in the Philadelphia militia in anything more than a nominal fashion. He was also active in the construction of the Philadelphia synagogue Mikveh Israel in 1782, to whose consecration he invited the president of Pennsylvania as he was then called.[6]

In any event, here is a remarkable record of the role of one Jewish merchant in the American Revolution at its very center in Philadelphia. Isaac Moses returned to New York in 1783 and resumed his peacetime business activity there. He was one of a group of some thirty merchants who addressed the New York legislature, proposing that the state reward their patriotism and compensate them for their losses by selling the Loyalists' estates. Subsequently Moses acquired several lots of land in New York City that had belonged to James DeLancey, the noted Loyalist. So did several other Jews, among them Hayman Levy (Moses' father-in-law), Jacob Mordecai, and Philip Jacobs. Among Moses' ventures was a partnership with the international trading firm of Samuel and Moses Myers and Marcus Elcan of Richmond, which did business with Amsterdam. In 1784 Moses even recommended Moses Myers as American consul in Amsterdam, where he was then living, but the request was "filed with similar applications." A year later, in 1785, the Myers' firm was in financial trouble, threatening the credit and solvency of its partner, Isaac Moses. He brought in Alexander Hamilton as his counsel, who interceded in his behalf with the New York creditors, assuring them that Moses was solvent. He estimated his assets at £98,000 and his liabilities at £90,000, which would indicate a rather close calculation and a precarious situation.[7]

The rise and fall of fortunes was not uncommon in this period, and the threat of bankruptcy hovered over many, if it did not overtake them all. It is demonstrated, for example, in the cases of both Haym Salomon and Aaron Lopez, whose estates, soon after their deaths, were discovered to be insolvent, despite their apparent earlier prosperity. Moses himself recovered from his financial troubles, as Hamilton predicted. He was successful as a general auctioneer in New York, and he died in 1818, leaving substantial property, including £129,600 worth of New York real estate, including a farm on Seventh Avenue valued at £25,000. He was a charter stockholder of the Bank of New York and a highly respected member of the Jewish community there.[8]

Other Jews besides Isaac Moses invested and engaged in privateering ventures during the Revolution. Michael Gratz, also of Philadelphia, was involved in many enterprises, especially in supplying the Virginia forces. He lived in Richmond for a time, and he operated the privateer, the *Rising Sun*, in partnership with Carter Braxton, a Virginia delegate to the Continental Congress and a signer of the Declaration of Independence. Gratz was one of the partners, with Robert Morris, in the privateers *Shippen* and *General Mercer.* Moses Cohen and Samuel Judah offered for sale a prize ship loaded with Irish beef intended for the British army. Moses Michael Hays, originally from Newport, was the first Jewish settler in Boston during the Revolution. He had an interest in the *Iris,* a Massachusetts brig armed with eight guns. He prospered in the field of maritime insurance during and after the war. Surprisingly, a Gideon Samson turns up in Exeter, New Hampshire, as the bonder of the *Wilks,* a New Hampshire sloop of ten guns. Its master was one Mendes, who is referred to somewhat cryptically as the younger son of a Jewish family.

Abraham Sasportas, a French Jewish merchant in the West Indies, lived in Philadelphia during the Revolution and is reported as the bonder of the two *Rachels*, a Pennsylvania privateer. Samuel and Nathan Bush and Jacob de Hart are also recorded as bonders of privateering vessels. Mordecai Sheftall, a prominent and active figure early in the Revolution in Georgia and South Carolina as the Commissary General of the forces there, made his way to Philadelphia after his release as a British prisoner. Here he tried his hand at privateering in 1781. He acquired the schooner *Hetty* and outfitted it on shares with partners. He directed its operations, and it brought in at least one prize, the sloop *Swift*. Moses Levy of Philadelphia shared the ownership of the six-gun schooner *Havannah* with Robert Morris, whose extensive private and public business activities are well documented.[9]

Illustrating at once the diversity of makeup of the Jewish community in America, as well as its dispersion and the variety of its contributions to the Revolution, is the contrast between Isaac Moses and Aaron Lopez, probably the two most active Jewish merchants in the country at the time. Isaac Moses arrived in New York from Germany in 1764. Here he married the daughter of Hayman Levy, a prominent merchant. He was established as a merchant in New York, but spent the war years in Philadelphia, where he attained success and importance. Aaron Lopez, on the other hand, was of Sephardic stock, born in Portugal, from which he escaped dramatically and arrived in Newport in 1752. Originally a Marano, he now assumed an open Jewish identity and became a member of the small but predominantly Sephardic community in Newport. He married as his second wife the daughter of Jacob Rodriguez Rivera, a leading Newport merchant and also a Sephardic Jew. The two families formed a powerful alliance, both economically and culturally. They played an important role in the local general community. Lopez acquired large interests in ships and maritime enterprises, which included both whaling and the slave trade. To these extensive mercantile activities was added the manufacture of spermaceti candles, in which Lopez's father-in-law, Rivera, pioneered. They figured prominently in the creation of a kind of industrial cartel, the first of its kind in America, controlling the distribution of spermaceti oil and the manufacture and sale of candles through most of the colonies. Their cartel embraced the principal producers, both Jewish and non-Jewish.[10]

Altogether, Aaron Lopez, by virtue of his origin and the substantial size and scope of his business, was rather more like a Mediterranean merchant prince characteristic of the Renaissance than an ordinary Jewish tradesman. The Lopez-Rivera families played a dual role, first as leaders in the Jewish congregation in Newport, Yeshuat Israel, which, though small, was host to visiting rabbis from the Holy Land. They were also prominent in the general community, as the friends and intellectual companions of the Reverend Ezra Stiles, minister in Newport and later president of Yale College. It was here that the most learned minister of a Jewish congregation in the country, Isaac Touro, taught Ezra Stiles Hebrew. It was perhaps not altogether accidental that the Newport Jewish community was the first to build a distinguished example of eighteenth-century architecture as its synagogue, now a registered historic landmark. It was the work of Peter Harrison, architect of many notable classical structures in Newport and other places.

All this background is essential for the understanding of the role of the Newport Jews and particularly of the Lopez and Rivera families during the Revolution. In the first place, the Newport Jewish community split sharply between Loyalists and Whigs. Only New York presented a similar division. Moreover, the Revolution and the accompanying war undermined the prosperity of Newport, which never recovered its position in trade. Its Jewish community virtually vanished after 1800, not to be revived until late in the nineteenth century.

Aaron Lopez was at first not clearly identified with the American cause. Perhaps the breadth and sweep of his business activities, embracing the West Indies, Africa, as well as America, lent a kind of international if not neutral character to his outlook. He did not sign any of the nonimportation agreements that ushered in the conflict of interests leading to war. He was able to persuade both the British and the Americans to permit his whaling vessels to depart on a long voyage at the outbreak of hostilities. Moreover, he became involved in a complicated effort to bring his considerable wealth out of Jamaica, which embroiled him with both sides. Thus, one of his ships, the *Hope*, en route from Jamaica ostensibly for Halifax, Nova Scotia, but actually for Bedford, Massachusetts, was seized in 1778 by two Connecticut privateers, and the British goods on board were declared a prize. Thus began a notable conflict, by which Lopez attempted to secure the release of the vessel, first in Connecticut courts and then through the Continental Congress. He employed James Wilson, the noted Philadelphia lawyer and a member of Congress, to argue the case for him. He won a judgment in Congress, but as late as 1781, Lopez was still suing in Connecticut courts for the return of the ship or its equivalent value at £3,000. Not until 1783, a year after his death, did the Lopez estate receive a favorable judgment in Connecticut.[11]

On 19 April 1780, James Wilson and William Lewis further requested and won from Congress a "protection" for Lopez and his factor, Captain Benjamin Wright in Jamaica, to authorize them to remove property from the island. Wilson pleaded that "the character of Mr. Lopez as a friend to the Liberties and Independence of the United States is clear and unimpeachable." Few had better reason for this privilege, he claimed, since "he is a merchant of extensive Business, is active, enterprising, and public-spirited." Thus did Lopez succeed in maintaining his reputation as a major figure in American business through the Revolution.[12]

Lopez was fortunate and important enough to have prominent friends to testify to his loyalty. On one occasion, he offered as evidence a document addressed by the legislature of Rhode Island to the legislature of Massachusetts, dated 23 August 1775, that "the whole tenor of Mr. Lopez's conduct as a merchant had been unexceptionable. . . ." This suggests that some question on this point had arisen. At a later date, in 1778, General John Sullivan, the American commander at Providence, wrote in connection with the seizure of Lopez's ship by privateers that he esteemed it his duty "to certify that on my first coming to take command in this department, I found from all the various declarations of all the friends of America that Mr. Lopez has ever proved himself by the most conspicuous and open conduct to be a warm friend to the rights of America . . . and that the whole tenure of his conduct has sufficiently evinced his zeal for the American cause and does not leave the least room for suspicion." There was almost too much protest in Sullivan's reiterated assertion that Lopez had not "the most distant inclination to do any act in opposition to the resolves of Congress . . . or even that he would countenance a trade advantageous to the enemies of America."[13]

Upon the British occupation of Newport with 8,000 troops in 1776, Lopez joined the general exodus from the town, first to Portsmouth, then to Providence, and finally to Leicester, Massachusetts, where his "principal object was to look out for a spot, where I could place my family, secured from sudden allarms [sic] and the cruel ravages of an enraged enemy." His extensive house and warehouse in Newport were abandoned to the British, who quartered, according to report, two hundred soldiers in it. Three related families, the Riveras, Lopezes, and Mendeses, totaling with their retainers some seventy persons, found a welcome and apparently happy refuge in the small inland town of Leicester, Massachusetts. Lopez wrote that he pitched "my tent, erecting a proportionable one to the extent of my numerous family on the summit of a high, healthy hill, where we have experienced the civilities and hospitality of a kind neighborhood, and moved in the same sphere of business I have been used to follow, which, altho much more contracted, it has fully answered my wishes." Interestingly, he had experienced the hospitality of Massachusetts much earlier, when in 1762 he crossed over the line and there received the naturalization that had been denied him as a Jew in his own home colony of Rhode Island.[14]

Their new home was much more ambitious than "a tent"; it was a "large and elegant mansion" located on an estate of thirty-one acres. It contained a store as well, which they kept closed on the Sabbath. His father-in-law, Jacob Rivera, occupied himself as a gentleman on an adjoining farm. The Lopez house in Leicester was acquired by the Leicester Academy many years later. The Lopezes missed their old home in Newport, and hoped they would all eventually be reunited there, "where . . . we shall soon . . . re-enjoy those habitations we have so long been deprived of, with all satisfaction." Unhappily this was not to be, for Aaron

Lopez was drowned in 1782, as he was dragged by his horse into a pond not far from Providence, on the way to Newport. The rest of the Leicester ménage returned to Newport in the following year, but never regained their prosperity. The post-Revolutionary era for the Jews of Newport was an unhappy one, as the town declined commercially, and the Jews again scattered, leaving their beautiful synagogue virtually unoccupied after 1800. Moses Seixas remained almost the last survivor of the community as the cashier of a bank in Newport.[15]

As Lopez himself noted, despite his prolonged troubles with the "rascally, peaked, bearded judges" of Connecticut over his forfeited vessel and its contents, he carried on a wide trade, although on a reduced scale. He traveled widely from his Leicester base and engaged in an extensive correspondence with merchants both at home and abroad. His surviving papers permit a comprehension of both the pattern and the trials of trade carried on during the Revolution, not only among Jews but also in the general community. A sampling of such letters indicates the character of this trade.

As early as 1776, he sold duck cloth for use on two frigates being built in Rhode Island. In the same year, the British seized his vessel *Clarissa*, which was loaded with lumber from Jamaica. On 28 April 1779 Jarvis and Russell of Boston informed Lopez of the money they held to his credit. A few months later a letter from Daniel Crommelin and Sons of Amsterdam acknowledged the receipt of a substantial sum from him in bills of exchange and made a further bid for business: "As it is very apparent that the intercourse between your continent and our country will much increase, we shall esteem it a particular favor when occasion offers your recommending our house to your friends . . . as we are fully acquainted with the American trade. We flatter ourselves to be able to give them as much satisfaction as any other house at this place." This firm, it was added, had the further advantage of doing business with St. Eustatius, a Dutch island in the West Indies important to the American trade, particularly during the Revolution.[16]

At home too, Lopez had frequent business dealings and exchanges of letters with Samson Mears of Norwalk, Connecticut. On 14 July 1779 Mears noted the slow sale of goods even at the lower prices; all that was sold included tobacco, gloves, a pair of buckram breeches, a sheepskin or two, and seven or eight bladders of snuff. Mears was concerned about his own affairs: "Sick and tired I am of an idle life and what to persue [sic]with an appearance of stability and advantage. . . . I am at a loss, and now appears new difficulties arrising [sic] to the southward and eastward by the threatening restrictions on trade, that adds to the confusion of the times. Is there nothing abroad that I can serve you and Mr. Rivera in?" He had heard favorable reports from St. Eustatius, and was ready to go there for a speculation. Later in 1779, Mears again wrote to Lopez, thanking him for "the Benevolence of your family toward the relief of the unhappy sufferers of Norwalk," which had been the object of a British raid. He had distributed the aid among the "Suffering Brethren," who included Asher Myers, his own brother, Myer Mears, M. Isaacs, S. Israel, and M. Judah. They were all refugees from New York, now living in Connecticut.[17]

Still later in 1779, Mears inquired of Lopez whether he would be interested in disposing of "100 boxes of Spermaceti Candles, deliverable at Norwalk for hard money or good bills of exchange." He was "reserving a preference to you or any of your friends," and must have an answer quickly. But he was still planning to leave the continent, "in pursuit of better fortune than I have met on it." Lopez was interested in hearing about the general state of business in many parts of the country, as is indicated in the letters he received, and they frequently included lists of current prices prevailing everywhere. Thus Moses Michael Hays, a former resident of Newport, who settled in Boston during the Revolution, wrote to Lopez in 1779 from Philadelphia: "A general disapprobation appears among the Trading People, it is no secret to say. That fixed prices are at an end, and what goods that are now selling is at the most enormous prices that have yet transpired in the course of the war. Every . . . article sold is now beyond all conception. Their [sic]appears a scarcity. Wether Real or Artificiall [sic] I have not had any opportunity to determine.[18]

A nephew of Aaron Lopez, David Lopez, lived in Providence and engaged both in business and correspondence with his uncle in Leicester. On one occasion in 1779 he wrote, reflecting the family sympathy with the Revolution: "Permit me Sir to congratulate you on the happy and important successes of the American Army, over the British forces at Charlestown." In later letters, David Lopez reported sales of wine and cloth, but noted that "business still continues dull and uncertain, tho' nothing except West Indian goods has yet fallen." On another occasion, in 1781, David Lopez reported that he was loading the wagon with rum, although there was not enough in the stills to fill four hogsheads. He was also sending a load of salt, "that article being on the rise." During the winter of 1780, Moses Seixas wrote from Newport that because of the severity of the season he had not yet received the goods. It was just as well, "as there is no demand for them at present, neither for specie nor paper."[19]

On 15 April 1781 Isaac daCosta, then in Philadelphia, wished Lopez a happy Passover festival, "with a succession of many more." He had sold the nutmegs Lopez left with him at what appeared to be a fantastically inflated price of $650 per pound. He had invested the total amount of more than $6,000 in two barrels of Muscavado sugar, whose price was on the rise and which was likely to yield a proper profit. The venturesome character of trade thus conducted in an era of inflation was equally revealed in a letter Jonas Phillips wrote to Aaron Lopez from Boston on 25 April 1781. He had great difficulty in investing his money in goods he wanted, and he had been obliged to buy a bag of pepper weighing 460 pounds. Pepper, Jonas reported, was selling at $80 per pound, and molasses was $41 a gallon. At the same time, Samuel Myers wrote to Lopez from Philadelphia that "all sorts of goods [were] plenty at Market," but "no other than Specie passing; there appears to be a total stagnation to the Paper Currency."[20]

A year later, in 1782, Benjamin Judah, who was clearing up his father's estate, asked Lopez to send him bills of exchange in payment for the pot and pearl ashes he had sold for him, and he wanted a report on the remaining twenty-two casks. He added his mother's greetings. At about the same time, Moses Michael Hays inquired of Lopez whether he would be interested in disposing of two hundred barrels of flour to be delivered at Hartford by Isaiah Doane and Samuel Emery: "I had you first in view in this negotiation, and would wish to know if it is agreeable to you to dispose of that quantity at current cash price . . . payable one half in cash immediately, the other half in two months." Aaron Lopez was thus the center of an intricate network of trade relations conducted on a wide geographical basis and in a great variety of goods under the uncertain conditions of war and monetary inflation. Among other activities he sold flour to the French army. This sampling of transactions illustrates clearly how Jews appeared to play a considerable role in business, amid great risks. One may wonder what skills of adjustment and adventure were required for success or even survival under those circumstances.[21]

Perhaps the most pathetic instance of the hazards and failures of trade in this period is communicated in a long letter from David P. Mendes of Jamaica, written on 15 August 1781. Somewhat cryptically, after noting the arrival in the island of his brother Abraham, who was a son-in-law of Aaron Lopez, David alludes to "the calamities which he has suffered from this cruel and unnatural war." He lamented that "my friendly admonition had no better effect upon his former conduct. Had he attended to them, the present calamities, as great as they are, would not have reduced him to that great degree of distress. It cannot be denied that I acted the part of an affectionate brother towards him. I did not only assist him with my council [sic], but my money too." What the calamities were is not explained, but Mendes proceeded to sympathize with Lopez himself:

It is not to be doubted but that this ruinous war must have affected you with heavy losses for which I am very much concerned. To be obliged to forsake one's house and seek an asylum at a distance of seventy miles from it with . . . a numerous family is truly deplorable. This island is far from being exempt of troubles. We suffer much by a total stagnation of trade, and the exorbitant prices of all kinds of commodities. . . . I pray Heaven to remove us from the horrors of war, and restore to us the blessings of peace.[22]

Mendes' predicted disaster was not far wrong. When Aaron Lopez died by drowning in 1782, on a trip to Newport, his estate later proved to be insolvent, despite his great business activity and presumed wealth, which was estimated at $100,000. His son, Joseph Lopez, took years to straighten out the estate. In 1789 it showed assets worth £13,536, but the net positive balance was only some £200. One note held by the estate was listed at $14,473 continental currency; it was settled for about £3-1/2, an incredible index of the rate of depreciation. Nor was Lopez the only merchant to experience such a fate in this period. He salvaged, however, his reputation even after death. Reverend Ezra Stiles, his friend of many years, eulogized Lopez as "a merchant of first eminence, for honor and extent of commerce probably surpassed by no merchant in America. . . . His beneficence to his family, connexions, to his nation, and to the world, almost without a parallel." A contemporary newspaper reviewed his attainments in almost extravagant terms: "He was a merchant of eminence, and of polite and amicable manners. . . . An ornament and a valuable pillar in the Jewish society of which he was a member. His knowledge in commerce was undoubtable; and his integrity irreproachable."[23]

The best known and most publicized personality in the Jewish annals of the Revolution was Haym Salomon. This may be partly accounted for by the fact that Salomon, as a broker for the Treasury, probably had the most direct and active role in the economic and financial affairs of the Revolution. This may be somewhat surprising, when contrasted with Lopez's long-time distinction in the American business world both before and during the Revolution. Salomon's origin was obscure, and his activity of short duration. How to account for this contrast between the two men is a problem in historical analysis. It is a problem of separating the known and the established contemporary facts of Salomon's career from the incrustation of myths that has gathered about it over more than a century thereafter, growing out of later claims. These have labeled Salomon somewhat extravagantly as the "Financier of the Revolution." There are thus two quite distinct parts to the historic account of Salomon's place in the Revolution. One is his actual role and achievement during the Revolution; the other is a later creation of myth-building, long after the event, which has a significant if somewhat arguable place in history. Each deserves to be recognized and analyzed separately.

The principal facts of Haym Salomon's life and work are well established in contemporary sources. He was born in 1740 in

Lissa (or Leszno) in what was then Poland, was later acquired by Prussia, and is now again a part of western Poland. He probably arrived in America in 1772, at the time of the first partition of Poland, which affected his home town. As a newcomer he was scarcely informed about the problems already troubling America, but it was later claimed that he was early acquainted with the Sons of Liberty organized in New York, and particularly with their leader, Alexander MacDougall, later a general in the war. If this is so, it would have offered an unusual introduction to America to one who was an alien unfamiliar with American affairs. Another tradition links Salomon with the romantic nationalism then characteristic of Poland, which was represented in America by Kosciuszko and Pulaski, heroes of the Revolution, whose friend he is supposed to have been. This too is unlikely, since any comtemporary mention of such an association is lacking. Nor does the later literature of Polish-American nationalism mention or recognize Salomon or any other Jews as in any way involved either in Polish nationalism or in the American Revolution.[24]

Haym Salomon's first service in the Revolution may have been that of a sutler with General Philip Schuyler's troops on Lake George. He was recommended for such a position by Leonard Gansevoort of Albany in a letter of 11 June 1776, as "having sustained the character of being warmly attached to America," for which no further evidence is given. On the occupation of New York by the British in the same year, following Washington's retreat across the Hudson River, Salomon was apparently again in the city. He remained there for two years, and was then married to Rachel Franks. His first son, Ezekiel, was born there. His conduct in New York was ambivalent during this period. Thanks to his knowledge of German and other languages, he became a commissary supplying the Hessian troops under General Heister, who valued his services greatly. He is, however, also reputed to have been an agent or even a spy for the Americans and to have helped in the escape of prisoners. Supposedly also he tried to subvert the Hessians. He was arrested twice by the British, and confined to the notorious Provost prison. He was even suspected of a part in a plot to burn the docks and British ships in port. He is reported to have been sentenced to death by the

British for this alleged role in the conspiracy. Altogether, Salomon's activity during this period was political as well as economic and somewhat mysterious in character.[25]

In 1778 this rather exciting phase of Salomon's career ended with his escape from New York, leaving behind his wife and child. He arrived in Philadelphia, it would seem not entirely unknown. In any event, on 25 August 1778 he addressed a memorial to the Continental Congress, in which he reviewed his activity. The document indicates either a brazen boldness or a merited right to the attention of Congress. In it he summarized his activities in New York and told how the Hessian General Heister had interceded with the British in his behalf and obtained his release. Salomon had then served as a purveyor to the Hessian officers and was also of great help to the American prisoners. His activities at last "rendered him so obnoxious to the British headquarters that he was closely pursued by the guards and on Tuesday the eleventh instant he made his happy escape from thence." He added that he had "most irrevocably lost all his Effects and Credits to the amount of five or six thousand pounds sterling and left his distressed wife and a child of a month old at New York, waiting that they may soon have an opportunity to come out from thence with empty hands." Salomon concluded by petitioning Congress "to grant him any Employ in the way of his Business, whereby he may be enabled to support himself and his Family."[26]

This key document, submitted to Congress, divides Salomon's revolutionary career into two almost equal parts. The first embodied his rather secretive activity, half-business and half-political, in New York under British occupation. The second part began in 1778 in wartime Philadelphia, in which he conducted himself more openly and certainly with great skill and patriotism. Without congressional assistance, he became a broker and commission merchant, as is indicated in a letter he wrote at this time to a merchant in Virginia. Salomon first referred to hats, writing that he would "defer sending them till I hear from you. They cannot be got for less than two and a half dollars. Silk stockings are grown scarce, and am afraid I shall not be able to send you the quantity you want. Goods are grown scarce, and from the number of vessels we have lost, and our capes are now swarming with enemy cruisers, we expect they will rise considerably." On 23

April 1782, Salomon wrote a letter in a similar vein to Jacob Cohen in Richmond: "The bay is full of privateers and there is much risk in shipping tobacco." Nevertheless, he instructed Cohen to ship twelve thousand pounds, when safe. He established an office on Front Street, and he advertised frequently in the *Pennsylvania Packet,* as did other Jewish merchants: "Bills of Exchange on France or any other part of Europe. . . . Likewise all kinds of Merchandize, and has it often in his power to procure Money on Loan for a short time."[27]

Aside from Salomon, other merchants who advertised at this time were Isaac Moses, Jonas Phillips, Isaac Franks, Moses Cohen, and Benjamin Nones. They all offered much the same services; Moses Cohen even advertised the opening of an Intelligence Office to supply servants. Salomon's advertisements appeared on occasion in French and Dutch, and they occupied a substantial part of a newspaper page, indicative of their scope and substance. In one respect Haym Salomon began to deviate from his other Jewish colleagues after 1781. His name began to appear frequently in the official diary kept by Robert Morris while Superintendent of Finance. Morris had been named to this post by Congress early in 1781, and he assumed a double function. In the first place, he was to put the Revolutionary government on an orderly business basis, both in the collection and disbursement of funds. Second, and this was more crucial, it became his function to raise funds to supply the needs of war in a country without adequate means or the ability to finance it. Morris' diary records the agony and struggles of the new financial officers to provide the funds required in the crucial year, 1781, which witnessed the final decisive Yorktown campaign. In addition to Robert Morris, there was also Gouverneur Morris, who served as his deputy, and with whom Salomon too had dealings. Gouverneur Morris had a long and distinguished political career during the Revolutionary era as well as thereafter.[28]

The chief sources of funds during this period were the substantial gifts and loans by the French government for the conduct of the war. There remained, however, the major problem of the transfer and disposal of the funds to America by the sale of French bills at adequate rates. This function brought into action Salomon's skill and service as a broker. It is indicated in the very first item in Morris' diary, recording Salomon's name. On 8 June 1781 an agreement is noted there with "Haym Solomon *[sic]* the Broker . . . to assist me in the sale of the Bills . . . his Brokerage to be settled hereafter, but not to exceed half a per cent." Salomon's experience is also indicated in the diary by the statement that "he had been employed by the officers of His Most Christian Majesty to make sale of their army and navy Bills." His knowledge of French was undoubtedly helpful, and he had become, as he claimed in his advertising, broker to the French army. Salomon was clearly an experienced and skilled broker in foreign exchange, and Morris used him in this capacity during his term of service as Superintendent of Finance.[29]

Salomon's name appears frequently in the Morris diary during 1781-1784, not only for the transaction of business and the sale of bills of exchange, but equally for consultation as to the state of the money market and the best terms to be obtained. Morris clearly had confidence in Salomon's expert judgment, and relied on his advice and skill in the execution of orders. One item in the Morris diary, dated 8 August 1781, illustrates admirably the broad nature of Salomon's services. It records that Morris sent for "Mr. Solomon" and "desired him to press the sale of Bills." The price was to be kept at six shillings per five livres, Pennsylvania currency. Salomon, however, informed him that sundry persons were selling French bills at lower rates. He was instructed to find out who was doing this by the next morning and "to urge them to keep up the price and to threaten them." It is not revealed how and what power Salomon had to threaten. Mr. Chaloner, the agent of the French army, was one of those reported to be underselling, and Salomon told how he had tried in vain to persuade the sellers to keep up the price. Morris gave him "a plan to press a sale on credit . . . and preventing others from selling."

Morris' problem at this time was to concentrate the sale of all bills in his hands or in those of an agent, to keep the price from being depressed. He discussed the matter with the French minister and apparently reached an agreement with him on the common purchase of supplies for both the American and the French armies, then preparing for the Yorktown campaign. A day or two later, Salomon reported the sale of 60,000 to 80,000 livres at 6 shillings for 5 livres on a credit of eight months, but Morris insisted on "four months, a part in hand and the remainder monthly." Salomon continued to make sales, but Morris objected that he had sold too many on credit: "However, as you have done it, I will not falsify your promises but in the future you must not sell on credit at all nor under six shillings for cash." On 2 April 1782 Morris instructed Salomon to deliver to Michael Hillegas, the United States Treasurer, "all the notes . . . for Bills 1-42, amounting to 500,000 livres sold for £34,758-18 s.-2d., Pennsylvania currency." He was further instructed to "render a separate account of your Brokerage (at 1/4%) to Mr. Mulligan, the Comptroller. On his certificate I will grant you a Warrant for the amount." All this was indicative of the substantial scale of Salomon's operation in this period.[30]

Moreover, the pattern of Salomon's business relationship to the Superintendent of Finance was now settled on a regular basis, and with it grew a bond of trust between the two men. The Bank of North America, the first of its kind, was established at this time, through the promotion of Robert Morris, who thought it "to be a most useful establishment to the public." Both he and Salomon were among its stockholders, and the latter kept a substantial account in it, out of which were made payments to the government. Morris continued to call upon Salomon all through 1782 for consultation and to commission him to sell bills. Thus, on 25 March 1782, he recorded in his diary that "as I shall want money for the opening of the campaign, I have given Solomon leave to make Sale of 400,000 livres to be drawn at 100 Days' sight . . . that they may be discounted at the Bank prices on these conditions seven shillings for five livres." The Yorktown victory of the previous fall had raised the value of exchange. On 11 July 1782, for example, Morris sent for Salomon "to consult with him on the ways and means of raising money to answer the present demands of the public and to provide for the first of August."

A critical situation for the government had arisen out of the discontent and unrest in the army, now relieved of combat and pressing for the payment of arrears of pay. At one time during 1782, a demonstration by some soldiers had forced the Congress and Morris to leave Philadelphia for Trenton and Princeton. Morris soon returned and celebrated July Fourth that year by releasing all of his personnel for the day to be "a leisure to

To the Hon'ble Superintendant of the Finances of North America;

when payable	Livres	Price	Penn'a Currency		
May 25th, 1782	100.000	a 7/.	7.000	„	„
D°.	60.000	a 7/.	4.200	„	„
D°.	21.500	a 7/.	1.505	„	„
D°. 26th	50.000	a 7/.	3.500	„	„
D°.	50.000	a 7/.	3.500	„	„
D°. 30th	50.000	a 7/.	3.500	„	„
D°.	10.000	a 7/.	700	„	„
	96.450. 6. 3	a 6/9	6.510	8	„
June 24th, 1782	20.000 „ „	a 7/.	1.400	„	„
July 3. 1782	34.635. 2. 5	a 7/.	2.424	9	2
May 1. 1782	4.000 „ „	a 7/.	280	„	„
May 30. 1782	3.414.11. 6	a 7/.	239	1	„
Livres „	500.000. „ „	£	34.758	18	2

Received of Mr Haym Solomon on the 4th instant the Six first mentioned Notes and this day the Six remaining Notes Specified in the above List, Amounting together to Thirty four thousand Seven hundred and fifty eight Pounds Eighteen Shillings and two pence Pennsylvania Currency for which am to Account Having signed duplicate Receipts this 10th. of April 1782

For the use of the United States   Mr Hillegas Cont^l Treas^r

Haym Salomon's account with the American Treasury, as of April 10, 1782. A page from Robert Morris' Diary, April 10, 1782.

Courtesy of American Jewish Archives

indulge those pleasing reflections which every true American must feel on the recollection that six years are now completed since that decisive step was taken in favor of the Freedom of their Country, and that they might each partake of the festivity usual on Holydays." The President of the Congress served a "Cold Collation" for the occasion, "to congratulate and be congratulated on the return of this day." Thus early began the national celebration of Independence Day, as recorded by Morris.[31]

At this time, too, on 12 July 1782, Salomon earned a great reward for his services in the public interest. Morris reported in his diary Salomon's usual visit "respecting Bills etc." He then added an item of special note and importance: "This Broker has been useful to the Public Interest and requests leave to publish himself as Broker to this office, to which I have consented as I do not see any disadvantage can possibly arise to the public service but the reverse, and he expects individual Benefits therefrom." The announcement had dual significance. In the first place, it revealed that Salomon had won official recognition after hardly more than a year's service as broker to the finance office. It defined Salomon's status and showed that he was also interested in carrying on private business with the advantage of a kind of public title. He used it to the full in his advertising. Thus, in announcing in the press a new partnership and business establishment in New York in 1784, Salomon publicly recited his services: "Broker to the Office of Finance, and honored with its confidence, all those sums have passed through his hands which the generosity of the French Monarch and the affections of the Merchants of the nation prompted them to furnish us with to enable us to support the expense of war . . . , and this is a circumstance which has established his credit and reputation; and procured him the confidence of the Public. . . ."[32]

Salomon was drawn into the midst of a public financial crisis in 1782, when a rebellious army and its officers demanded payment of overdue salaries. A settlement was effected with an agreement to meet the officers' demands by 1 August, at least in part. As the date approached, Morris became concerned over his ability to meet the demands and frequently called Salomon into conference, expressing "my anxiety to provide for the regular discharge of Paymaster General's notes which fall due the first of August. . . . My time is principally consumed in forming Contrivances to pay some Debts and to parry the payments of what I cannot accomplish." Interestingly, Morris' financial difficulties were as great after the war was over as they had been earlier. The needs were still there to be met, but not the funds to pay them. The amount due the officers on 1 August was some $140,000, of which Morris still lacked $101,000. Salomon owed £15,000, equal to $37,500, for bills already sold, and the remaining sixty-odd thousand dollars had to be raised somehow. On such a slender thread hung the credit and security of the United States. Morris, however, was certain that "the hopes and expectations of the malicious and disaffected will in this instance be disappointed." Morris thereupon "directed Solomon the Broker to sell more Bills to provide for the balance. . . ." This was apparently done, and the solvency of the United States was restored.[33]

Salomon also performed regular merchandising functions for Morris and the United States government. On 16 August 1782 Morris sent for Salomon and handed him a "Waggoner's Receipt for twenty dry Hides sent from South Carolina and desired him to sell same to the best advantage of the United States." He also instructed Salomon to take charge of a few casks of pot and pearl ashes, the property of the United States government, and "to sell the same to the best advantage." In September 1782 occurred a transaction that involved some dubious practices by a French seller, of which Salomon seemed to be an innocent victim. A Monsieur Caure offered Morris some soldiers' shirts, which the latter had reason to believe had been sold to him by Salomon. Salomon was called in, and he explained that the shirts were indeed the same. He sold them for Monsieur deBrassine, but a M. Balmy had also sold them to Caure, while Salomon was negotiating for them with Morris. They were now being sold to Morris a second time.[34]

Salomon's unlikely possession of large funds to help finance the government, as often claimed in subsequent unsubstantiated accounts, is well illustrated in an episode that occurred in August 1782. Morris had just resolved the army pay crisis requiring funds on 1 August, when a new one arose. Morris needed $20,000 to repay a loan made by Mr. Chaloner, treasurer of the

French army. In this stress he sent for the "broker Haym Solomon, for William Bingham and John Ross, being informed that the two last named gentlemen have money by them." In desperation he attempted to convince them that they should advance their money to the government. When Bingham demurred that he had other uses for his money, Morris told him, "I would not offer him an interest of 5 percent per month as is now the practice, but hoped he would exert his patriotism." He promised to repay the debt as soon as possible. Morris made a similar appeal to Ross, but only Bingham complied with the request. Salomon obviously could make no such advances and was not even asked.[35]

Morris had serious trouble with some of the French agents then resident in Philadelphia. There occurred a rather unsavory conflict over an exchange transaction with the director of the French hospital in Philadelphia, in which Salomon played an important role as an unwitting victim. He had sold this agent some bills on credit, which were now repudiated. Morris had complete faith in Salomon's integrity and authorized him to prosecute the case. This resulted in the conviction and punishment of the French agent. On 5 February 1783 Morris instructed Salomon to take the necessary action to recover the money due from deBrassine on the latter's notes. DeBrassine had given them to him while acting as agent for Monsieur deMars, the director of the French hospital, in the purchase of bills of exchange. DeMars now attempted to evade payment by disclaiming deBrassine's transaction completely. Of a heated discussion at a meeting of all parties on 15 February 1783, Morris reported: "We had a good deal of altercation and finally M. deMars says he will not fulfill the engagements of M. deBrassine, so that I shall be forced to have recourse to the Law."

Morris further commissioned Salomon to collect information about the relations between these men. The Intendant of the French army peremptorily refused to honor the notes amounting to £3,514, 6s., 3d., payable to Salomon on or before 1 November. Monsieur deMars, chief of the Hospital Department, also refused to honor them. Morris concluded that Salomon had made the sale in good faith, and that the Frenchman involved had used the King's name and credit for "private pursuits in which they were jointly interested." He authorized Salomon to have deMars arrested and "to pursue all proper steps to prove that deMars either authorized deBrassine or was interested in his transactions. . . . I must here in justice to Haym Solomon *[sic]* declare that altho' he has endorsed the note I consider him only as a Broker in this business, and not liable to pay as an Endorser thereof." Morris employed lawyers, including the celebrated James Wilson, "to advise and assist, being determined if possible to obtain Justice for the United States in this business. . . ." Ironically, the case came to trial in March 1783, just as Morris reported that "glorious news that a general peace was concluded at Paris, January 20, 1783," for which the French were entitled to credit. The government won the case, and deMars and deBrassine were ordered to pay £3,500, which Salomon collected. He was also authorized to defray all expenses in the case, including the lawyers' fees.[36]

During the summer of 1783 still another crisis developed as a group of soldiers marched from Lancaster to Philadelphia "to seek for justice and demand back pay." Congress removed itself to Princeton, and Morris retired briefly to Trenton. The National Credit was so low that the Bank of North America refused to renew a loan for $100,000 unless they received better security than the credit of the United States. Salomon visited Morris frequently at this time, protesting his inability to sell bills. "I cannot sell at present," he reported on 11 September 1783. Morris shifted to bills on Amsterdam, and Salomon was able "with some difficulty to sell 40,000 guilders at three shillings per guilder at ninety days' sight." Isaac Moses, a prominent merchant already dealt with earlier, came to the rescue and bought "bills for 50,000 guilders and 10,000 livres on Paris, part in cash, part in Notes." Salomon continued to report the dull state of the market to the end of 1783. Morris now became weary of this thankless and troublesome office and planned to leave it, but not before he had put the government finances into some kind of order. He was especially determined to clear the long-standing debt of $100,000 to the Bank of North America.[37]

On 5 March 1784 Morris sent for Salomon and asked him to offer bills totaling $50,000 on Charleston, Richmond, and Annapolis: "The pressing demands of the Bank render this step necessary." At this time, too, Salomon brought word to Morris that a new bank was being promoted in opposition to "the national bank." This was to be the Pennsylvania Bank and was promoted by some Quakers, headed by Miers Fisher, a Tory Quaker of Philadelphia. Salomon reported its progress to Morris, and he became embroiled personally in a bitter polemic with Fisher in the press, which had anti-Semitic overtones. Fisher argued that the new bank would lower interest rates and protect the people against the Jews and their usurious practices. Salomon rose to the defense and addressed a letter to the *Independent Gazetteer* on 13 March 1784. He condemned Fisher's attack on the Jews: "I am a Jew; it is my own nation and profession. I also subscribe myself a broker." He was hopeful that Jews would eventually win equal rights, and he expressed this view publicly on several occasions: "I do not at all despair . . . that we shall still obtain every other privilege that we aspire to enjoy along with our fellow citizens."

Salomon took the offensive against Fisher; the Jews, he wrote, were "early, uniform, and decisive Whigs, and were second to none in our patriotism and attachment to our country." But where were Fisher and his fellow-Quakers: "Who traded with the enemy? Who first depreciated the currency? . . . Who did not pay any taxes? Who has now the public securities in hand?" Salomon thus turned the tables and accused the Quaker financiers of having introduced excessive interest rates and similar extortionate practices during the Revolution.[38]

During 1784 Salomon began to plan his return to New York. He established a new brokerage enterprise there in partnership with Jacob Mordecai. He visited New York several times and offered to serve as an emissary to Robert Morris there. Both Morris and he left the government service during the year. Morris noted on 15 September 1784 that nine years of neglect had left his private affairs "in a state of confusion as to threaten a loss of Property and Reputation." Morris' diary ends abruptly on 30 September 1784. Salomon, too, now concluded his valuable and meritorious service as a financial consultant and broker to Morris, which had begun in 1781 and endured through a critical period in public affairs.[39]

Another aspect of Salomon's contribution to the Revolution deserved recognition and notice, provided it is put in proper perspective and without the exaggerated importance assigned to it in later years. Contemporary evidence substantiates the fact that Haym Salomon advanced funds for the support of some Revolutionary leaders. The evidence for this is primarily to be found in the papers of James Madison. In 1827, answering an inquiry from Salomon's son, Haym M., Madison wrote: "Among other members of Congress from Virginia whose resources, public and private, had been cut off, I had occasion, once, perhaps twice, myself to resort to his pecuniary aid on a small scale for current wants. We regarded him as upright, intelligent, and friendly in his transactions with us." Money was indeed tight during the Revolution, as the delegate from Virginia once noted: "It is not always that money can be had on any terms." They begged the governor of Virginia, Benjamin Harrison, to relieve them from "the distressing and degrading situation in which we are placed, from the scantiness and uncertainty of our supplies in which our private credit can avail us nothing, and prices are immoderate and ruinous."

In such circumstances, Madison's grateful acknowledgement of Salomon's help, both immediately and in his reminiscences thereafter, takes on special significance. As he once wrote to Edmund Randolph of Virginia in September 1782: "The kindness of my little friend in Front Street will preserve me from extremities, but I never resort to it without mortifications as he obstinately rejects all recompense. The price of money is so usurious that he thinks it ought to be extracted from none but those who aim at profitable speculations. To a necessitous delegate he gratuitously spares a supply out of his private stock." There is, nevertheless, a note of condescension in his allusion to "my little friend in Front Street," since Madison, himself a short man, could scarcely describe the other as "little."[40]

Virginia apparently repaid Salomon's advances, in tobacco, if belatedly and grudgingly. Thus, in July 1782, Joseph Jones, the treasurer of Virginia, informed Madison that he had "never heard from Mr. Salomon whether the waggoners delivered to him the tobacco carried here . . . in payment for loans by him to delegates who had pledged their overdue salaries as security." Later in the same year, Randolph wrote to Madison that, unless Mr. Ross should need too much, "there can be no objection to the application of the balance [of tobacco] to the relief of the little

Levite." (Note again the condescending reference to the "little Levite.") In another letter to Madison, Randolph enclosed "a note to a Jew . . . in Market Street. . . . He knows me well and my punctuality too. His partner in Richmond knows me also." In the same letter, Randolph, somewhat cryptically but disparagingly, also wrote: "I feel most sorely at this moment the wounds of Haym Salomon and divers other Jews," probably in reference to their pressuring Virginia for payment.[41]

How many other public figures enjoyed Salomon's largesse during the Revolution is not clear for want of contemporary records, despite the long list offered in later, eulogistic, but scarcely substantiated accounts of Salomon's unrestricted generosity. An unexpected testimony appears, however, in a letter from Don Francisco Rendon, Spain's unofficial agent in Philadelphia, to the Governor-General of Cuba in 1783: "Mr. Salomon has advanced the money, for the service of his Most Catholic Majesty, and I am indebted to his friendship . . . for the support of my character as . . . agent here, with any degree of credit and reputation." It is a strange tribute from the representative of Spain's monarch to the philanthropy of a Jew. Similarly, Alexander Hamilton's Cash Book for April 1784 contains an entry for £150 Pennsylvania currency "by a draft to H. Salomon," but it is not clear whether it was in repayment of a loan. Unquestionably, Haym Salomon served the fiscal needs of the Revolutionary government ably and even unselfishly and deserved well of the country, and his contributions do not need to be exaggerated by later fictions.

Salomon apparently also prospered as a broker, as he wrote somewhat boastfully to a correspondent in London: "My business is [that of] a broker, and in bills of exchange, and so very extensive that I am generally known to the mercantile part of North America."[42] The scope of his private business is suggested in a number of his transactions. In one, dated 7 June 1783, Salomon instructed one Daniel Cormick of New York to sell for him 845 cases of fine gin that had just arrived from Holland. At the same time he wrote to Eliezer Levy of Baltimore to buy depreciated certificates. In the previous year he had answered an inquiry from Joshua Isaacs of Lancaster that he would supply all the money needed to buy bills of British officers being held as prisoners: "Draw on me for any sum."[43]

Salomon's private life and role in the Jewish community of Philadelphia during the later years of the Revolution were equally notable. While still in New York and relatively obscure, he had married Rachel Franks, member of a prominent American family. Her brother was Isaac Franks, who served ably as an officer in Washington's army. Another kinsman was Lieutenant-Colonel David S. Franks, an important Jewish figure in the Revolution, who has already been dealt with. Aside from Salomon, however, the Franks clan was so much affected by intermarriage and assimilation that Salomon's two sons and two daughters were apparently the only descendants to carry on its Jewish tradition and loyalty. Salomon maintained an active role in the Philadelphia Jewish community. He was a prime mover and major contributor to the erection of a new synagogue for Mikveh Israel, and he bore the brunt of a long controversy over it with Jonas Phillips, another prominent figure here.[44]

Salomon renewed relations with his own family in far-off Poland after the war. He advanced substantial sums for their support by means of long-range exchange transactions. To his father, Solomon, he wrote that, despite his lack of learning, his practical knowledge of languages had been most useful to him in business, and he recommended that the children be educated in "the Christian languages." He would, however, help out should his "brother's children have a good heart to learn Hebrew." To an uncle in London, to whom he also sent some money, he wrote earnestly in 1783: "Your bias of my riches are too extensive. Rich I am not, but the little I have I think it my duty to share with my poor father and mother.... Whatever little wine I can squeeze out I will give my relations, but I tell you plainly and truly that it is not in my power to give you or any relations yearly allowances." In strikingly modern fashion, he warned them not to "expect any idle and golden dreams that can never ... be accomplished." He discouraged his relatives from coming to America: "I desire no relation may be sent." He added in a rather crude and quaint Yiddish that there was "*vinig Yidishkayt*" (little Jewishness) here.[45]

Salomon took a strong stand on Jewish rights in the American community after the Revolution, and he joined others in the forceful assertion of this position. Aside from his single-handed defense of his Jewishness against the aspersions of Miers Fisher, as described earlier, Salomon was one of a half-dozen Jewish leaders in Philadelphia who spoke out boldly as early as 1783. Rev. Gershom Seixas, Barnard Gratz, Simon Nathan, Jonas Phillips, Asher Myers, and Haym Salomon addressed the Pennsylvania Council of Censors, petitioning them to remove from the state constitution the Christian test oath required of all officeholders: "Your memorialists . . . with great submission apprehend that a clause in the Constitution which disables them to be elected by their fellow citizens to represent them in the assembly is a stigma upon their nation and their religion, and it is inconsonant with the second paragraph of the said Bill of Rights." They called attention to the fact that "the Jews of Pennsylvania, in proportion to the number of their members, can count with any religious society whatsoever the Whigs among them. They have served some of them in the Continental Army; some went out in the Militia to fight the common enemy; all of them have cheerfully contributed to the support of the Militia and the government of this state." They warned that otherwise the Jews would go elsewhere, and indeed some were already returning to their prewar homes. The protest failed in 1783, but in 1790, following the example of the new federal Constitution, Pennsylvania repealed the objectionable clause and thus became one of the first states to establish religious equality in the political realm.[46]

This was Haym Salomon's last public action, combining his two major interests, national independence and religious equality. Less than two years later, on 6 January 1785, long in failing health, he died prematurely, not yet forty-five years old. The *Pennsylvania Packet*, in which he had advertised frequently, announced his death, which occurred "after a lingering illness. An eminent broker of this city, he was a native of Poland and of the Hebrew nation. He was remarkable for his skill and integrity in his profession, and for his generous and humane deportment." It was a well-merited tribute to a figure who played a notable role both as a Jew and as an American patriot.[47] Salomon's estate came to a substantial amount (some $353,000) but was largely in government currency and certificates of indebtedness, which were then greatly depreciated. A final evaluation in 1789 revealed that Salomon was actually insolvent; his debts of $45,292 exceeded his assets of $44,732 by $560. His family was left virtually penniless, but his widow was remarried in the year following his death to

David Heilbron. Another daughter was born to the couple, who later moved to the Netherlands.[48]

Such posthumous insolvency was not uncommon in the post-Revolutionary era. Aaron Lopez, an even wealthier merchant, suffered the same fate after his death by drowning in 1782. Salomon's patron, Robert Morris, experienced an even greater mortification, when, following hectic speculative activity, his career ended in bankruptcy in 1797. Morris spent several years in a debtors' prison and died impoverished and almost forgotten. It is ironic that Morris' services as a financial genius and financier of the Revolution have remained largely unremembered and inadequately recognized. Salomon's achievements, however, have been greatly expanded into virtually mythical proportions as part of the process by which the modern Jewish community in America has sought honorific recognition for its role and contributions to the Revolution. Salomon became the focus and principal beneficiary of this historical development, which will be considered separately and subsequently in a later chapter. It constitutes, as it were, a later stage and sequel to the Revolution, comprising several significant trends and claims, of which Salomon himself would probably have been unaware.

6

Other Economic Activities

The previous chapter closed with a discussion of the extensive enterprises and services of Haym Salomon, generally accepted as the most significant single Jewish contributor to the economics of the Revolution. The present chapter opens with the account of the business affairs of a less well-known but noteworthy merchant, Simon Nathan. If Haym Salomon represents a high degree of cooperation with the Revolutionary government, Nathan illustrates an equally high level of controversy and confrontation with a state government. Nathan's business was exceedingly intricate; its history constitutes a long and complex process of negotiation and opposition between the state of Virginia and a militant Jewish businessman. We still do not know whether and to what extent justice was finally done in this conflict of unequal parties.

Simon Nathan, founder of a large and important Jewish family in America, had obscure beginnings. Born in England in 1746, Nathan migrated to Jamaica, where he became a merchant of considerable scope. Whether from sympathy for the American cause or for merely business reasons, he shipped cordage, canvass, and powder to America early in the war by way of a neutral port. When discovered, he fled from Jamaica, first to Havana, and from there he went on to New Orleans, both places then under Spanish jurisdiction. They were important centers of trade with America during the Revolution. In New Orleans, during 1778-1779, Nathan invested heavily in bills of exchange on Virginia issued by George Rogers Clark and his agents. The proceeds went to finance General Clark's venture to conquer and acquire the Northwest Territory.[1]

Thus began a series of transactions that involved Nathan in a long-lasting dispute with Virginia over the payment of these bills. Other business enterprises complicated the relationship between Nathan and Virginia, one of which endured beyond the Revolution and was apparently never fully resolved. Drawn into the controversy were such important figures as two governors of Virginia, Thomas Jefferson and Benjamin Harrison; the principal delegate to the Continental Congress, James Madison; the Attorney-General, Edmund Randolph; and others. Their extensive correspondence over many years did not always clarify, but in fact further mystified the various claims of all parties. Altogether, this is an amazing example of the character and intricacies of business generated by the Revolution, in which Jews were involved.

Nathan's relations with Virginia began amicably enough. In the winter of 1780 he came to Richmond, where he lived for a time. In a letter dated 18 July 1783, Jefferson, who was governor of Virginia in 1780, outlined the whole association with Nathan over the years to Edmund Randolph, then the state Attorney-General. It began when Nathan presented his bills for payment, claiming to have paid "a hard dollar for every one named in the bill," and the total amounted to more than $50,000. "The bills appearing fair," Jefferson accepted them and agreed to pay in tobacco. Warrants were issued for ten hogsheads of tobacco as well as for other payments in cash and bills. This may have been a premature action, since Jefferson now wrote to General Clark for verification. He also consulted two justices of the Court of Chancery, who split on the merits of the case. Edmund Pendleton upheld Nathan's claims, but George Wythe ruled that he must prove he paid par for the bills. Clark's reply was that the bills were negotiated for "paper dollars," which, of course, had had a declining value.[2]

The issue that thus arose was whether Nathan had bought the bills at depreciated rates and was now claiming full face value. The Virginia legislature repudiated the earlier settlement. Jefferson's recollection of the situation was that Nathan seemed "to act candidly enough with us." This remained his position, perhaps because he had made the first settlement with Nathan, and he was subsequently humiliated at the repudiation and the failure to fulfill contracts. Nathan continued to protest that he had paid silver dollars at Havana and New Orleans, "without knowing they had been drawn at a depreciated rate," and he insisted on his right to full payment.[3]

In 1780, furthermore, Governor Jefferson negotiated with Nathan to supply clothing to the troops at Fort Pitt, writing on 9 June: "Your obliging offer of serving the state in the purchase of supplies for the officers and men stationed at Pittsburgh is accepted." Nathan's business in Richmond was closed out because Virginia failed to accept protested bills. He moved to Philadelphia, where he remained for the duration of the war. Thereafter he went to New York, as did so many others. One Virginia bill was for 15,000 livres on a French firm, Penet and Company. Unhappily the firm became bankrupt, and the bill was unpaid. Nathan now had an additional claim against Virginia for this bill, which remained unresolved for a long time.[4] In July 1781 Nathan resorted to a desperate device. A magistrate in Philadelphia issued to him an attachment on fifteen bales of merchandise, shipped by Monsieur Penet from France on the vessel *Franklin*. The Virginia authorities became both incensed and alarmed at this legal attack on a sovereign state. They protested to the Supreme Executive Council of Pennsylvania that "great evils may ensue to the particular state, and the Union in general, if individuals be allowed to arrest the military supplies of one state imported into or passing through another in time of war."[5]

Here was a constitutional issue of first magnitude. Joseph Reed, president of the Pennsylvania Council, acknowledged that the case might "tend to establish a precedent of great importance." The state supreme court rescinded the attachment and ordered the goods restored to Virginia. Madison and other Virginia delegates to the Continental Congress commended the action and advised clemency and no further action against the perpetrator, "as this is the first instance known to us in which it has been necessary to assert the sacredness of the property of a confederate state. . . ." Nathan appeared before the Pennsylvania Council and pleaded ignorance of state rights; he had acted merely "as a matter supposedly of right."[6]

Nathan, nevertheless, persisted in his efforts to collect from Virginia what was due him. In 1782 Jefferson appealed to Governor Benjamin Harrison for protection against a possible private suit by Nathan under an assumpsit of Virginia's public debt. He feared it would "leave me exposed to shipwreck where there never was anything in the nature of a private assumpsit [assumption of debt]." Amazingly, he expressed fear on this account to travel to Philadelphia, and "to leave a state by whose laws I must certainly be protected, and trust myself in another where that protection would be doubtful." Governor Harrison assured Jefferson he would be protected in the event of a suit by Nathan. Somewhat improperly, he introduced the charge that "Mr. Nathan's transactions may be fair for what I know, but so many frauds have been practiced in that quarter that I am led to doubt everything."[7]

An element of prejudice had entered the case, as Thomas Smith, Nathan's agent, complained when he made a plea for his client's rights and expressed the hope that "notwithstanding his former imprudence," the council would "throw aside the prejudices against this unfortunate man, altho' a Jew, and afford him relief, for the sake of his innocent family." Governor Harrison gave substance to the charge when he instructed the commissioners to investigate the western accounts, and urged them to hurry: "Nathan is so extremely pressing that I think he is conscious of the unjustness of his demand and hopes to worry him into payment before your report reaches me." Nathan's plea, however, was that Governor Jefferson had accepted his bills totaling £15,000, as drawn by Colonel Clark and Todd for Virginia. As to the issue of depreciation, he argued that he could prove the bills were purchased in silver for the full amount. He was now reduced to depending on them for his living: "That in fact he had no other resource." He was willing to accept arbitration or to receive one-third or one-fourth now and have the rest on interest to the end of the war. He hoped for a quick decision, "as he has long lain out his money ... at Havana and New Orleans thro' his attachment to the cause of America and the high ideas he entertained for the United States, and is now suffering, for want of the money."[8]

The outcome at this stage of the encounter was that Nathan, in Richmond in December 1782, agreed to arbitration of his claim in Philadelphia. Each party was to designate an arbitrator, and their judgment was to be binding. Joseph Reed and William Bradford were named as arbitrators, and Nathan entered bond for £30,000, but Virginia argued that its credit as a state was adequate to cover it. In February 1783 the arbitrators found for Nathan, and ruled that he should be paid fully as for specie. Governor Harrison apparently accepted the award and wrote to Jefferson that "no funds are yet established for that purpose. I shall lay the award of the arbitrators before the next assembly, who will no doubt provide for the payment." A committee of the Assembly of Delegates recommended the payment of the full sum with interest at 6 percent to May 1783.

Nathan's triumph was, however, short-lived. The assembly again repudiated the settlement and called for a new one, to the dismay of James Madison. As he wrote to the Attorney-General: it will "require all your eloquence I fear to shield the honor of the state from its effects. The agency which the Delegation (to the Congress, including himself) had in the affair will impart no small share of the mortification. I suppose the feelings of Mr. Jefferson and Mr. Harrison also will not be much delighted by it." Somewhat unhappy over all this, Randolph nevertheless accepted his assignment, "to prop the reputation of Virginia for good faith and to submit to hear just and copious reproaches thrown upon her." Randolph betrayed a note of bias in concluding sardonically that Virginia would receive no other satisfaction than to learn that "a Jew merchant, unconnected with America, took up bills on Virginia from pure magnanimity or affection for her."[9]

A second arbitration was, in fact, arranged, and the arbitrators met in Baltimore this time, as agreed, on 10 August 1783. The arbitration was indecisive and adjourned to Alexandria. Apparently nothing came of this meeting either. As late as 1789 Nathan's claims were still outstanding, including the protested bill on Penet and Company, which had been taken over by his creditors and presented to Virginia for payment.

Nathan had still another unhappy encounter with Virginia, in relation to western land grants. He was one of the stockholders of the Indiana and Illinois companies that had acquired large areas of western land after the French and Indian War ended in 1763. Nathan was a latecomer in these ventures, whose originators and promoters included a number of Jews, principally Joseph Simon,

David Franks, Michael Gratz, and Levy Andrew Levy, the last two Simon's sons-in-law. Nathan had acquired three hundred shares and was thus one of the plaintiffs suing Virginia for recognition of their rights. That state had conquered the Northwest Territory during the Revolution and had canceled all previous grants. In 1793 the case reached the Supreme Court and was rejected since it involved a sovereign state. Interestingly, a similar case involving Georgia at this time (*Chisholm v. Georgia*) led to the adoption of the Eleventh Amendment to the Constitution recognizing the rights and immunity of states from suit in federal courts.[10]

Despite Randolph's slur on Nathan's motives, his patriotism was unimpeachable. In a letter written to President Thomas Jefferson many years later, applying for a public appointment as a commissioner of bankruptcy, Nathan recited that, aside from his business with Virginia, he had also supplied clothing to the troops of South Carolina in a time of dire need. Although lacking any military background, Nathan enlisted in Captain Andrew Geyer's company of the Fourth Battalion of Pennsylvania militia, but there is no record of his active service. In Philadelphia Nathan married Grace Mendes Seixas, a sister of Rev. Gershom Seixas, who was the minister of Philadelphia's Mikveh Israel during his patriotic self-exile from New York. Nathan himself was prominent in the Jewish community, serving as president of the synagogue in 1782. He was one of the group, including Seixas and Salomon, that petitioned the Pennsylvania Council of Censors in 1783 for the repeal of the Christian test oath required of public officials. After the Revolution, Nathan moved to New York, where he encountered financial difficulties at first, but subsequently prospered in business and was prominent in community affairs. He died in 1822, and his only son, Isaac Seixas Nathan, fathered a large family, whose members became linked by marriage with such other leading families as the Gratzes, Cardozos, and Hendrickses. They produced a distinguished progeny long prominent in both the general and the Jewish community.[11]

Nathan's Revolutionary career sharply contrasted with that of another Jewish merchant, American-born but pro-British in sentiment. This was David Franks, born in New York in 1720, whose family, of German origin, had probably accompanied

George I, the Hanoverian King, on his accession to the English throne. The Franks family engaged in business on both sides of the Atlantic all through the eighteenth century, and some of them settled in America. They supplied the British army during the French and Indian War. One of their ships, the *Myrtilla*, ironically brought the famous bell to Philadelphia in1752, later known as the Liberty Bell. Two of David's brothers, Naphtali and Moses, lived in London and were partners in a large army contract firm, Colebrook, Nesbit, and Franks. David Franks was the American agent of this company in Philadelphia, where he lived before the Revolution. Surprisingly, he was a signatory there of the non-importation agreement in 1765. As early as 1758 Franks did business with George Washington, who was then a Virginia militia officer serving in a British colonial war. Washington instructed Franks to procure "as much green thicks as will make indian leggings for 1,000 men; if green cannot be had, get white; if there is not enough of that, get any colour." For his own use he commissioned "two English packs for carrying field baggage, a traveling letter case, a pair of light shoe-boots, a haircloth trunk to go under a field-bed, half a dozen china cups and saucers. Must have the articles to hand speedily or they will be useless to me." Franks executed the order promptly; in a later letter he acknowledged the receipt of £196, 15 s., 2 d. and wished Washington "a successful campaign." Eventually, it led to the conquest of the West from the French, in which Franks thus had a modest part.[12]

During the Revolution, however, David Franks had conflicting loyalties, and his course of action was not a smooth one. In contradictory fashion, he stayed on in the American zone but performed services for the British with American sanction. This proved in time too delicate a posture to maintain; he was banished to the British side in 1780, and he spent the remainder of the war in Britain. In the accepted manner of the time, Franks early became commissary of British prisoners, a role approved by the American government, but he, or rather the family firm in London, was reimbursed by the British for his outlays. Known to Washington from earlier dealings, Franks received his instructions in a letter of 9 February 1776. Writing to the Continental Congress from his encampment at Cambridge, Mass.,

Washington expressed the wish that Franks would send a deputy to see that the prisoners received what was allowed them by Congress: "It will save me much time and much trouble. . . . If there were persons to superintend this business, that their wants would be better attended to . . . and the whole could be then brought into proper account."[13]

In May 1776 Congress adopted rules to govern the operations of David Franks as commissary of prisoners. He was to "supply rations, wood, and money allowed to officers and sell his Bills for such sums of money as were necessary. An officer was to visit the prisoners monthly to count the prisoners so victualled and supplied." Prisoners might practice their trades and were not to be recruited for the army. In November 1777 Washington wrote to Congress, pointing out certain flaws in the arrangements made for prisoners. Franks, as agent for the British, had sent six thousand Continental dollars to Mr. Richard Graham of Virginia for the subsistence of Hessians and other prisoners in that state. Washington questioned the propriety of "a policy of suffering the enemy to support themselves with money which they refuse themselves and which they attempt to depreciate in every instance they possibly can." Moreover, he added the fear that "it may be counterfeited." Washington also challenged the British policy "as to our prisoners in their hands. Nothing will do for their support but hard money. If the enemy were obliged to furnish the same, the quantity with us would be greater. . . . I do not know what consequence a Prohibition against receiving continental money or the currency of any state from them might involve. I think the subject is worthy of the consideration of Congress."[14]

In January 1778 the Board of War reported to Congress, complaining of the bad treatment of the American prisoners in New York, by comparison with the British prisoners in American hands. Bills of exchange amounting to £600 had been purchased from Franks and sent to New York for the American prisoners, but "every obstacle was thrown in the way to prevent negotiation of these bills and, after a delay of two months . . . were returned to Mr. Boudinot, the American commissary of prisoners." They were treated cruelly and denied food, then tempted to enlist with the new levies in order to save their lives. By contrast, Myer Hart, a Jewish merchant of Easton, serving as agent for Franks to supply the British prisoners stationed there, reported that they were well treated and received one pound of bread and one of meat daily, although the meat allowance had recently been reduced to twelve ounces. They had freedom to move about and to work out at one dollar per day. Officers were on parole, and surgeons were designated to care for them.[15]

David Franks was apparently acquitting himself successfully as a commissary in the care of the British prisoners. Nevertheless, he experienced increasing difficulties in this anomalous position. He remained in Philadelphia during the brief British occupation of Philadelphia in 1777 and was, therefore, subsequently subject to suspicion and distrust. After the British evacuation of Philadelphia, many Tories were accused and convicted of treason for their conduct under the occupation. There was, however, not one Jew among them, and even Franks was acquitted by a jury with a verdict *ignoramus* ("we do not know") on a charge of giving information to the enemy. Interestingly, his beautiful and brilliant daughter, Rebecca Franks, figured prominently in the entertainment of the British officers in Philadelphia. She played a conspicuous role in the notorious Meschianza or fancy dress ball given in honor of the departure of General Howe for England. She was the daughter of a mixed marriage between David Franks and Margaret Evans. Eventually she herself married Sir Henry Johnson, a colonel in the British army, and subsequently she lived and raised a family in England.[16]

Greater troubles lay ahead for David Franks. One episode involved his niece, a Miss Hannah Levy, who was granted a pass by General Benedict Arnold, commander of Philadelphia after the occupation, to go to New York on the excuse of collecting a debt from a British officer. Arnold's relations with the Pennsylvania Executive Council under the radical Joseph Reed were troubled on many grounds, and Arnold's suspicious conduct and alleged economic exploitation of his position as commander ultimately led to a court-martial, in which he was found guilty and reprimanded. In the Levy case too, the council charged that her projected trip to New York was really improper and in the interest of her uncle, David Franks. She was denied a pass, and this gave rise to a constitutional issue of rival military and civilian jurisdictions in Philadelphia. Significantly, Arnold was then transferred by Washington to the command of West Point, where he attempted his notorious and treasonable betrayal. It ended with his flight and desertion of the American cause.[17]

In 1778 final disaster struck David Franks directly. On 26 October Washington informed General Clinton, the British commander in New York, that Congress had canceled Franks' appointment as commissary of prisoners. Clinton was asked to name a successor. Franks himself had been arrested by order of Congress on the charge of "clandestine correspondence" with the enemy. The provocation was a letter he had written and sent to his brother Moses in London, by way of his brother-in-law, the Tory officer General Oliver DeLancey, which had been intercepted. It revealed "a disposition and intention inimical to the safety and liberties of the United States." He had reported the galloping inflationary prices in Philadelphia. Moses attempted to intercede for his brother by appealing to Lord North, the Prime Minister of Britain, in behalf of "my unfortunate brother, . . . whom the tyranny of Congress has caused to be arrested and thrown into jail in that city." He hoped Sir Henry Clinton would exchange him, but "God knows whether he will be alive when such an act of benevolence and mercy shall reach him." The brother's alarm was somewhat exaggerated, since Congress soon released Franks to the jurisdiction of the Pennsylvania Supreme Council for further action. A trial jury acquitted him in Philadelphia, and Franks was freed and remained in the city nearly two years longer.[18]

The Pennsylvania Supreme Council finally ordered his expulsion on 6 October 1780. Perhaps it required some time to liquidate the property of a wealthy merchant, such as Franks obviously was. Rosenbach, the noted Philadelphia book dealer, discovered a brochure of 1780, advertised as a "Catalogue of a Collection of Valuable Books to be sold at the House of David Franks, Nov. 1, 1780." At this time, too, the Board of the Treasury reported that a house was available, recently occupied by David Franks. It was large and could be rented for £300 gold per annum. It was recommended as a proper dwelling for the President of the Congress.[19] In any event, David Franks went first to New York and then to England, where he entered a claim for compensation, avowing a loss of property estimated at £20,000, besides land valued at £6,000. He was allowed an annual pension of £100, which was scarcely liberal. His family ties with the Loyalist cause were close. Aside from his daughter, Rebecca, who married a British officer, his sister, Phila, had eloped and married Oliver DeLancey, of a prominent New York family, who became a Loyalist general in the British army. A son of David Franks, named Moses, was also in England and became an ensign in a British regiment.[20]

Franks did not prosper in England. In 1783 he wrote to Joseph Simon, a Jewish merchant of Pennsylvania, at Lancaster, and a former partner in land operations, that he was hard up. He intended to return to America, where he had land interests. By 1785 he was back in this country, bearing an introduction to Benjamin Franklin from a Richard Frankland of Dublin. It expressed the hope that Franklin's "countenance and advice will be of the most essential service to him." Past sixty-five now, Franks never regained his position and property, and he died in the yellow fever epidemic of 1793 in Philadelphia, in a sense a casualty of the Revolution. An episode occurring many years later, in 1816, relates to Lady Johnson, formerly Rebecca Franks, David's daughter, and adds a sad final note to the annals of the family. General Winfield Scott, a hero of the War of 1812, visited England in 1816 and met Lady Johnson at Bath, where she lived in great state. According to his account, she confided to him: "I have gloried in my fellow Americans! Would to God I too had been a patriot!" When chided by her husband, Sir Henry Johnson, she explained that she did not regret her marriage, but "I ought to have been a patriot before marriage." Scott concluded: "Hers were the only dry eyes in the party."[21]

As already indicated, Joseph Simon had been an associate of David Franks over many years in various enterprises, particularly western land operations. Simon's sympathies were, however, wholly with the Revolution. A contemporary of Franks, he was born in Germany and settled in Lancaster, on the Pennsylvania frontier, in 1740, barely a decade after its foundation. He remained a lifelong resident there and gathered about him a group of fellow Jews, who constituted a small quasi-community. Several married his daughters; among them were Michael Gratz and Levy Andrew Levy, who were his associates in land acquisition. One daughter, Shinah, married Dr. Nicholas Schuyler, of Albany, a military surgeon during the Revolution. Simon was an Indian trader and operated the largest store in Lancaster. By the extent and variety of his business, as well as by its strategic location, he was in a position to contribute greatly to the conduct of the war. Thus the firm of Simon and Henry supplied rifles, ammunition, blankets, and provisions to the army. Already on 2 November 1775, the Committee on Claims of the Continental Congress acknowledged a debt of over $2,300 to Simon for materials. Another bill was for $426.66 to pay for blankets delivered at Fort Pitt for use at the hospital. In 1778 Simon was paid $302 for arms supplied to the Thirteenth Virginia Regiment.[22]

Josph Simon, among his many activities, was also associated with David Franks as his agent for the supply of British prisoners in Pennsylvania. In January 1778 he wrote that, as soon as he heard from Franks, he would visit the various places where the "prisoners are under my department." In somewhat illiterate style, he instructed an associate, Elijah Etting: "You'd please to speak to some of the gentlemen members of Congress to know if we may continue as Yousual *[sic]*. Till I here *[sic]* from Mr. Franks, it is not in my power to make payments. I have to this day some thousands of pounds due me from Mr. Franks."

In November of 1778, Simon addressed the Board of War, reporting that Franks had directed him "to stop issuing provisions etc. to said prisoners . . . agreeable to a resolve of Congress discontinuing his acting in said office." Simon requested further instructions to supply the prisoners "with provisions, wood, Straw, Tobacco, Soap, Candles, etc." He accounted altogether for 285 prisoners, among them 140 at Fort Frederick, "Fredericktown 50, Winchester about 30, Lancaster 40, and Easton 25." He asked the board to appoint him as the successor to Franks, and promised "to give satisfaction on as good terms as any other person whatever." There is no evidence that he received this assignment. Simon was now advanced in age, although he lived on until ninety-two and died in Lancaster in 1804. In a broad sense his was a national business career, comparable to that of Aaron Lopez, and not limited to any one place, although Lancaster was his lifelong home for more than half a century. In this frontier location, it was natural that he should have been involved in the formation of the Indiana and Illinois companies for the acquisition of western lands, along with David Franks, the Gratzes, Whartons, and others from Philadelphia.[23]

One other Jewish merchant should be included with the group of leading figures engaged in business related to the Revolution. This was Jonas Phillips, who enjoyed the additional merit of being a prominent and zealous member of the synagogues both in Philadelphia and New York. He was also the founder of an important Jewish family in America, noted for his son, Naphtali, a newspaper publisher in later years, and particularly for his grandsons, the two brothers, both professional naval officers, Uriah P. and Jonas Levy, and Mordecai Manuel Noah, the versatile practitioner of many professions. They will be dealt with elsewhere as extraordinary and colorful embodiments comprising the new Jews who reflected the mixed Jewish and American elements in the post-Revolutionary era. Moreover, Phillips himself added an intellectual dimension to the role of the Jews in America, proclaiming their equal political and religious rights. His importance thus transcended the mercantile contribution alone.

German-born in 1736, Phillips was in New York by 1756, where he established himself as a retail merchant and auctioneer. He married into a Sephardic family, more accurately one of Portuguese origin; his wife was Rebecca Machado, daughter of the *hazzan* of Shearith Israel. On the outbreak of the Revolution, he chose the patriotic side and left New York with his family, urging that others do the same rather than live under tyranny. In Philadelphia he became a merchant and also an active member of Mikveh Israel, of which he was president as well as an ardent promoter. In 1778 he enrolled in Captain John Leviton's company of the Philadelphia militia, although he was already past forty.[24]

Phillips' mercantile sense and role are well indicated in an informative letter he wrote on 28 July 1776 to a Gumpel Samson of Amsterdam. It was intercepted by the British and is preserved in the Record Office in London. Written in Yiddish, the German dialect, it referred to an earlier lost letter, to which there had been no reply, a not uncommon occurrence in wartime. Phillips included a bill of exchange for his mother and added that Dutch wares would be in great demand, for want of English goods. He indicated that profits might be as high as 400 percent, and he listed the commodities in demand: linens, sheeting, Osnaburgs, Russian duck, ivory combs, needles, pins, sewing silks, drugs and medicines, worsted stockings, woolen blankets, and other woolens. Here was a virtual spectrum of manufactures America did not as yet make at home but needed to import. Despite its commercial content and tone, the letter closed optimistically on a political and patriotic note: "The war will make all England bankrupt. The Americans have an army of 100,000 and the English only 25,000 and some ships. The Americans have already made themselves like the states of Holland. The enclosed is a declaration of the whole country. [The allusion is to the Declaration of Independence, of which he enclosed a copy.] How it will end, the blessed God knows. The war does me no damage. Thank God."[25]

Perhaps overly optimistic in his initial prediction, Phillips nevertheless persisted and was quietly successful, if not in the grand style of an Isaac Moses or Aaron Lopez. He was among those who offered unsolicited advice to Robert Morris, the Superintendent of Finance. In 1783 he proposed a lottery, which Morris, according to his diary, "could not approve either as reasonable, feasible, or just, therefore returned it to the author." Whether from an inclination toward a more intellectual orientation, or perhaps because of his position of leadership in the Jewish community, Phillips rose above the mere merchant's level and expressed himself strongly on the broad question of Jewish rights and emancipation. In 1783 he joined with several leaders of Philadelphia's Jewry in petitioning the Pennsylvania Supreme Council for the removal of the religious test from the Constitution.

On 7 September 1787, back in Philadelphia, after a brief stay in New York, Jonas Phillips, this time by himself, addressed the Constitutional Convention, then completing the preparation of the federal Constitution, and appealed to it in behalf of the Jews: "All men have a natural and unalienable right to worship Almighty God according to the dictates of their own conscience and understanding." He reminded them that "it is well known among all the citizens of the thirteen United States that the Jews have been true and faithful Whigs, and during the late contest with England they have been foremost in aiding and assisting the states with their lives and fortunes. They have supported the cause, have bravely fought and bled for liberty which they cannot enjoy." He concluded with the hope that the Convention would change the religious oath required of officeholders: "Then the Israelites will think themselves happy to live under a government where all religious societies are on an equal footing." Happily, the Convention had already written into the Constitution precisely such a clause, forbidding all religious tests for public office. Pennsylvania followed suit in 1790, and other states thereafter.[26]

There were numerous other Jews, not otherwise well known, whose business activity impinged at some point on the course of the Revolution and therefore left some mark on it, however slight or ephemeral. Thus, even before the Revolution, Isaac Adolphus, who died in 1774, advertised in the *New York Journal* in July 1769 that he had available wares "equal in price and superior in goodness to British goods of the same patterns, which if the patriotic Americans should approve large quantities can be readily furnished. . . ." This call to national economic independence was consistent with the sentiment stirred by the nonimportation agreements following the Stamp Act and other repressive British measures. It persisted in American patriotic thought well after the Revolution. A similar interest motivated Samuel de Lucena, born in New York, the son of a functionary in the congregation Shearith Israel. He may have learned the art of soap-making from a kinsman, Moses Lopez, in Newport. In 1765 he was in Norwalk, Connecticut, whose legislature he petitioned for a privilege to manufacture potash. During the Revolution he turned up in Philadelphia, where he addressed Congress for financial help to search for sulfur, an essential commodity in war. He was denied on the ground that it would set a bad precedent, since he would profit by discovery. It was admitted, however, that he was "well affected . . . to the American cause," and that he "might have been prompted by a desire to serve the public." There is no evidence that he was successful in his effort. Others of the same name, however, James and John Charles Lucena, were Loyalists and left America because of the Revolution.[27]

In Pennsylvania the Etting family achieved a creditable record in all aspects of the Revolution, economic as well as military. There were two branches of the family, founded by two brothers, Asher and Elijah, respectively. Asher's son, Reuben, as already recorded elsewhere, died of privations of war as a prisoner of the British. His daughter was Esther, the heroic wife of David Hays, a farmer and merchant in Westchester County, New York, whose exploits against the Tories there have already been related. Asher's brother, Elijah Etting, was an Indian trader in York, Pennsylvania, who supplied blankets to General Hand for the hospital at Fort Pitt, for which he was authorized payment of $426. Elijah died in 1778, and his family split up for the duration of the war. The widow, Shinah, and her five daughters were among the first Jewish settlers in Baltimore. Two sons, Solomon and Reuben, remained in Pennsylvania but were too young for service in the war. After the war they also came to Baltimore, where they performed distinguished service in the general and Jewish life of the community. Reuben was important in military activity during later wars and was a prominent Jeffersonian politician. Solomon played a leading role for many years in the agitation for the repeal of Maryland's law requiring a Christian test oath of all officeholders. This was a kind of sequel to the Revolution. The so-called Jew Bill of 1826 brought about final repeal, and Solomon Etting was immediately elected to the Baltimore City Council and was chosen its president. He was joined as a member of the council by Jacob I. Cohen, a wealthy banker of Baltimore, who had also participated in the repeal movement and with justice protested that "in a time of peril and war the Jews had borne the privations incident to such times . . . in defense of the common cause." Both Etting and Cohen were thus the living embodiment of the process of political and religious emancipation that grew out of the Revolution and spread, however slowly, into state after state. They also founded families distinguished in Baltimore Jewish and general history.[28]

Another early Jewish settler in Baltimore was Benjamin Levy. He came from Philadelphia, where he had signed the nonimportation agreement of 1765. In Baltimore he was designated by the Continental Congress as a signer of the Bills of Credit issued there. It is not clear whether such a signature entailed the assumption of liability for their security or was merely indicative of patriotic support for them. Levy was well-connected with prominent military and political figures of the Revolution. Already in May 1775 he was writing intimately to the then Major Horatio Gates, later the commanding general at Burgoyne's surrender in 1777 at Saratoga. Levy wrote that he would have answered earlier, "but my mind has been agitated for some time past with the various scenes of British policy that I could think of nothing else. Your sentiments are so generous and liberal in favor of America that if you had no other merit that alone would lead me to gratify you in every intelligence in my power." He was sending some sundry goods amounting to some nine pounds, and he added friendly sentiments for Mrs. Gates and Master Bob, all indicative of a close personal relationship.[29]

A year later, in December 1776, Levy was writing to Robert Morris in Philadelphia, whom he appears to have known well. The British were threatening the city, and should they take it, Levy invited Morris and his family to take refuge with him in Baltimore. He had "very good rooms on our first floor . . . ; our house is good and large, and could accommodate all your children and three or four servants, but sincerely pray that you may not be under the necessity of leaving your home, and that we shall soon hear of the enemy retiring." Happily the battles of Princeton and Trenton intervened, the danger passed for the time being, although the British did take and hold Philadelphia briefly during 1777. As a sequel to the wide Levy acquaintance-ship, a letter from Mrs. Rachel Levy, widow of Benjamin, was addressed many years later to President George Washington, "a former acquaintance." She asked him for a position for her son, Robert Morris Levy, who was "nearly of age, brought up for a merchant," but without capital. There is no evidence that the request brought an appointment for young Levy, but it is one of many such applications, which indicate the rising political aspirations of Jews in post-Revolutionary America. They will be treated later as a significant manifestation of the Jewish interest in serving in government after the Revolution. A brother of Robert,

Nathan Levy, was the United States naval agent in Haiti in 1798, during the undeclared war with France.[30]

Another Jewish merchant, Jacob Hart, was an early settler in Baltimore. Born in Germany, he was on the American and patriotic side during the Revolution, although others of the same name in Newport were not. In 1781 Lafayette, on the way to Virginia for what was to be the decisive Yorktown campaign, stopped in Baltimore. He needed funds badly, and £5,000 was raised, of which Hart is reported to have contributed £2,000. Congress later expressed its thanks to the contributors, and Robert Morris as Superintendent of Finance repaid the debt. In 1786 occurred an episode reminiscent of post-Revolutionary obligations often not honored. A Mrs. Rachel Hart petitioned Congress to redeem a certificate given to her husband, Noah, for the payment of medical services he had furnished to British prisoners in Maryland. Despite the names, it is not altogether demonstrable or certain that they were Jewish, a not uncommon dilemma in the period.[31]

Among the Jewish merchants who abandoned New York for Philadelphia early in the Revolution, one of the most widely experienced was Hayman Levy. Like many others, born in Germany, he had lived in New York since the 1740s and had engaged in extensive and diverse business activities, among them the supply of military goods to the British army and the operation of a privateer during the French and Indian War. With the collapse of the wartime boom, he went bankrupt, a not unusual experience in this era of wide political and economic oscillation. Later Levy turned to the fur trade and was even reported to have employed young John Jacob Astor as a fur beater. He was one of some ten Jewish merchants who signed a nonimportation agreement in 1765. In 1776, while still in New York, he was directed by James Mease, Clothier-General of the Continental Army, to send the goods purchased by New York to General Washington, then in Massachusetts. Almost immediately thereafter, however, Congress instructed Mease to return these goods for the use of New York.

Levy was one of the patriots who, according to the recollection of Naphtali Phillips, son of Jonas, "fled from New York to Philadelphia after the battle of Washington Heights . . . into a voluntary exile during the time New York was in the hands of the British." His son-in-law, Isaac Moses, left New York too and became a merchant of great consequence in wartime Philadelphia, as detailed elsewhere. During the remainder of the war, Levy continued to supply clothing to the army. Both Moses and Levy returned to New York after the Revolution and assumed a prominent role in the rebuilding of trade as well as the restoration of Shearith Israel there. Interestingly, a Levy Marks petitioned Congress in 1777 "to be appointed to superintend the clothing making up for the troops." The petition was referred to the Clothier-General.[32]

Manuel Josephson was another refugee from New York, who escaped across the bay in a small, leaky boat, as did so many other Jews. He settled in Philadelphia and became a broker. His name appears in Robert Morris' diary, although not as frequently as that of Haym Salomon. On one occasion, Josephson, the diary relates, "brought in sundry Bills protested by Mr. Jay, then United States minister in Spain." Josephson visited Morris several times, "respecting the payment of the Bills. . . . I offered new bills on Spain, and he desired to wait until he can hear from his Principal." In the end, Josephson accepted the bills on Madrid, and thus the matter ended. A somewhat unusual episode of the Revolution concerned Moses Franks of Philadelphia, a kinsman of both David and David S. Franks, who played important roles on opposite sides of the Revolution, as already narrated elsewhere. In 1776 Moses Franks was designated by Congress as one of three men, including Thomas Hanson and John Donaldson, for the mission of conveying $250,000 in funds to General George Washington at Cambridge, for the conduct of the campaign against the British in Boston. The task was executed successfully, for which they were paid some eighty-nine pounds. No more is recorded about Franks, except that he was a private in the First Company of the Fourth Battalion of the Philadelphia militia, in which a number of other Jews also served.[33]

As the political and economic center of the Revolution, Philadelphia and indeed the state of Pennsylvania as a whole provided many and varied opportunities for trade and attracted many merchants, Jewish and others. One of these who was especially active was Aaron Levy. He came from Amsterdam in 1760 and was a pioneer settler in the town of Northumberland. He was one of the small but important group of Jewish traders who carried their business into the interior of Pennsylvania. They also became land proprietors on the frontier. Joseph Simon and his son-in-law, Michael Gratz, were among those who operated out of Lancaster. They have been dealt with earlier. As early as 1775, Aaron Levy supplied goods to the Pennsylvania troops and was paid some forty-four pounds. During the Revolution he lent a sum of money to Robert Morris, Superintendent of Finance, always in need of funds, who authorized the Treasurer of the United States to issue interest-bearing loan office certificates to him. After the war Aaron Levy acquired land in Centre County, Pennsylvania, and laid out the town of Aaronsburg, the first in the county.

An unusual episode of 1782 further illustrates the activities of Jewish merchants in central Pennsylvania. There had been British prisoners kept in this area all through the Revolution, and Joseph Simon had been an agent of David Franks in supplying them. The Yorktown surrender of 1781 brought more prisoners to this area. A Jewish merchant of Lancaster, Joshua Jacobs, entered into a correspondence with Haym Salomon about their maintenance, and particularly about the sale of bills issued by British officers kept there. Salomon's reply was ambitious in tone and scope: "Draw on me for any sum by post or express, and it shall be honored at sight, let the sum be ever so great. The bills may be drawn on New York, (still under British occupation) or London, if they are endorsed by their commanding officer."[34]

Among the most enterprising Jewish merchants during the Revolutionary era and after were the Gratz brothers, Barnard and Michael. They too were born in Germany, whence they migrated first to London, where they had an uncle, under whom they served an apprenticeship. They then came to Philadelphia, Barnard as early as 1754 and Michael in 1759. They began their business careers during the French and Indian War, Barnard as a clerk of David Franks, and Michael as an apprentice to Joseph Simon, one of whose five daughters he married. They became part of that group of merchants, embracing Jews like Simon and Franks, and others, not Jews, in Pennsylvania, such as George

Groghan and the Whartons, who acquired land grants on the frontier and formed the early Indiana and Illinois companies. In 1765 both Gratz brothers signed the nonimportation agreement, and their anti-British sentiment, as in the case of others, was undoubtedly motivated by their frontier expansionism. During the Revolution Michael Gratz became associated with Robert Morris and others in the outfitting and operation of privateers. He also traded extensively with Virginia, and for a time lived in Richmond. Thus, as early as 26 March 1776, the Virginia Committee of Safety authorized the payment of £2,800 for sundry goods purchased from Gratz, and in June of the same year another warrant for £708 was issued to him for "sundry Broadcloths furnished to the public." Later in 1776, Michael Gratz purchased a ship for Virginia. He was a partner of Carter Braxton, a signer of the Declaration of Independence from Virginia, in privateering and other ventures. Gratz also handled the financial affairs of the Virginia delegation in Congress. One advance he made them in 1780 was for $30,000 in continental currency, actually worth only $400 in Virginia money. In 1781 Michael Gratz furnished £1,500 in supplies for the proposed Clark expedition against Detroit, which never materialized, and he had to wait three years before he was reimbursed in tobacco.[35]

Significantly, on the conclusion of the war in 1783, and for several years thereafter, the merchants of Philadelphia experienced a period of depression and financial difficulty, in part owing to speculative activities, particularly in land. Some Jewish merchants were in distress and even went bankrupt. In 1789 Michael Gratz petitioned the city for a broker's license. He described himself as an "old resident of Philadelphia, who had resided there upward of thirty years." He pleaded that "owing to the late Revolution among other causes, he has sustained considerable injuries and is at present without any fixed Employ or Business." He had ten children to provide for. Incidentally, one of them was Rebecca, who was to become in later years the first notable Jewish woman in America, widely known and highly regarded both in the non-Jewish world and also among Jews as an articulate voice of Jewish interests and causes. Significantly, as late as 1833, a bill in Congress authorized the payment of continental loan office certificates issued to Michael Gratz in 1779 for goods imported from the West Indies. The bill did not pass; but it offered further evidence of Gratz's extensive revolutionary activity in the economic sphere.[36]

Among the Jews who left New York for Connecticut, a significant contributor to the Revolution was Solomon Simson. He was the son of Joseph Simson, born in Germany in 1686, who survived the Revolution and died in 1787, at a hundred and one. Solomon was established in New York as the owner of a spermaceti candle factory, which the British seized when they occupied the city. He served in the New York militia and in 1778 petitioned the state legislature to compensate him for "certain common and other articles taken into public service." He lived in various towns of Connecticut during the Revolution, but returned to New York thereafter and continued to play a prominent role even then. In 1785, for example, John Jay, the Secretary for Foreign Affairs, transmitted to Congress a proposal from Solomon Simson, whom he recommended highly "as a Whig citizen and an honest man." The document outlined a plan for a national mint, and Jay added that "the subject appears to me of sufficient importance to merit the attention of Congress, and this paper if committed may possibly be the means of putting that business in proper order."[37]

In later years Simson was active as the vice-president of a New York Democratic Society. He was attacked by the ex-Loyalist and conservative journalist, James Rivington, as a "Shylock," which brought the retort from Simson that he was proud to be a Jew. Interestingly, this was only one instance of a number of public slurs against Jews after the Revolution. They perhaps represented a reaction against the political progress and recognition of Jews in the post-Revolutionary era, to be dealt with later. Among Solomon Simson's more unusual contributions was a Hebrew letter he addressed to the Jews of China. In it he described the Jewish community of New York as consisting of some seventy-two families, and he asserted that the "Jews live in great security . . . and sit in judgment in civil and criminal cases just as do Gentiles."[38]

Solomon Simson's dedication both to Jewish and to American interests was carried forward by his son Samson. He was born in Danbury, Connecticut, during the family's exile from New York.

He attended and was graduated from Columbia College in 1800, and he presented on this occasion an unprecedented thesis. It was written for him by the Rev. Gershom Seixas, the patriotic Revolutionary minister, who was now a trustee of Columbia. Dealing with the history of the Jews in America, it may be regarded as an expression of Jewish pride and self-awareness at this early date, by both minister and student. In it young Samson waxed eloquent and patriotic: "In the year 1776, at the time when the people of this country stood up like one man in the cause of liberty and independence, every Israelite that was among them rose up likewise and united in their efforts to promote the country's peace and prosperity." While not literally accurate, it was, nevertheless, a proper affirmation of loyalty, combining it with faith in Judaism. This was a major consequence of the American Revolution and the role of the Jews in it, as expressed by the Seixas, Simson, and many other contemporary Jewish families.[39]

Another wartime Jewish refugee from New York to Connecticut was Samson Mears, who settled in Norwalk. In 1777 the town was raided and pillaged by the British, and the Jews suffered severe losses. Aaron Lopez, from his refuge in Leicester, Massachusetts, came to their help, and Mears thanked him for "the benevolence of your generous family toward the relief of the unhappy sufferers of Norwalk." Mears dated the raid as in the ninth of Ab season, commemorating the destruction of the Temple, and compared that event with the attack on Norwalk. In even bolder spirit, the residents of Norwalk, among them Myer Myers, Solomon Simson, and Benjamin Jacobs, petitioned the Council of Safety for a vessel of eight guns to protect Long Island Sound against the repetition of raids. Simson conducted an extensive trade, and he once suffered the seizure of a shipload of salt by Connecticut privateers.

Samson Mears, however, complained of his depressed state and voiced a desire to move to the West Indies in letters to Aaron Lopez, with whom he carried on business transactions. The extent of his commerce is suggested in the *Journals of the Continental Congress*, which contain an order for $1,666 to be paid to Mears for goods supplied to William Aylett, Deputy Commissary General for Virginia. Aaron Lopez bore a specially close relation to several Jewish merchants in Connecticut, with whom he carried on a correspondence and business. David Judah, the son of a Jewish father named Michael or Meir and a Christian mother, was born in Norwalk in 1756. During the war Connecticut seized some sugar of his, but released it to him. In 1780 he wrote to Lopez, complaining of monetary depreciation and its depressing effect on business. He had lost his means of livelihood and appealed to Lopez for a supply of goods. Similarly, a Joseph De Pass, living in Woodstock, also wrote to Lopez at this time, complaining of his distressed condition and requesting a stock of fresh goods for his store.[40]

Myer Myers, the famous silversmith of New York, and his brother, Asher, a brass worker, both moved to Norwalk during the Revolution. Here Myer was considered for an appointment as reducer, to melt lead into bullets, but the British confiscated his tools, as well as his brother's, in their raid on Norwalk. They declined their share of Aaron Lopez's financial assistance, but received an abatement of taxes for their losses, along with others. In another capacity, as a revolutionary patriot, Myer Myers participated in an unusual episode with one Peter Betts in October 1776. They filed a complaint with the secretary of the Connecticut legislature against Ralph Isaacs of New Haven, who was probably of Jewish origin and a graduate of Yale College. They reported hearing Isaacs talk in a Norwalk tavern to the discredit of the American forces as being always in retreat from the British. "The people of Long Island had submitted to the British, and so will all others," said Isaacs, whose "conversation was very discouraging with respect to success on the Continental side." Isaacs, a suspected Tory, was at first detained and confined to a fixed place of abode, but was finally allowed to take an oath of loyalty and to live undisturbed on his estate, perhaps because of his advanced age and family connections. After the war, Myers returned to New York, where the congregation of Shearith Israel designated him as one of a committee of three to present an address of welcome to Governor George Clinton and to express their joy in their new-found freedom.[41]

In Rhode Island the prosperous Jewish community of Newport was disrupted by divisions of loyalty as well as by the early British occupation. The Lopez and Rivera families, as already related elsewhere, found refuge in Leicester, Massachusetts, and carried on their extensive business operations from there. Those of a Loyalist conviction, of whom there was a considerable number, as will be dealt with later, either stayed on or, in the case of a few more determined ones, fled later to New York under British occupation. Early in the Revolution, however, the General Assembly of Rhode Island accepted three four-pounder cannon from Jacob Isaacs and voted to pay Aaron Lopez twenty-two pounds in lawful money for four half-barrels of gunpowder and one whaleboat for the use of the state.

Jacob Isaacs, scion of an old New York family, appears again in the public documents after the Revolution, as late as 1791. He was the author of a petition to Congress requesting compensation for developing a process to desalinate seawater and thus make it suitable for use on ships at sea. Congress referred the matter to Thomas Jefferson, then Secretary of State, regarded as a kind of unofficial scientific expert. After an investigation, Jefferson recommended its rejection as impractical. The Isaacs family continued to be important in Newport after the Revolution. A brother, Moses, who had served as an army officer during the Revolution, entertained President Washington when the latter visited the town in 1790. During Washington's visit the famous letter in support of religious rights was presented to him on behalf of the Jewish community by Moses Seixas, to which Washington made his equally famous reply, to be discussed later.[42]

In the dispersal of Newport's Jewry early in the Revolution, Moses Michael Hays went to Boston, where he was the first permanent Jewish settler and prospered in the insurance business. Two nephews came to Boston with their widowed mother, Hays' sister, and lived with him. They were Abraham and Judah Touro, sons of the Reverend Isaac Touro, the famous *hazzan* of Newport, who was a Loyalist and who had gone to Jamaica where he died prematurely. Abraham Touro became a prominent merchant in Boston, and his brother later migrated to New Orleans, where he acquired a considerable fortune. Both brothers left their large estates for distribution among a great variety of public causes and were thus the early models of large-scale American philanthropy.

Hays himself was an active Mason, as were many other Jewish merchants in this period. Significantly, Masonry in the late eighteenth century provided a broad means of assimilation for many Jews in America, especially through its liberal tradition and links with the Enlightenment. Hays was the founder of several Masonic chapters in various parts of the country and rose to the rank of Deputy Grand Master. In 1782 Hays offered financial advice to Robert Morris, then the Superintendent of Finance, but the details are not specified in the Morris diary, which reports the episode. Morris politely declined his proposal; the present state of public business, he wrote "does not require the assistance you have so kindly offered. If I should find it necessary to adopt the measure you propose or any similar one my views thereon will be fully communicated to Mr. Lovell, the receiver." A clue to the proposal is perhaps contained in an earlier letter of Morris to Hays, commenting on a plan to collect taxes from the states, to establish a "fund of money as you propose in the hands of the Continental Receiver, Mr. Lovell, so that he will be enabled to exchange money for Bank Bills or my Notes. . . ."[43]

In the South as in the North, Jewish merchants played some role in supplying the economic needs of war, despite the restricted scope of trade generally. This was partly due to the limited character of the population and the plantation economy, but more especially because of the military and naval activity of the British and their Loyalist allies in occupying much of the territory and the principal towns, such as Charleston and Savannah. Available funds were low, and the country resorted to many kinds of paper money. The troubled fiscal relations of Simon Nathan with Virginia during the Revolution have already been explored, as have also the business transactions of Michael Gratz. There were others, too. An Isaac Levy appears as a provisioner of the Virginia forces on the frontier. With two partners, Gratiot and LaCroix, obviously of French origin, he engaged in trade in the Illinois Country in 1779, in order "to furnish . . . provisions and other necessary things . . . to empower them better to carry out their patriotic design." In 1781 Levy complained he had been paid with worthless currency by Virginia.[44]

In the lower South too, Jewish business activity appears not uncommonly. An unusual petition in the Georgia colonial documents records that several women, including Abigail and Sally Minis of Savannah, addressed James Wright, the royalist governor, and council of Georgia. Belonging to the Whig Party, they complained that they were persecuted, and they asked permission to go to Charleston. They were allowed to leave, and Mrs. Abigail Minis carried on trade in Charleston, despite her advanced age, while her son, Philip, was busy with Revolutionary matters, such as advising and guiding the French invaders of Savannah in 1779.[45] Other Jews of Savannah, particularly the Sheftalls and Cushman Polock, were early known for their Whig sentiments and patriotic activities, as already related elsewhere. In 1781 Governor Wright, in a communication to Sir George Jermaine, Secretary for America in the British government, remarked on "the great number of sculking [sic] rebels and disaffected persons in this province," and he made special note of the Jews: "For these people, my Lord, were found to a man to have been violent rebels and persecutors of the King's loyal subjects." He advised that they should not be allowed to return to Georgia. In fact, however, a number of Jewish craftsmen and traders remained in Savannah under British occupation and had to be exculpated by special circumstances in the investigation that followed the British evacuation at the end of the war, as is explained elsewhere.[46]

Ironically, the very fact that some Jews had left Savannah for a more hospitable refuge in Charleston brought an accusation by "An American," in the *South Carolina American General Gazette* in December 1778, that the Jews were deserting their state for business in South Carolina. This brought a rebuke from "A Real American and True-Hearted Israelite," otherwise unidentified, refuting this charge. Only the wives of Jews and their children were in Charleston, and some were carrying on business. The men, on the contrary, had left for Georgia on 22 November, "on being informed of the enemy landing . . . and proceeded post haste to Georgia, leaving all their concerns unsettled, and are now with their brother citizens in the field, doing that which every honest American should do. . . . The Charleston Israelites have hitherto behaved as the other citizens of this state." The inference was left that the Southern Jews were subordinating their business interests to their patriotic, military obligations. This has already been amply illustrated in an earlier chapter on Jewish military activities.[47]

The wide travels and tribulations, including the imprisonment of the Sheftalls of Savannah, are illustrative of both the military and the economic role of the Jews in the South. They have been recounted at length elsewhere. Others, however, had similar if less dramatic experiences, and a certain number of Southern Jews, like the Sheftalls, ultimately found refuge in Philadelphia, where they were a notable addition to the wartime expansion of Mikveh Israel. Isaac daCosta refused to accept British protection on the capture of Charleston and suffered the loss of his property. He arrived in Philadelphia in 1781, and he petitioned the Continental Congress for the redemption of some Loan Office Certificates, pleading that he had no business or other means of livelihood. Congress, however, had no funds for the purpose. Cushman Polock was another refugee from the South in Philadelphia. Congress authorized payment of $1,287 to him by James Mease, the Clothier-General, for the supply of goods, and also to Minis and Cohen, another Georgia firm, for $5,496.[48] Abraham Cohen helped to furnish clothing for General Pulaski's Legion in the South. Cohen, born in London, was the son of Moses, the first functionary in the Charleston synagogue. He later lived and prospered in Georgetown, South Carolina, where he was named deputy postmaster in 1789. He was also an auctioneer and commissioner of streets and markets. His nephew, Jacob Myers, succeeded him as postmaster in 1801. Jacob's father, Mordecai Myers, had been a purveyor to General Francis Marion, the famed "swamp fox" of South Carolina.[49]

An unusual episode involved Solomon Bush and his brother Nathan in a claim against South Carolina. On 30 March 1780 Solomon petitioned Congress for compensation for his brother's schooner, the *Speedwell*, impressed into service by South Carolina. In the following year, the Admiralty Office recommended, after an examination of the case, that Bush be paid $45,000 in South Carolina currency, agreeable to an appraisal. After the Revolution South Carolina acknowledged other claims and issued "indents" or indentures for payments to a number of Jews, indicative of the extent and variety of wartime supplies. Thus Isaac daCosta was allowed more than £126 for salt acquired in April 1780. One Isaac Laney was paid some £7 for sundries supplied to the military forces. Solomon Cohen was awarded £54 for "an hogshead of rum" impressed for the use of the garrison at Georgetown in December 1782. Jacob Minis was allowed nearly £10 for "sundries" for the Continental Army and militia in 1779.

Joseph Alexander was paid for 720 pounds of flour, supplied to the militia in 1779. He illustrates the problem of identification, since he may not have been Jewish. He lived on Wadmalow Island rather than Charleston, where namesakes of his were prominent and active Jews, particularly Abraham Alexander, who was *hazzan* of the synagogue and an officer in the militia. An Aaron Alexander, who may have really been Abraham, was allowed £38 for militia duty in 1779 and 1783, while Joseph Myers was paid £8 for beef supplied to the militia in 1781. Other indents were in favor of Philip Hart, Joseph Markess, and Solomon Polock, an express rider, all of Charleston. Some also served in a military capacity, probably in the Charleston militia.[50]

North Carolina, too, acknowledged various Revolutionary debts by the issuance of certificates to claimants in 1783-1784, but the purposes were not specified, although it must be assumed that they were primarily economic in character. The amounts were both large and small; they provide a sampling of the scope and scale rather than the totality of wartime business in which Jews seemed to be involved. Thus Abraham Moses was allowed £3,000 with interest of £180. Joseph Laney was granted some £109. In Georgia, Moses Nunez of Savannah had served as "Linguist to the Indians" as early as 1778. In 1782 he petitioned Governor Martin to be named "Commissary and Interpreter to the Indians and also Clerk of the Market in Savannah, in consideration of the losses he has sustained in these times." Interestingly, other appointments of Jews to public office, usually of an economic nature, were made at this time, although there is no indication of their being in recognition of or compensation for wartime services. In 1784 Daniel Nunez was sworn in as Harbor Master for Savannah, following his appointment by the legislature. Abraham daCosta was granted a license by the governor and council as vendue master or public auctioneer.[51]

Of special interest in this connection is the fact that some

Canadian Jews too claimed recognition and compensation for their services to the Revolution, some long afterwards. This may have been partly because the Jews in Canada were largely recent arrivals from America in the years between the last French and Indian War and the American Revolution. Their kinship and sentiments may have still been linked to the Jews south of the border, whence they came. As will be shown later, Jewish loyalty on the American side too was sharply divided between Britain and America. In the main, however, loyalty was primarily to the region where they lived, whether British or American. There were exceptions, as already indicated, such as the unusual example of David S. Franks, who was born and grew up in Philadelphia but was settled in Montreal before the war. He left Canada, however, with the American army, which had invaded it unsuccessfully early in the Revolution. Franks pursued a military career in the American army and attained the relatively high rank of lieutenant-colonel. His was, however, a special case.

Nevertheless, several claims were made by Canadian Jews for services rendered to the American forces. One such was by Levy Solomons, who was married to Rachel, the sister of David S. Franks, which may possibly have had some bearing on his attitude toward the Revolution. In any event, Solomons addressed a petition to Congress on 15 November 1784, in which he outlined his services as a basis for compensation. He related how General Montgomery had named him purveyor of American hospitals in Montreal in 1775. He furnished several houses for the purpose and supplied them. When the army retreated, Solomons evacuated the sick by providing carriages for them. General Arnold's troops carried off some goods belonging to him at La Chine. As a result he was exposed to "insults and injuries from people of every denomination."

General Burgoyne subsequently persecuted Solomons as a disloyal person, and he was compelled to leave his house. He concluded his petition that "notwithstanding the persecution your Memorialist has suffered he has uniformly adhered to the American side, and as his affairs have taken a more favorable turn he has been enabled from time to time to lend his assistance to such prisoners as have been brought in here." Solomons thus claimed some degree of sentiment and loyalty to the American cause, and he sent along $1,400 in continental currency for redemption by Congress. He had received it from General Wooster on account when the army left Canada. It was now worthless, but he had no doubt that "his real advances will be reimbursed to him, . . . his services and sufferings rewarded and compensated, and that the justice and a candour of Congress will oblige him to consider it his duty to pray for the prosperity of the United States of America." Written from far-off Montreal, where Solomons continued to live and presumably to give his loyalty to Canada, this plea for compensation was ignored by Congress, as were many other similar requests, even from Canadian petitioners in America.[52]

Another unsuccessful Canadian petitioner for compensation from America was Aaron Hart. He was the first Jew to arrive with the British army in Canada by 1760. He settled at Three Rivers on the Saint Lawrence River and was probably the wealthiest and most prominent Jew in the country at his death in 1800. In 1786 Hart submitted a claim for compensation for supplies furnished to the American army in 1775. He sent his son Moses to visit relatives in America, but incidentally to press Congress for cash, securities, or land. He was also to find out how to exchange continental currency for cash. There is no evidence that Moses was successful in his venture.

An even stranger case is that of Barnard Judah, who made his claim for compensation as late as 1824. He was then living in New York and was the father of nine children. He was out of work, and he sought the assistance of John Taylor, a prominent Democratic politician and former governor of New York, to obtain a position as a clerk of customs. In support of this claim he cited the service of his father, Samuel Judah of Montreal, in 1775, nearly half a century earlier. As he put it, this happened "during the time which tried men's souls at Montreal during the Revolution." His father was "I beleeve [sic] one of the best friends to the cause of the Americans . . . and lost his all in aid of our blessed country." There is no precise explanation of how this happened, and it could hardly support a claim for compensation except for a government position in grateful recognition of some vague service performed. Here is a late echo of the Revolution that went unheeded. There were other such Jewish claims at this time for compensation or pensions, as a kind of sequel to the Revolution, which will be considered more fully elsewhere.[53]

To conclude, the amazing medley of recorded items relating to the business and social role of the Jews during the Revolution is significant, in part because the number is not inconsiderable, in part also because of the great diversity of activities. In view of the small total Jewish population, these ranged widely from petty and local merchandising to relatively large-scale enterprises in trade and shipping, performed throughout the country, from north to south, both at the center and in peripheral, outlying places. The Jews had acquired the necessary experience and means of doing business during a long period of more than a century preceding the Revolution. They also adapted themselves to the new situation and carried on their life and business somehow under the uncertain conditions of war, the shortage of goods, the depreciation of currency, and the inflation of prices. Their economic contributions to the conduct of war were notable and valuable.

In a composite, pluralist America, comprising many elements other than those of English origin, the Jews fully and early appreciated the special import and promise of the Revolution as an instrument of their emancipation and integration into American society on the basis of equal rights. This, together with the necessity of survival, made them willing and ready to perform not only many military services but also to carry on equally the ordinary functions of trade and the supply of goods and fiscal services. The result was a mixture of the unusual actions required by war and the practical, prosaic, daily affairs of business that make up the pattern of all wars.

COL. ISAAC FRANKS (1759-1822)

Born in New York, but left for Philadelphia. Continental Army officer who became a colonel in the Pennsylvania Militia after the Revolution. President Washington's landlord in Germantown in 1794.

Portrait by Gilbert Stuart

LT. ABRAHAM ALEXANDER (1743-1816)

English-born. Reader in the Charleston synagogue and Revolutionary officer in the South Carolina Militia.

Portrait by Lawrence Sully

Courtesy of Hannah London Collection and American Jewish Archives

MORDECAI SHEFTALL (1735-1797)

Born of an old founding family in Savannah, Georgia. Commissary General of Issues for Georgia and patriarch of an important Jewish Southern family.

Portrait by unknown painter

Courtesy of Mrs. B. H. Levy, Savannah, Georgia, Hannah London Collection, and American Jewish Archives

MAJOR BENJAMIN NONES (1757-1826)

Born in Bordeaux, France. Patriot and volunteer soldier in the Revolutionary Army; major in the Pennsylvania Militia after the Revolution.

Portrait attributed to John Ramage

Courtesy of Hannah London Collection and American Jewish Archives

REV. GERSHOM MENDES SEIXAS (1745-1816)

Born in New York of Sephardic stock. Revolutionary patriot and spiritual leader of both Shearith Israel of New York and Mikveh Israel in Philadelphia, which he served during the Revolution.

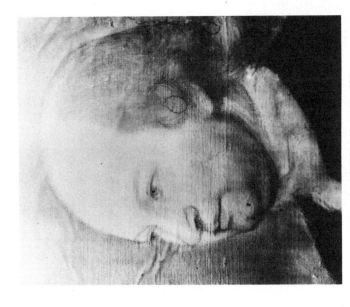

REV. ISAAC TOURO (1737-1783)

Born in Curaçao of Sephardic stock. Minister of the famed Newport Rhode Island, synagogue, and an ardent Loyalist, who took refuge and died in Jamaica.

Portrait by Gilbert Stuart

Courtesy of Hannah London Collection and American Jewish Archives

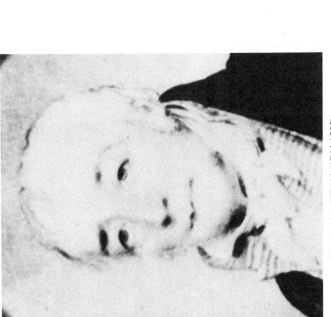

SIMON NATHAN (1746-1822)

Born in England, he left Jamaica to join the American cause in Philadelphia. Prominent Revolutionary merchant and soldier in the Pennsylvania Militia. Founded an important Jewish American family.

Portrait by Henry Inman

Courtesy of Hannah London Collection and American Jewish Archives

ISAAC MOSES (1742-1818)

German-born, who left New York for Philadelphia during the Revolution. Patriotic merchant and Revolutionary privateersman, who also served in the Pennsylvania Militia.

Portrait by John Wesley Jarvis   *Courtesy of Hannah London Collection and American Jewish Archives*

LT. COL. DAVID S. FRANKS (1743-1793)

Born in Philadelphia, but lived in Montreal until the outbreak of the Revolution. Continental Army officer and diplomatic agent.

Portrait by Charles Willson Peale
Courtesy of Hannah London Collection and American Jewish Archives

JONAS PHILLIPS (1736-1803)

German-born. Patriotic merchant and soldier in the Pennsylvania Militia, who left New York for Philadelphia and was active in both cities.

Portrait attributed to Charles Willson Peale   *Courtesy of Hannah London Collection and American Jewish Archives*

7

Jewish Loyalists During the Revolution

A complete record of the Revolution must consider persons of every persuasion, the pro-British as well as those who were pro-American. Dr. Benjamin Rush's sweeping dictum that the Jews were Whigs was not strictly true for them, any more than it was for the general population. It was not a matter of being for or against independence. There was instead a wide spectrum of opinion, ranging from conviction for either side to acquiescence or indifference. Most Jews were aligned with the patriotic side, since they were predominantly non-English in origin and had no particular attachment to Britain. It applied even to recent arrivals in America, such as Francis Salvador and Haym Salomon, although the former was English-born. Their interests were American, and they responded to the challenge of Revolution and war, especially since the opportunity of active participation was offered to them.

Nevertheless, a number of Jews chose the British side of the conflict, often because they found themselves in British-controlled areas and it was more convenient to remain than to leave. Aside from those in New York and Newport, there were already some Jews in Canada, who had gotten there following the British conquest and were settled in Montreal and other places. They remained loyal to England, although a few claimed to support the American invasion of Canada in 1775. The Jew who attained the highest military rank in the American army, as a lieutenant-colonel, was a Canadian from Montreal, David S. Franks, who had been born in Philadelphia. Active Loyalism must be applied specifically only to those Jews who lived in one of the American

colonies and made their choice voluntarily. Many were undoubtedly modest people, such as craftsmen or tradesmen who
continued to ply their trades wherever they were and whatever
the difficulties. They lived in all the towns where the British were
in control at one time or another.

The identification of Loyalism is, however, most certain and
most meaningful in cases where it became a question of taking an
oath of allegiance or where it required an outright choice of sides.
These might be called the legal or activist Loyalists, who frequently fled to British lands, such as Canada, the West Indies, or
England proper. There were not many of these, but their record
is illuminating. Both types of Jews, patriotic and Loyalist, were
often displaced and were affected considerably by the Revolution. Many never regained their prewar status and prosperity,
especially those Loyalists who returned to America after the
Revolution to resume life and business, often in reduced
circumstances. An important example is that of David Franks, as
has already been indicated.

Others remained in British lands and submitted claims to the
government for compensation, which were not always acknowledged or else were rewarded only grudgingly by Britain.
An early doubt as to Jewish patriotism appeared in the writing of
Rev. Ezra Stiles. Self-styled friend and companion of the Jews of
Newport, especially of Aaron Lopez and Rev. Isaac Touro, Stiles
nevertheless accepted without question the Jewish separation
from the general American community and voiced early suspicion of their loyalty. Thus, already in his diary of 1770 he
recorded that the Jews of London were operating a "secret intelligence office" in America for the British ministry: "It is entirely a Jewish affair." In 1777 he further noted that "the Jews are
very officious in informing against the inhabitants," although he
gave no specific details. In truth, the Newport Jews were divided
in their loyalty, and among them were eventually some Loyalists.
The split began to appear in 1776 when the Rhode Island
legislature adopted a resolution requiring an oath of allegiance to
be taken by all suspected Tories. Seventy-seven Newport individuals were thus tested, including four Jews, who refused to
take the oath. They offered highly plausible social and religious
reasons in support of their objections.[1]

One of the Jews who thus rejected the required oath was Moses Michael Hays, a Newport merchant and an active Mason. He subsequently affirmed his loyalty to his native land and proved it by his services. Now, however, he denied being "inimical to my country. . . ." As a Jew, however, he was not allowed to vote, and "never had the Continental Congress or the legislatures taken any notice . . . respecting the society of Israelites to which I belong." Moreover, he protested to the Rhode Island legislature against discrimination in his being pressed to take the oath while others were left free. In the end, Hays yielded and took the oath, promising "to heartily assist in the defense of the United Colonies." Hays later left Newport and established himself in Boston, virtually the first permanent Jewish settler there. He prospered in the insurance business and achieved national prominence in Masonry, then a social and intellectual bond joining Jews and Gentiles in their common devotion to the Revolutionary cause. Interestingly, a predecessor of Hays in Boston, Abraham Solomon, is reported to have been convicted there for seditious utterances, although he may have earlier served at the Battle of Bunker Hill.[2]

Reverend Isaac Touro, the spiritual leader of the Newport congregation, also refused the oath of allegiance on the ground that he was an alien by virtue of his birth in Curaçao. He was unequivocally pro-British in his views, and he stayed in Newport under British occupation only until 1779. He then moved with his family to New York, where the British extended financial assistance to him. He maintained a semblance of religious activity there at Shearith Israel for the benefit of the Jews who had remained during the British occupation. In 1782 Touro took his family to Jamaica, where he died within a year. His widow, a sister of Moses Michael Hays of Boston, returned to America with her two sons, Abraham and Judah. They were brought up by their uncle in Boston and later prospered as merchants, Abraham in Boston and Judah in New Orleans.[3] Judah fought and was wounded in the Battle of New Orleans in 1815.

Two other Newport Jews refused the oath of allegiance. Myer Polock alleged that it was contrary "to the custom of the Jews," and Isaac Hart declined it until and unless the oath was required of all. These two brothers-in-law, who became active Loyalists, paid a heavy penalty for their choice. Both later left Newport with their families and joined the British in New York. They were assigned some land on Long Island. Here a number of Loyalists built Fort St. George as a rallying point. It was attacked by a band of Americans from Connecticut in 1780, and Isaac Hart was killed and reported to have been mutilated by the attackers. According to *Rivington's Gazette*, a Loyalist newspaper, he was "inhumanly fired upon and bayoneted . . . in fifteen parts of his body . . . and died of his wounds a few hours after, universally regretted by every true lover of his kind and country." The entire Hart family of Newport was Loyalist, including Moses, Samuel, Jacob, and Naphtali. Perhaps the explanation of this general defection lies in their important business association with the British during the earlier French and Indian War. They had engaged in supplying the army and in privateering, and Isaac Hart had been a partner of Governor Wanton in this business. Wanton was banished from the state by an act of the legislature during the Revolution; Isaac's brother, Jacob, was allowed rations and one dollar per day by General Guy Carleton, the British commander at New York. After the war, almost destitute, Jacob Hart went to England with his family and applied for compensation. He was granted an annual pension of forty pounds.[4]

The Hart family continued to press for compensation for their loyalty to the British crown. Jacob Hart's son, Moses, presented a petition to the Royal Commission on Loyalists in London after the war. His father was now dead, and a memorial was dedicated to him in Whitehall. Moses Hart had never signed or taken any American oath: "They were by this means obnoxious and quitted the Island with the British troops and went to New York." He was enrolled in the Loyalist militia of New York. With all this to his credit, Moses Hart received a pension of twenty pounds annually, scarcely a lavish reward for such loyalty. He later acquired some land in Canada, and a town was named for him.[5]

Myer Polock, the fourth member of the Newport group, also became an avowed Loyalist. His unhappy experience served as a subject of recrimination against British ingratitude on the part of Edmund Burke, the noted Whig conciliator, in a speech in Parliament in 1781. Polock had been stripped of his possessions and evicted from Newport because he had imported tea, in defiance of the boycott. Polock was with his brother-in-law, Isaac

Hart, on Long Island, when the latter was killed at Fort St. George. His own brother also died of hardships. Polock went to the Dutch island of St. Eustatius, which the British Admiral Rodney captured and plundered. His object was to destroy this center of contraband trade with America. According to Burke, the British seized nine hundred Johannes, a monetary coin, from Polock who was thus mistreated by both sides. This was a surprising tale of Jewish woe to be recited in Parliament by a leading British critic of the war.

Other Jews, less prominent or less zealous Loyalists, stayed on in Newport during the British occupation. After the American recapture of Newport in 1779, a list of fifty alleged Loyalists was compiled, which included Haym and Simon Levi, Isaac and Jacob Isaacs, Benjamin Myers and his mother, Rachel, and Isaac Eliezer and his son. Ezra Stiles added Moses Seixas and Moses Levy to the list and charged that some on the list had been informers for the British. In 1781 Rachel Myers, a Newport widow with nine children, fled to New York and appealed for help to the British General Clinton in behalf of herself and family. Rachel also fled from New York on its evacuation by the British and went to Canada. She later returned to the United States, and her son served patriotically in the War of 1812. This is not the only such case illustrating the persistence of Jewish attachment or return to the American scene, even if for a time that person had chosen the British side. Many others reverted and returned to America after the Revolution, and their offspring became loyal Americans. In reverse, however, Hannah Hays wrote to Benjamin Franklin in 1789 for help to recover property, since she wished to return to her children and friends in Britain.[6]

The Jews of Canada present a special problem with respect to their role in the Revolution. They first arrived there from America as suppliers to the British army during the French and Indian War. Such was the case of Aaron Hart, who had come on the staff of General Amherst in 1760. By 1768 there were enough Jews in Montreal to found Shearith Israel congregation. Some of them were among the first Jews to go as traders to the frontier, where they encountered Jews from the American colonies. Thus Ezekiel Solomons was at Mackinac as early as 1761; his cousin, Levi Solomons, who later helped supply hospitals for the

American army in Montreal, and Chapman Abrahams both traded at Detroit. Significantly, the Jews in Canada participated in early efforts to obtain self-government for Canada similar to that enjoyed by the colonies to the south. Thus, as early as 1764, Eleazer Levy signed a petition for an elected assembly in Quebec, and Aaron Hart was similarly a signer in 1770. In 1774, following the Quebec Act, which established an appointed Legislative Council, some fifteen Jews, among them Aaron Hart, Samuel Jacobs, Isaac Judah, and David S. Franks, signed a petition for an elective assembly. Franks later left Canada and became an officer in the American army.[7]

The Canadian Jews were thus, like their kindred in America, strongly for self-government, even though for the most part they remained loyal to Britain. Aaron Hart served as a commissary officer to General Haldimand. He became the most prominent Jew in Canada and was known as the Seigneur de Bécancour at Three Rivers, where he settled. His brother, Moses Hart, was on the muster roll of the British Legion in 1778; in 1795 he petitioned for a land grant in Lower Canada. Samuel Jacobs was an Assistant Commissary in Quebec, and Isaac Judah was in the Canadian militia. He subsequently received a land grant in Upper Canada. Chapman Abrahams provided supplies for several Canadian regiments during the war and served personally as a volunteer against the American army at Three Rivers.

After the war the movement for self-government was revived. In 1784 some twenty-five of the signatories to a petition were Jews. Thus a similarity of political outlook and experience existed between the Jewish communities in America and Canada, despite the difference of allegiance. Their problems were similar too. Aaron Hart's son, Ezekiel, was the first Jew elected to the Quebec assembly, but was denied his seat on religous grounds. In the same manner, Jacob Henry was denied a seat in the North Carolina legislature.[8]

Loyalty was thus largely a function of location and the fortunes of war, among Jews as among others, whether from necessity, convenience, or mutual conviction. New York, in particular, as the center of British operations throughout the war, became a gathering point for Loyalists, Jewish and other. Those who remained in New York signed an address of loyalty to the crown and presented it to General Howe. The Jewish signers included Abraham and Moses Gomez, Jr.; Barrack and David Hays; Uriah Hendricks; Levy Israel; David, Nathan, and Isaac Solomon. In all, there were some sixteen Jews among nearly one thousand on this list. Some were more zealous than others in avowing their loyalty, supporting it with positive action.

Perhaps the most notorious among the latter was Barrack Hays, merchant and auctioneer. He was originally a lieutenant in the New York Whig militia but subsequently switched to the royalist side. He was an "officer of scouts" for both Generals Clinton and Carleton. After the war, Hays made his way to Canada and petitioned Governor Haldimand to appoint him vendue master or auctioneer in Montreal. As he wrote to the governor, he had received five shillings per day as "officer of guides" and wished to have his pay continued, since he had a large family to support. He had been an auctioneer in New York for twenty years, and he would function as one in Montreal. He was prepared to take a French-speaking partner, one Samuel Davis, probably also a Jew. After much wandering, he died in the West Indies. Barrack's son, John Jacob Hays, later turned up in the Northwest, at Vincennes, Indiana. Here he intermarried, became sheriff of St. Clair County, and was later postmaster of Cahokia, Illinois. Interestingly, a cousin, Jacob Hays, who also intermarried, was for many years high constable or police chief in New York City.[9]

Other Jews who lived in New York under British occupation, but who probably represented a more lukewarm type of loyalty, were Uriah Hendricks, Alexander Zunz, and Henry Moses. All stayed on after the war under an act restoring rights and allowing them to live "without any molestation." Zunz and Moses first came to this country during the Revolution, one as sutler and the other as a soldier with the Hessian forces. Zunz became highly respected in the Jewish community in New York; he had helped to keep Shearith Israel going during the war. Moses settled as a merchant in Charleston after the war. Moses Gomez, Jr., served as an officer in the Loyal City Militia, while a related branch of the family, headed by the patriotic Daniel Gomez, spent the war in Philadelphia. Rachel Pinto, originally from Stratford, Connecticut, whose three nephews served with the American forces, came to New York in 1779, and took the oath of allegiance to the crown. She remained in New York after the war and died there in 1815. Others who came to New York during the Revolution and who probably had pro-British sentiments were James Lucena, Jacob Louzada, and Abraham Florentine, the last two from New Jersey. Lucena and his son, John Charles, both from Savannah, belonged to the Catholic branch of the family and eventually returned to Portugal. Florentine went to Nova Scotia in 1783 and from there to England. He made a claim for compensation of nine hundred pounds in losses, which was neither recognized nor awarded. Many years later he was back in New York and was employed as a street inspector.[10]

Some thirty Jews remained in New York under British occupation, but they represented different social levels and degrees of loyalty, difficult to define for want of specific evidence. Among them were Levy Simons, Moses and Lyon Hart, Samuel Lazarus, Samuel and Isaac Levy. The last-named Levy is supposed to have entertained British soldiers with "dexterity of hand." A Moses Levy traded with England, and a ship of his arrived in New York in 1780. Above all there was Dutch-born Uriah Hendricks, who came to America as early as 1755. He was actively engaged during the French and Indian War in supplying the army and in outfitting privateers; these activities may perhaps account for his pro-British inclinations. Described as a "Loyalist in politics and a loyally-conforming Jew in religious practice," Hendricks was, nevertheless, able to stay on in New York after the war. Although he had signed an Address of Loyalty to General Howe and the British crown, he also joined with other Jews in an address of welcome to Governor George Clinton after the war. He married successively into the Gomez and Lopez families. His son, Harman, became the founder of the important copper smelting industry in New Jersey and the head of a prominent family in the Jewish community of New York.[11]

Of Samuel Lazarus, who also lived in New York during the war, an interesting episode is recorded. In 1777 he was married by the patriotic Rev. Gershom Seixas, then living in Connecticut, who slipped into New York for the purpose, wrapped in a coat which hid his face, except for his aquiline nose. That Seixas was willing to run such a risk bears testimony either to his zeal for his professional calling or to his friendship for the man. Lazarus also stayed on in New York after the war, which would indicate that he, too, was not actively identified with Loyalism. His son, Eleazer Lazarus, was the editor of the first Hebrew and English prayerbook published in America. His great granddaughter was Emma Lazarus, the author of the "New Colossus," the famous poem inscribed on the base of the Statue of Liberty in New York harbor.[12]

During the British occupation of New York the fate of the synagogue, Shearith Israel, was in doubt. It had been abandoned by its patriotic members who left the city, and by its minister, Rev. Gershom Seixas, who took its sacred objects with him to Connecticut. Those who remained were anxious to keep it open and in use. For a time the British designated the building as a hospital, and on one occasion it was vandalized by some British soldiers. It is perhaps indicative of Jewish influence that they were punished for this action. Barrack Hays, one of the leading Loyalists in town, persuaded the British to return it and allow a resumption of religious services. Lyon Jones, a furrier and a Loyalist, became its provisional head. Another who joined in this endeavor was Alexander Zunz, who was its president when the Whig Jews returned to New York after the war. He then resigned and restored the synagogue to the former leadership, as is recorded in the minute book of Shearith Israel. Zunz himself became a respected member of the Jewish community and was a broker and a founder of the New York Stock Exchange.[13]

The synagogue also acquired a new spiritual leader during the war in the person of Jacob Raphael Cohen, who came down from Montreal. In 1784, on the return of many of the patriotic Jews and former members from Philadelphia, an exchange was effected by which Gershom Seixas regained his old post at Shearith Israel, while Cohen went to Mikveh Israel in Philadelphia. Seixas, the first American-born minister, introduced sermons in English and Americanized the service. He was the first Jewish Regent of the New York State educational system and a trustee of Columbia College.[14]

The case of David Franks as a Loyalist is a very special one; it has already been described fully elsewhere, and need only be summarized here. It was unusual in that he was able to remain on

American territory while serving the British in an important capacity as commissary of British prisoners until 1778. Although he was then dismissed from that office, Franks had remained in Philadelphia during both the British and American occupation and was not finally expelled until 1780. His two brothers were members of an old British supply firm. David Franks executed his office as the fiscal agent of this firm, but with the assent of Washington and by appointment of the Continental Congress. His son was an officer in a British regiment, and his daughter, Rebecca, married a British army colonel in America. His sister, Phila, was married to Oliver DeLancey, a New York Loyalist and British general. All the family associations were thus completely Loyalist. The anomaly was only partially clarified when he and his daughter finally moved to New York and from there went to England. Here the daughter spent the rest of her life as the wife and mother of an English family that belonged to the gentry, as did also his sister, Phila, wife of an American Loyalist, General Oliver DeLancey, until her death at eighty-nine. David Franks claimed losses of £20,000 in a petition to the British commissioners on Loyalists but received an annual pension of only £100. He returned to Philadelphia in later years and died there in the fever epidemic of 1793, an impoverished and forgotten casualty of the Revolution.[15]

A unique example was Abraham Wagg, a Loyalist of positive intellectual convictions about the Revolution. His position was one of choice rather than chance. His remarkable attempt to intercede and influence the peace negotiations, however impractical, was certainly unusual, presumptuous, and unhappily nonproductive. His was apparently the only recorded instance of a Jew in America who offered the British a program and advice on policy regarding the Revolution. There was also Isaac de Pinto, a Dutch Jew and a publicist of some note, who published his views about British colonial policy. This will be dealt with subsequently. The two were quite different personalities, but they supplement each other remarkably, and both were supporters of Britain during the Revolution.

Abraham Wagg was born in London in 1719, the descendant of an old German-Jewish family originally from Frankfurt, where its name was Bachrach Zur Wage (meaning "at the sign of the

scale," used for weighing gold), later Anglicized to Wagg. Wagg
came to New York some years before the Revolution and
established himself as a wholesale grocer and manufacturer of
chocolate. Here he married twice, into the prominent Sephardic
Gomez and de Lucena families. For Wagg the outbreak of
Revolution presented a problem of allegiance, which was
resolved conveniently by the British occupation of New York in
1776. He declared his loyalty to Britain and joined the Loyal
militia; he also served on the voluntary fire patrol to combat fires
reportedly set by the revolutionists. Already in his fifties, Wagg
incurred a lameness when he was injured during service in the
Night Guard "for preventing and discovery of fires." In a later
petition of 1786 to the Royal Commission on Loyalists in London,
he wrote that "having sentiments and taking a decided part in
favor of Great Britain, he was early recommended as a Loyalist to
the protection of General Sir William Howe." In consequence of
"your Memorialist's attachment to the British government, . . . he
became obnoxious to the American states, liable to their acts of
proscription . . . and was reduced from affluence to mere penury.
. . ." Despite such clear-cut losses directly attributable to his
loyalty, Wagg's claim was not acknowledged, and the record
shows no compensation for him.[16]

Wagg's principal contribution as a Loyalist took the unusual
form of two documents he prepared and submitted to the British
government during the war. It is noteworthy that such private
proposals for bringing peace should have come from a Loyalist
rather than a patriotic source, and most surprisingly, from a Jew.
The first version of Wagg's views, dated 22 August 1778, was
entitled "The Sentiments of a Friend to Great Britain and
America." It was addressed to the three British Commissioners
for Peace who arrived in America in 1778 to explore the possibility of a settlement at a time when the French and Americans had
concluded a treaty of alliance in the wake of the great Saratoga
victory over General Burgoyne the previous year.

Wagg was strongly conscious of the French role in the relations
between Britain and America. The peace mission failed, but
Wagg's advice, unsought and unheeded by the British, is an
interesting reminder of the occasion; Wagg predicted that it
would take a British force of 9,000 men for each of the thirteen

colonies, or a total of 117,000 men, to subdue America. One wonders how a Jew arrived at such a strategic military calculation, but he concluded it was a highly unlikely possibility for Britain to raise and provide such a force. Wagg, therefore, advised Britain to withdraw from the American states and to concentrate on the preservation of British rule in Canada and the West Indies. In a continued war by Britain against an alliance of France, Spain, and the Netherlands, she might even lose Jamaica, Florida, and Gibraltar, a prediction that was indeed partially fulfilled later on, at least as regards Florida.[17]

Such a war was unnecessary and should be avoided, Wagg reasoned, since the Americans were only using France to win their independence. Their "natural alliance" would in the long run be with Britain for economic if no other reason. The British commissioners had been authorized only to feel out the situation and the likelihood of a compromise, but not to negotiate for independence. They were repudiated by the American radicals. The war had to run its course, and it is doubtful that either side was ready for Wagg's proposal, even had they known about it. In 1779, unfit for further duty, and with the permission of the British commander in New York, Wagg, his wife, and three children left for England. He remained there the rest of his life, dying in 1803 at eighty-three. The family was in want and depended for support on the bounty of a wealthy cousin in England, a Mrs. Judith Levy. This information is derived in part from a letter written by Mrs. Wagg to her nephew, Harman Hendricks of New York, son of Uriah Hendricks. It is interesting evidence of the international bonds of kinship between European and American Jewry.

In 1782 Wagg addressed another letter to Lord Shelburne, the foreign minister, while peace negotiations were proceeding. He was, however, concerned less with peace than with the problem of the French alliance. His letter was entitled "Private Suggestions on a Plan to Dissolve the Connection of America with France." As in his earlier proposal, Wagg again argued that the Americans must incline toward Britain rather than France after the war, not only for economic but for sentimental reasons as well. Thereby Wagg anticipated more broadly the views of Lord Sheffield's

Observations on the Commerce of the United States, published in 1784, which argued for the continued American dependence on England. Only the radical Congress was pro-French, according to Wagg; the country itself was anti-papist and anti-French. The American army too was jealous of the French army.

Wagg again advised the recognition of American independence, and he foresaw renewed Anglo-American friendship based on a common culture and trade. Thereby he suggested the subsequent split in American politics between the pro-British Federalists and the pro-French Jeffersonians during the period of the French Revolution. "Britain," Wagg reasoned, "will derive more extensive and more durable advantages from such a natural alliance than from their former connections, when self-interested governors and placemen [political appointees] had it in their power to cause feuds and animosities." Should such an alliance materialize, "the Americans will throw off the mask and tell France and Spain that the law of nature and nature's God entitles America . . . to be perpetually allied with Great Britain by the nearest ties of consanguineity, being of the same religion, speaking the same language, and remembering their former intercourse. . . ." Here was an amazingly long-range prophetic view presented by an obscure Jew who belonged to both Britain and America by virtue of birth and residence. This proposal of Wagg's, too, went unnoticed, despite its far-sighted anticipation of coming events.[18]

Another equally unusual analysis of the Revolution was made by a contemporary Jew who was neither British nor American. He was Dutch-born, of Portuguese origin, named Isaac dePinto, a Jewish name common to both Europe and America. He was an economist and publicist of considerable reputation in Europe, who was even compared with his contemporary, Adam Smith. A product of the Enlightenment, he wrote in French but was translated into other languages, including English. As early as 1776, with the Revolution scarcely begun, he wrote "Letters Concerning the Troubles in America," addressed to Mr. S. B., a physician at Kingston, Jamaica, otherwise unidentified. DePinto was anti-Revolutionary if not anti-American, and his earlier pro-British writing had earned him an annual pension of five hundred pounds from the English East India Company. He could hardly be advertised as one "who must necessarily be disinterested" because he was Dutch, not English.[19]

DePinto began by condemning "those who are blinded by the passions of commercial jealousy, envy, or national prejudices." He argued that the American colonies had no ground for complaint against Britain, since they had profited greatly by British support and generosity. Britain had defended them at great expense, and they paid barely a small fraction of the cost in taxes. DePinto deplored the spirit of Cromwell abroad in the colonies, and he declared that the war was "at once the most unavoidable and the most just that ever was undertaken" by the British. However, foreseeing already in 1776 the possibility of French intervention, he believed that the young king of France was too wise to become embroiled in it. He was served by too many wise men to be misled by propaganda. Within two years, however, France was allied with America and at war with Britain.[20]

In a second letter, dePinto developed the more theoretical and extraordinary aspect of his argument, pleading for a united Europe against the colonial revolt. It was his strange but nevertheless plausible reasoning that the principal empires of Europe should unite and not divide in order to preserve and protect their possessions. If there must be war, why not one against the Barbary corsairs and pirates who infest trade, or even for the liberation of Greece from Turkey? These, he granted, "are political dreams." Europe, he argued, needed the West Indian trade to provide bullion for Asian commerce. Unless Europe hung together to resist the colonies, they would win their independence. He urged further, in fact, that "America will sooner or later become either wholly or in part independent of Europe." The time was, however, not yet ripe. Moreover, in a prophetic mood, dePinto foresaw that North America would "invade and subjugate Mexico and Peru," and all the West Indies would "pass under the dominion of the continent." Here was a shrewd prediction of a kind of American expansionism later proclaimed under the name of the Monroe Doctrine, as formulated in 1823. The European empires should, he insisted, therefore unite to retard, not advance, American independence. Otherwise the Eastern and Western Hemispheres would be separated as before

Columbus, and "it would be the severest convulsion ever experienced in Europe."[21]

In a spirit perhaps characteristic of a publicist who was also a Jew, and hence above national prejudice, dePinto concluded that "my great aim in all my writings has always been to cure national hatred and to remove those jealousies which are the springs of it, and which are always founded on interest ill understood." With some vanity he noted that certain celebrated authors had already adopted his views, and "I should with still more pleasure see sovereigns convinced of those truths, as there would certainly result from thence the greatest benefit to mankind."[22]

DePinto thus expressed what might certainly be considered a world view of historical evolution, resting it on European unity and benevolent world imperialism rather than on a more combative concept of the prospects and promise of revolution and the creation of new nations in a divided world. The latter has actually transpired since the nineteenth century, whether with or without happy consequences. Quite correctly, he judged that it depended on the other European empires to determine whether and when the colonies might achieve independence. With much wishful thinking, he believed that England would ultimately triumph on this occasion. There were many faithful subjects who opposed the conflict; only New England was most revolutionary and possessed by the spirit of Cromwell's intolerance and recalcitrance, said dePinto. The other colonies were more politic and more divided.[23]

The British seized on this work by dePinto and had it translated into English, and it was published and circulated widely. Benjamin Franklin, then in France, wrote that a Swiss publicist, W. F. Dumas, would be employed to refute "the Jew Pinto whose venal pen has been employed in the most insolent manner against the Americans." Despite its illiberal tenor, however, dePinto's writing must be acknowledged as the most highly intellectualized appraisal of the Revolution made by a contemporary Jew. It was by a European Jew, since there was probably none in America capable of such an intellectual effort. At most, theirs was a sentimental expression of loyal attachment to the American cause.[24]

An unusual type of Jew who came to America during the war

must somehow be fitted into the pattern, since he belongs neither to the Loyalist nor to the patriotic category. There were several German Jews who arrived with the Hessian troops as sutlers, provisioners, or even soldiers, and were thus presumably British partisans. But they probably had no particular attachment to Britain and, indeed, stayed on in America after the war and were easily integrated into the Jewish community here. There was, for example, Alexander Zunz, mentioned earlier, who operated in New York and remained here after the war. Zunz married a Jewish woman and established himself as a prominent member of both the business and the Jewish community in New York. Another Hessian Jew was Joseph Darmstadt, who settled in Richmond, where he commanded great respect in the community despite his heavy German accent. He was both a Mason and an observant Jew, indicating the remarkable ability of many contemporary Jews to combine what might have been considered disparate qualities. In 1789, for example, he composed a doggerel skit on Purim, the first of its kind in America.

Other Hessian Jews who came to America as sutlers were Henry Moses, Samuel Levy, and Levy Solomon, who were in Charleston during the British occupation, but remained in the city after the war and became part of the Jewish community. They were Loyalists only in a nominal sense.[25] An even stranger case was that of Samuel Prado, who lived in London and was never in America. He was, in fact, married to the widow of Francis Salvador, an early Jewish casualty of the Revolution on the South Carolina frontier in 1776. Like the Salvadors, he held claims to land in South Carolina, which he lost during the Revolution. His application for compensation from the British government was rejected. He may, therefore, be considered as a Loyalist *in absentia*, who suffered losses as a result of the Revolution. Interestingly, Salvador's uncle, Joseph, came to Charleston after the Revolution to claim his lands. He died and was buried there.[26]

The experience of the South with loyalty and Loyalists, both Jewish and other, was rather special in character. It arose out of the fact that both Savannah and Charleston were captured by the British between 1779 and 1780 and were held for the rest of the war. British control in the South seemed complete, and American resistance was at once bloody and almost hopeless. Although some sought refuge elsewhere, many people stayed on and made the best of the situation, from necessity more than from loyalty. It is doubtful how genuinely Loyalist such persons were. In 1780 a committee of Loyalists in Charleston approved some 166 citizens as acceptable residents, including several Jews: Joseph Myers, Abraham Alexander, Moses Eliazer, Philip Cohen, Marcus Lazarus, Saul Simons, and Philip Moses. Some of these, Lazarus, Alexander, and Moses, for example, had served in the South Carolina militia, especially in Lushington's so-called "Jew Company" of Charleston. They all signed an address of loyalty to Sir Henry Clinton, the British commander.

The *Royal Gazette* and *Royal South Carolina Gazette* named other Jews as resident and doing business in occupied Charleston, among them Joseph and Emanuel Abrahams, Jacob Jacobs, Abraham and Gershon Cohen, and Isaac deLyon. Interestingly, a century later, Rabbi Barnett A. Elzas, the historian of Charleston's Jewry, himself English by origin and education, defended the Loyalists and argued with perhaps an excess of zeal that "concerning these Loyalists, it should be remarked here that there was just as true patriotism in them as there was in the most ardent Revolutionists. Their conduct was actuated by just as high motives." Survival in a difficult time was undoubtedly one of the motives. It should be noted, however, that a number of other Jews remained as prisoners or were expelled from Charleston as rebels and found their way to Philadelphia, where they reinforced the membership of Mikveh Israel. Among these were the daCostas, Philip Moses, Jacob Cohen, Abraham Sasportas, Abraham Seixas, and Israel Jacobs.

There were also probably some true Loyalists among other Southern Jews. One such was the strange case of Myer Franks of District 96 in South Carolina. He was known as "an old Tory," and a company of Whigs raided his smokehouse. After the war, Franks sued the commissary for the loss of the supplies, but the case was thrown out of court. Barnard Moses was another loyal subject who fled from Charleston to Jamaica in 1783 and applied to General Sir Guy Carleton for relief.[27]

Savannah, too, under British occupation during much of the latter part of the war, had a similar record of a division of loyalty among the Jews. Some escaped to Charleston and some, like the

Sheftalls, were later taken prisoner at the British capture of Charleston. James Wright, the royalist Governor of Georgia, wanted the Jews banished permanently from the province because of their rebellious conduct. A few, however, remained in Savannah and subsequently presented claims as Loyalists. Thus the Lucenas, both the father and the son John Charles, as well as Moses Nunez, avowed their loyalty. As early as 1775 they joined in a declaration that "oppressed as we are in our civil and religious rights by those unconstitutional bodies [Parochial Committees of Safety], we think it our duty to testify our allegiance to His Majesty." Although the Lucenas were themselves at least of Jewish origin, they, together with Nunez, complained of the parochial committee, whose chairman and one or more members were "persons professing the Jewish faith." The chairman in question was Mordecai Sheftall. Nunez subsequently reverted to the Revolutionary side.

In 1782 a patriotic assembly in Georgia proscribed James Lucena. He returned to Lisbon, whence he had fled as a Marano in 1761, like his cousin Aaron Lopez. Lucena returned to Catholicism, as did his son, John Charles, who settled in London. Here he made application for compensation as a Loyalist but was rejected by the Commission on Loyalist Claims. He too abandoned Judaism, to which his attachment had been slight. He served as Portuguese consul-general in London, thanks to his father's influence. Here is an interesting indication of how the course of Jews was not always out of Catholic Portugal but on rare occasion also back to Portugal; and this, too, was in a sense, a consequence of the Revolution.[28]

Thus was the American Revolution, like all revolutions, fought not only on the battlefield but also in the hearts and consciences of men who were not necessarily combatants in the field. They were displaced, and many suffered great hardship as the fortunes of war shifted. After the war some of Loyalist convictions left either for British lands in Canada, or the West Indies, or England itself, where they entered claims for compensation. Others remained and were subject to judgment and reprisal by local committees or even legalistic action. These judgments were contemporary and were thus closer to the events; the judges were thus better able to determine motives and suitable punishments.

In the case of the Jews, a considerable number came into question as suspected Loyalists, as has been indicated. Only a few were proscribed, however, or punished, perhaps because they were not thought important enough to warrant severe treatment. Most of them apparently stayed on or, if they had left, returned later to America, and accepted or adjusted to the new condition of independence. Their children even fought in later American wars, as will be illustrated subsequently.

One case of an early change of heart and conviction was that of a Philadelphia Jew, Mordecai Levy. The Philadelphia Committee of Safety as early as 1775 concluded that his "disrespectful speeches about Congress proceeded from the most contracted notions of the British Constitution and the rights of human nature. Better instructed, he asked for pardon in the presence of a large crowd in the College Yard." As Mordecai Levy himself described the dramatic incident, on 17 July 1775 he took the required oath of loyalty along with other Jews, and assured the committee that "whereas I have spoken disrespectfully of the General Congress as well as of those military gentlemen who have associated for the Liberties of America, I now take this opportunity of declaring that my conduct proceeded from the most contracted notions of the British Constitution and the rights of human nature." After this admission of a kind of perverse political theory, Levy confessed: "I am sorry for my guilt and am ashamed of my folly. I now believe all assemblies to be legal and institutional which are framed by the united suffrage of a free people and am convinced that no soldiers are as respectable as those who take up arms in defense of liberty." He added that kings were only to be feared and obeyed when they executed just laws. Levy's repentance was coupled with a profound wish that the "counsels of Congress may be always directed with wisdom and that the arms be crowned with success. And I pray that every man in America who behaves as I have formerly done, may not meet with the lenity which I have experienced, but may be obliged to expiate his crimes in a most ignominious manner."[29]

This episode of an early conversion of a tentative Jewish dissident to American principles reveals a number of conditions affecting the status of the Jews in America at an early stage of the Revolution. In the first place, there were Jews in America who seemed to have theoretical doubts as to the propriety or legality of early anti-British actions. It seemed important, in the second place, to bring such deviationists to account and to a correct view, whether freely or by some measure of coercion is not clearly indicated. The Jews too were thus apparently considered part of the total community, and their compliance with the general sentiment was thought desirable. In either case of conformity or nonconformity, their opinions and position were judged essential and were to be brought into line with the rest of the community. This specific case happened in Philadelphia, where the actions and ideas ultimately leading to the Revolution were being generated and precipitated. Levy died in 1783, as the war ended, and thus did not live to enjoy or savor the fruits of American emancipation.[30]

Whereas Philadelphia offered an early example of reconversion of a dissenting Jew to the proper patriotic sentiment, Savannah illustrated how those who were of questionable loyalty were handled subsequently. This occurred at the end of the Revolution, when Savannah was evacuated by the British after an occupation of several years. Many people, including some Jews, had stayed in the city and had presumably accepted the British regime. After the war some were proscribed by act of the state legislature; they were to be banished and their property confiscated. Two were Jews, Isaac deLyon and Levi Sheftall, brother of the patriotic Mordecai. Levi had been active on the American side earlier in the Revolution, but found himself in British-occupied Savannah at the end. Thanks to the intercession of his influential brother, Mordecai, both men were restored to citizenship but were denied the right to vote or hold office for fourteen years, and their property was made liable to a fine of 12 percent.[31]

In Charleston, too, during the painful siege of 1780, the population became divided over the outcome. Many residents, both soldiers and civilians, petitioned General Lincoln that further resistance was hopeless and urged surrender. There were a number of Jews among the so-called addressers. After the capture, many stayed on in the city under British occupation, whereas others were treated as prisoners, or were evicted from Loyalist Charleston. After the war and evacuation of Charleston, those who had remained in the city were examined by a patriotic committee for their collaboration with the enemy. They were acquitted and excused on various grounds, and some were vouched for by others. Thus General Thomas Sumter himself praised Myer Moses as one who was "friendly and attached to the American cause. . . . His treatment of the American wounded and prisoners was such as to entitle him to the good wishes and gratitude of all those who had the success of the Revolution at heart."

Jacob Jacobs and Gershon Cohen were not arraigned or questioned, perhaps because they had fought in the defense of Charleston. Instead, they testified to the good character of other men, who had not helped the enemy and should not be punished. Thus Mordecai Lyon, they assured the committee, was a "Polander" and a tailor, who had been in Charleston only fourteen months. He had "done nothing against the American cause." Henry Cohen was a Prussian Jew who had never assisted the British. Levy Solomon and Samuel Levy were both sutlers with the Hessians, who had recently come to Charleston and were considered honest, inoffensive men. Similarly, Montague Simons; Henry Moses, another Hessian sutler, but more probably a soldier; Henry Harris, a tailor; and Haym Solomons, who had come to Charleston with a cargo of skins only four months earlier, were exonerated of the accusation that they had assisted the British.[32]

Evidently Loyalism was a broad category, which covered all degrees of collaboration with the British. It ranged from those who made a conscious choice and commitment to the crown to perhaps a larger number who found themselves forced to remain under British authority in occupied places. This was true of the Jews as it was also of the general population in America. Nevertheless, it must be recognized that the Jews too had their choice of a broad range of thought and action during the Revolution. The significance of this diversity perhaps lies in the fact that they were able and willing to entertain such varied opinions and positions in this critical period. They had to that degree become an accepted part of the total community, and their attachment to the American cause, or their defection from it, was considered important enough to be judged by the general community.

8

Post-Revolutionary Effects on the Jews in America

The Revolutionary War ended with a peace treaty in 1783, but the American Revolution, in its broader sense, continued for at least another half-dozen years. Its subsequent stage led to the creation of a new federal union and government in 1789. Revolution thereafter erupted in France, embroiling all of Europe for a generation. The age of Revolutions was thus extended to the Jews of Europe, where emancipation now became a major issue. It also affected the United States internally and externally. The French Revolution stimulated a political division in America between a conservative pro-British Federalism and a more radical pro-French Jeffersonianism. In all the confrontation of internal and external forces that ensued, the few thousand Jews who had lived through and shared in the trials of Revolution and war were scarcely noticeable or noticed. They represented a small element, for whom, however, the recognition of their rights to both political and religious equality was real and important, if scarcely visible to the rest of the country. Hence the test of the following post-Revolutionary period was whether the Jews would succeed in achieving an equalization and integration promised inherently in the doctrinal concept of the Revolution, as embodied in the Declaration of Independence and the federal Constitution.

The winning of equal rights as a result of the Revolution was basic not only for the Jews but also for the whole country. It testified to the reality and lasting quality of the Revolutionary promise, in the face of counterforces that operated in the nineteenth century. One was internal and was the outgrowth of

156

state and regional pressures, particularly over slavery as between North and South. The other was external and took the form of a great wave of migration in the nineteenth century, which affected the Jews as much as others in the population. The question was one of how fast and in what form the incorporation and integration of the many new and diverse elements would occur under the impact of equality inherent in the Revolution, on the one hand, and xenophobic prejudice on the other. The goal of *e pluribus unum* (out of many, one) was the ultimate criterion of American society, not only politically as regards its component states, but also socially and culturally with reference to its many racial and religious components. Interestingly, the Revolution had already provided a kind of early melting pot for the Jews who comprised diverse elements derived from many sources in Europe, as represented by the Portuguese Aaron Lopez, the German Jonas Phillips, and the Pole Haym Salomon.

For the Jews, as for the rest of the country, the Revolution therefore extended beyond the War of Independence. The test was whether they would fulfill and realize their equality of rights and develop a consciousness of belonging to and being a part of America. Conditions in the states were diverse and variable with respect both to the numbers and to the status of the Jews. Progress was neither even nor smooth, and the problems and handicaps persisted well after the Revolution. One favorable factor was perhaps the relative stability of the Jewish population, which scarcely doubled between the Revolution and 1826, at the semicentennial of the Revolution, and before the great nineteenth-century flow of immigration began.

The Jews in the post-Revolutionary era were primarily the survivors of the Revolutionary generation and their descendants. It was predominantly a native-born generation, much more so than was to be the case for a century thereafter, as a result of later immigration. The Jews were a mobile element, probably as much so as the rest of the population. They spread out from the original few settlements along the Atlantic seaboard, forming new communities in Boston, Baltimore, Richmond, and elsewhere, and moving individually westward to the frontier. They carried trade and skills wherever they wandered, but they also engaged in land speculation, which was a common enterprise of the period.

Significantly, the Jewish community retained its integrity, socially and religiously, even as it became an integral part of general society. This fact shows the essential multiplicity and diversity of American society, even as it was achieving political unity. The record of the post-Revolutionary generation in America, both Jewish and other, is thus a direct outgrowth and product of the Revolution itself and must be treated in such terms.

Significantly, already in January 1790, as the French National Assembly was considering the adoption of a Declaration of the Rights of Man, the French Jews addressed the National Assembly and cited the example of the American Jews, pointing out that "America has rejected the word toleration from its code" in preference for "equality." It is noteworthy that in August of the same year, President Washington, in acknowledging the warm greetings of the Jewish community of Newport, also stressed the fact that "all possess alike liberty of conscience and immunities of citizenship. It is now no more that toleration is spoken of, as if it was by the indulgence of one class of people that another enjoyed the exercise of their inherent natural rights." Despite his conservatism, Washington, as much as Jefferson, was here espousing the radical doctrine of the Enlightenment.[1]

Equally, as shown already during the Revolution, the Jews developed the habit and practice of participation in national affairs ceremonially as well as practically, both by group action and individual effort. Thus in 1782 the patriotic spiritual leader of Mikveh Israel in Philadelphia, Rev. Gershom Seixas, delivered a special "prayer for the government," invoking the grace of God on "His Excellency the President and Delegates of the United States in Congress assembled, on his Excellency, George Washington, Captain-General and Commander-in-Chief of these States." As early as 1781, Gershom Seixas had begun the collection of state constitutions and their analysis for discriminatory provisions against the Jews, which he cited at the end of each one. It was the first such comparative political study by a Jew, and probably by anyone for this purpose. Again in 1783, ten Jewish signatories, among them Haym Salomon, Issac Moses, Jonas Phillips, Isaac Franks, and Moses Levy, all then residents in Philadelphia, joined some eight hundred others in an address to

Congress urging them to return to the city despite the mutinous threats and demands of the army for arrears of pay.[2]

The American Jews, or at least their leaders, repeatedly pressed upon the government of both states and nation the recognition and confirmation of their rights, not always successfully. In 1783 some of the prominent Jews in Philadelphia, such as Phillips, Salomon, Simon Nathan, and Seixas, petitioned the Supreme Executive Council of Pennsylvania to repeal the religious clause limiting Jewish rights to office in that state. It was then denied and not granted until 1790. In New York, too, in 1783, the Jewish leaders, many only recently returned, addressed a warm welcome to the newly arrived Governor George Clinton and asserted proudly: "Though the society we belong to is small, when compared with other religious societies, yet we flatter ourselves that none has manifested a more zealous attachment to the sacred cause of America in the late war with Britain." The climax of these early assertions of hope and expectations occurred in 1787, when Jonas Phillips appealed to the Continental Convention, then concluding its labors in Philadelphia, to give recognition to the principle of equal religious rights under the new government. Happily, the Convention had already included a clause in the Constitution, forbidding religious oaths, thereby fulfilling the wishes of the Jews.

Through Phillips, as it were, the Jews had a small part in the consideration of the Constitution. Phillips promised that "then the Israelites will consider themselves happy to live under a government where all the religious societies are on equal footing. I solicit this favor for myself, my children, posterity, and for the benefit of all the Israelites through the thirteen United States of America." Moreover, he invoked God's blessing upon the Convention: "May the almighty God of our fathers, Abraham, Isaac, and Jacob, imbue this noble assembly with wisdom, judgment, and unanimity in their counsels."[3]

Despite such expressions and hopes of religious equalization, progress was slow and uneven during the post-Revolutionary years. Here and there in the country, anti-Jewish sentiment emerged and was expressed publicly, as will be indicated later. A counterresponse was called for, and an appeal was made to the principles and promise of the Revolution. Sometimes, this was done by the Jews themselves, occasionally by voices from the general public. Thus, in 1783, the *South Carolina Gazette and General Advertiser*, which had already reproached such prejudice during the Revolution, now again reproved those Christians who were antagonistic to Jews: "He who hates another for not being a Christian is not himself a Christian. . . . The Jews have had a considerable part in our late Revolution. They have behaved well throughout. Let our Government invite the Jews to our state and promise a settlement in it. It will be a wise and politic stroke, and give a place of rest at last to the tribe of Israel."

Despite this note of implied condescension, the Jews in South Carolina prospered and multiplied after the Revolution and made up the largest community in America for a generation. Significantly, aside from those living in Georgetown, Camden, and other such small places, the Jews of Charleston produced an active community under new leadership, which was American in origin and orientation. Governor Moultrie and other state dignitaries attended the dedication of a new synagogue in 1794. Other new synagogues were built in the years after 1782, for example, in Philadelphia and Richmond, and were evidence of growth and a new self-assurance and security. In later years, such figures as Isaac Harby, the journalist and dramatist, and Penina Moïse, the poetess, both of Charleston, exemplified the new integrated Jewish and American character. This phenomenon was best illustrated in the Reformed Society of Israelites, promoted by Isaac Harby in 1826. The movement had strong native American and even Southern traits. It proved short-lived, particularly as the centers of Jewish cultural and economic activity shifted and settled in the North, to be fed and reinvigorated by the new immigration.[4]

A measure of Jewish equalization and integration into American society is to be found in the progressive but piecemeal and uneven abolition of religious test oaths and restraints in the several seaboard states following the adoption of the Constitution. In fact, some states, such as Pennsylvania, Delaware, New Jersey, and Maryland, adopted test oaths during the Revolution and did not repeal them until years later. The process of repeal, however, began then too and proceeded gradually. New York abolished its restrictions as early as 1777, in its first state constitution. Virginia followed a decade later, in 1786, and Georgia in 1789. Pennsylvania, which had adopted a religious test oath in 1776, repealed it in 1790, and was followed by Delaware and South Carolina in 1792. Other states were, however, more dilatory. Maryland became the major case in which the confrontation of two opposing views on this matter began as early as 1797 and continued until 1826, when the "Jew Bill" finally repealed the test oath for public office. Considerable pressure was exerted for repeal by two leaders of the small Jewish community in Baltimore, Jacob I. Cohen and Solomon Etting, both of whom had experience in the Revolution. These men were elected members of the Baltimore City Council immediately after repeal, and both Etting and Cohen served as its president for many years.[5]

In the remaining states the imposition of religious tests or other restrictions was removed even more gradually, perhaps because there were relatively few Jews in those states. Such gradualism also marked the relatively slow separation of church and state. Whereas Massachusetts required a religious oath for public office as late as 1820, Connecticut and Rhode Island did so until 1842, despite Rhode Island's long tradition of religious toleration since Roger Williams' time. North Carolina repealed its religious test only in 1868, and New Hampshire, which had few Jews, as late as 1876. By contrast, the new Western states, organized under the Northwest Ordinance of 1787, forbade religious discrimination immediately. This was linked with the Jeffersonian principle of natural right and equality, which was also incorporated into the federal Constitution of that year. It is significant that leadership and direction in this field derived from the national rather than state governments.[6]

The hope and promise held out by the Revolution to the Jews, even in Europe, are suggested in an obscure but interesting episode that occurred in Germany in 1783. An anonymous German writer addressed an appeal to the President of the Continental Congress. This was published in the *Deutsches Museum* and was reprinted as a pamphlet in 1787. The identity of its author is still unknown, although it has been attributed even to Moses Mendelssohn, the great contemporary leader of the Jewish

intellectual emancipation in Europe. Most probably the appeal
was the work of Christian W. Dolin, a liberal Christian and founder and editor of the *Deutsches Museum*; it may never have reached
America. The intent was perhaps to improve the status of the
Jews in Germany by proposing an escape for them.

The United States, according to the writer's argument, was
possessed of much vacant land, which would require more than a
century for occupation. Why not open it to Jews from Germany?
As many as two thousand families might be ready to emigrate at
once: "Your religion does not forbid you to open your waste lands
to us to build up. You already tolerate Jews in your country."
Emanating from Germany, this proposal was an early harbinger
of the great German immigration, both Jewish and non-Jewish,
which occurred during the mid-nineteenth century. It was an
early prototype and anticipation of the famous plan for Jewish
emigration from Europe proposed by Mordecai M. Noah of New
York in the 1820s, for which he offered the site of Ararat on an
island in the Niagara River. Noah's project too was premature;
clearly the subsequent torrent of migration was not to be confined
within any plan or program.[7]

The early participation of Jews in civic and scientific affairs is
revealed in an unusual if minor episode of 1784. There was then
great popular excitement and interest in the possibility of balloon
ascents. The *Pennsylvania Packet* of 29 June 1784 reported a
project for such an event in Philadelphia, sponsored by a civic
group. Its costs were to be borne by subscribers, among whom
were Haym Salomon, Jonas Phillips, and Benjamin Nones, who
had all played conspicuous roles in the Revolution just concluded. A flight was to be attempted by Peter A. Carnes, which,
however, failed to materialize. There was not to be a successful
ascent in America until almost a decade later, in 1793, by the
Frenchman Jean-Pierre Blanchard.[8]

The Jews participated fully and freely in the public celebration
of the ratification of the Constitution by Pennsylvania. There was
a great procession in Philadelphia in 1788, and the Reverend
Jacob R. Cohen marched in it, arms locked with other clergymen.
The Jews had a table of refreshments set up at the end of the
parade. According to the recollection of Naphtali Phillips, the
fifteen-year old son of Jonas Phillips, who described the event in

1868, when he was ninety-five years old, it was laden down with "soused [pickled] salmon, bread and crackers, almonds and raisins," but no liquor. It was tended by an old cobbler, Isaac Moses, not to be confused with the more famous Revolutionary War merchant of the same name.[9]

More significant undoubtedly was the role played by Rev. Gershom Seixas as one of the thirteen clergymen who participated symbolically in the inauguration of George Washington as President on 30 April 1789 in New York. They all marched in closely marshaled rank in the procession that followed. David S. Franks, a lieutenant-colonel in the Revolution, was one of the three marshals who were in attendance at the inauguration. This may have been recognition for an acquaintance of Washington, but Seixas undoubtedly served officially as a Jewish clergyman. Equally noteworthy was the presentation and publication of "A Religious Discourse Delivered in the Synagogue in this City [New York], November 29, 1789," in honor of President Washington's proclamation of a "Day of Thanksgiving." It was the first of its kind in Jewish-American history, and Seixas was the most appropriate person for the honor. Sixteen pages long, written and delivered in English, as was Seixas' practice, the publication contained appropriate prayers for the government as well as a sermon on the times.[10]

Peculiarly notable and noteworthy both in its ceremonial symbolism and practical, political import was the famed exchange of sentiments between President Washington and the existing Jewish congregations between 1789 and 1790. It was further significant as the first concerted effort by the Jews of America to act publicly in unison. Difficulties of communication and delays disrupted the movement, and in the end, several messages were presented by separate congregations at different times. It may, nevertheless, be considered as a unanimous, if not united, expression and exchange of views on the issue of religious rights that concerned the Jews particularly. Despite its special character, it is, nevertheless, a significant symbolic manifestation of the integration of the Jews into American society following the Revolution.

It would appear that the congregation of Shearith Israel in New York initiated a proposal for a single statement of loyalty by all the Jews in America, on the occasion of Washington's inauguration as President. Rather surprisingly, the first action was taken by the most remote congregation in Savannah. As early as 6 May 1789, only a few days after the inauguration of President Washington, Levi Sheftall, scion of an old Jewish family in Georgia and president of the congregation, addressed a letter of congratulation to President Washington, wishing him happiness and success in behalf of the Savannah Jews. The very remoteness and isolation of this Jewish group may account for its independent but no less important action.[11]

On 2 July 1790 Moses Seixas of Newport wrote to the New York congregation complaining of the delay in formulating a common address. The inauguration was now more than a year past and the suitable opportunity would appear to have been lost. In August 1790 an appropriate occasion presented itself for action by the Jews of Newport. President Washington visited Newport, and at a large reception on 18 August, to which prominent Jews were invited, Moses Seixas presented his famous letter, which employed language that was at once happy and ringing. Moses Seixas was a brother of Rev. Gershom Seixas, and there may have been a family gift for language, if he indeed composed the letter. There is no evidence to the contrary. Unlike his brother, the minister, who patriotically left New York when the British occupied it during the Revolution, Moses had remained in Newport under similar circumstances. He was, however, left undisturbed after the British evacuation and served as the first cashier of the Bank of Rhode Island, which had its offices in his house until his death in 1809. He was also Grand Master of Rhode Island Masonry and in 1790 was president of the Newport synagogue, when he delivered his greetings to President Washington, both as a Jew and as a Mason.

The Seixas message had a touch of eloquence, as it hailed the new government, "erected by the majesty of the people, a government which to bigotry gives no sanction, to persecution no assistance, but generously affording to all liberty of conscience and unanimity of citizenship." Washington answered in kind, repeating in fact the key phrases, "to bigotry no sanction" etc., as if he not merely agreed but could not improve the language. In this ceremonial and official exchange of a common faith in religious equality, the first of its kind in political history, was sounded at the very birth of the American nation a belief in equality and not merely toleration, as Washington made sure to assert and reaffirm the distinction. This was a direct outgrowth of the American Revolution and one of the ideas it had generated.[12]

At this very time, too, in July 1790, Charleston's synagogue, Beth Elohim, addressed a letter to President Washington. Each congregation was apparently acting on its own, despite the original intention of concerted action. This diversity of communication significantly reveals a diversity of expression if not of view and a remarkable gift for composition among the relatively few Jews then living in America. The Charleston letter was composed by the president, Jacob Cohen, a veteran of the Revolution, and it recited the blessings and benefits of the new government in three long pages, of which a small selection must suffice to illustrate the style and content:

> To the equal participation and enjoyment of all these [the natural and inalienable rights of human nature] it has raised us from the state of political degradation and grievous oppression to which partial, narrow, and illiberal policy and intolerant bigotry has reduced us in almost every other part of the world. Peculiar and extraordinary reason have we, therefore, to be attached to the free and generous Constitutions of our respective states, and to be indebted to you, whose heroic deeds have contributed so much to their preservation and establishment.

Here was voiced a new civic patriotism, perhaps the first expression of it by Jews to a secular regime in the modern world.[13]

Three other congregations, New York, Philadelphia, and Richmond, joined also by Charleston, despite its earlier address already cited, agreed on a common address to be presented to President Washington. The government was now located in Philadelphia, and on 13 December 1790 Manuel Josephson delivered it in person. Washington was careful to answer this as he had replied to the others with a proper expression of appreciation and gratitude. The fact that all the congregations had written or joined in letters is significant evidence of the harmony of thought and sentiment among the Jews of America on the subject of a common interest in religious freedom and their deep loyalty to the United States after the Revolution. The exchange of correspondence was published in the *United States Gazette* of 1790.[14]

Despite such an auspicious beginning, anti-Jewish prejudice existed during this period and received public expression here and there. It stemmed from economic and political friction perhaps more than from religious antagonism. Some of these episodes have already been cited elsewhere as occurring during the Revolution proper. Only one such episode deserves review at this point, partly because it occurred in 1784, in the intervening years between the Revolution and the new government established in 1789, and partly because it involved Haym Salomon's activities, and thus hit at the very core of Jewish participation. Salomon then had less than one more year to live. The attack was made by a Quaker banker, Miers Fisher of Philadelphia, who was a sponsor of a new Bank of Pennsylvania soon to be chartered by the legislature in competition with the Bank of North America, which had proved so useful in financing the Revolution in its last phases. Gratuitously, Fisher dragged in the Jews as he argued that the new bank would lower interest rates and protect the people against the Jews and their usurious practices.

Salomon rose to the defense in a letter published in the *Independent Gazette* on 13 March 1784 in which he condemned Fisher's calumny against the Jews. He took the offensive and denounced Fisher and his fellow Quakers as the true culprits who had traded with the enemy, did not pay taxes, and depreciated the currency. By contrast, Salomon argued, the Jews were "early, uniform, and decisive Whigs and were second to none in our patriotism and attachment to country." It is noteworthy that, at the close of the Revolution, Salomon did not believe that full equality had yet occurred. As indicated, this religious liberation passed into law and practice quite slowly, over the ensuing post-Revolutionary period. At the same time in 1785, in far-off Georgia, Mordecai Sheftall also found occasion to send a letter to the *Georgia Gazette*, signed "a real citizen," defending the role of the Jews during the Revolution.[15]

Significantly, the most troubling episode of anti-Semitism occurred at the close of the century. The French Revolution, which had been on for a decade, cast its shadow upon this country, severely dividing its internal politics. In 1798 occurred the so-called undeclared war between France and the United States, which was predominantly maritime in character. Internally, too, political passions ran high between the pro-British Federalists, still further divided between the warlike Hamiltonians, the more pacific followers of President John Adams, and the pro-French Jeffersonians, who were to take power after the bitter presidential election of 1800. It was also the time of the notorious Alien and Sedition Acts. Interestingly, the Jews expanded their participation in public and political affairs during this decade. Diverse individuals became active politically, and some began to aspire to and achieve public office, both elective and appointive. They were more important on the state than on the national level, but the scale and scope of their efforts and attainment must not be exaggerated. It was, however, a new and significant phenomenon, and it was especially noteworthy that, living in cities for the most part, the Jews were most involved in Democratic or Jeffersonian politics. In their sympathies, too, they were most compatible with popular Democratic goals.

There were, however, some prominent Jewish Federalists; one of them, in fact, bore the brunt of the first major political attacks, as will be seen. The political integration of the Jews thus began in a difficult time, both internally and externally, and produced some unfavorable reactions. To counter this, however, it must be noted that the wars of this period, in 1798 and 1812, provided opportunities for considerable military service by young Jews, who were, in an active sense, the sons of the veterans of the Revolution. Thereby they confirmed the right of the Jews to a proper place in the American historic record.

One of the episodes that reflected the violent journalism of the time was directed against Moses Levy, a lawyer of Philadelphia, who was counsel to Benjamin Rush. He had helped Rush in a libel suit against William Cobbett, a reactionary former British journalist, writing under the name of Peter Porcupine. Although Levy was a Federalist and a Christian by conversion, this did not keep Cobbett as Peter Porcupine from deriding Levy in a malicious and faked Anglo-Jewish dialect.

More serious was an attack in *Fenno's Gazette* in 1800 against

Benjamin Nones and other Jewish merchants in Philadelphia. Nones was a French-born Jew who came to America during the Revolution. He fought in the war in the South and won the commendation of General Pulaski in whose corps he served. Later he acquired a major's rank and subsequently settled as a merchant and broker in Philadelphia, where his business fortunes fluctuated. He was one of the first Jews in America to seek public office under President Jefferson, as did several of his sons, who also fought in the War of 1812. This will be dealt with in the proper place, and is mentioned here only to illustrate the man's full adaptation to life in this country. Nevertheless, as an ardent Jeffersonian, he became a victim of slander and aspersion generated in an atmosphere of political division and partisanship.

Nones, however, rose to the occasion and published a remarkably eloquent reply in William Duane's *Philadelphia Aurora*, the leading Republican journal. Ironically, he listed and admitted the triple charges "of being a Jew, of being a Republican, and of being poor." He asked pointedly: "How then can a Jew but be a Republican in America especially?" He reviewed his career "as an American throughout the whole of the Revolutionary War in the militia of Charleston and in Pouleskey's [sic] legion. I fought in almost every action which took place in Carolina and in the disastrous affair of Savannah, shared the hardships of that sanguinary date, and for twenty-three years I felt no disposition to change my political any more than my religious principles." As for being poor, Nones argued somewhat whimsically that it was no disgrace even in a Jew. He admitted having been bankrupt, but he had paid his debts. He was a "democrat because I was a Jew."[16]

Even in far-off Charleston, charges were made in the press in 1800 that the Jews had indulged improperly in politics during their religious services, when a candidate for office distributed his tickets. This was denied in a Charleston newspaper of 16 October 1800, and the writer launched into a eulogy of Jewish conduct during the Revolution, which was still fresh enough to warrant honorary citation: "Their steady adherence to the American cause, and their continued submission to the government and laws of their country are substantial proofs of their patriotism and attachment." In 1819 a Charleston historian, J. L. E. Shecut, paid tribute to the Jewish role in the Revolution: "When the War of the Revolution commenced, all of this nation [Jewish] who were in South Carolina, able to bear arms, zealously joined in their country's martial ranks for the great but dubious contest. The prize to be acquired in the event of a successful issue, religious and political freedom, was great enough to induce the free offering of every patriotic exertion, and even of fortune and life in the undertaking."

Interestingly, in 1824, a Colonel Worthington, who was making a speech in the Maryland legislature for the repeal of the religious test oath required for public office, recited the same events of the Jews' role in the Revolution in Charleston. He told how a company of Israelites was formed in Charleston in 1779, all living in King Street. This was the "Jew Company," commanded by Captain Richard Lushington, which fought under General Moultrie at Beaufort and in defense of Charleston. Worthington cited as authority Jacob I. Cohen, who had been a member of this company and was now a resident of Baltimore and a strong advocate of the proposed act for religious equality in Maryland.[17]

The Jews in New York were early attracted to the Tammany Society, one of the first democratic organizations that were social as well as political in purpose. Isaac Gomez, Isaac Levy, and Isaac Seixas were members of the Tammany Society; Naphtali Judah was a sachem, and Solomon Simson was a founder and vice-president. James Rivington, a Loyalist in the Revolution and now a Federalist journalist, attacked Simson as of the "tribe of Shylock" and indulged in similar diatribe. It is noteworthy that in 1798, Rev. Gershom Seixas, the patriotic clergyman of the Revolution, delivered a sermon on the occasion of a National Fast proclaimed by President Adams. In it he struck a pro-French note, contrary to the official Federalism. He reminded people how the French had helped America win independence "from an enraged enemy," whom the Federalists were now assaulting.[18]

Despite such occasional outbursts of anti-Jewish sentiment, the Jews of the post-Revolutionary generation persisted in their effort to become integrated into American society politically and socially. They sought political office on all levels of government and were remarkably successful, especially in the South. They participated actively and significantly in the post-Revolutionary wars, both in 1798 and 1812. Their political activity and achievement were most abundant and striking on the local and state levels, less so in the federal government, perhaps because there were few federal political offices, for which competition was keen and largely politically oriented. The Jews could scarcely expect to have great political weight or influence at this early date in the sphere of elective office nationally. They were few, and their principal preoccupation as well as occupation was as yet business. A surprising number of them, however, were already engaged in the professions of both law and medicine, proportionately perhaps more than was to be the case for a century to follow. The Jewish political and military record during this early post-Revolutionary period was, nevertheless, both extensive and diverse, and will be reviewed in the next chapter.

9

Political and Military Services in the Post-Revolutionary Era

The quest for public office began with a few Jews while the Revolution was still going on, and affected veterans of the war, although they enjoyed slight success. Two, in particular, have already been dealt with earlier; their quest was a direct outgrowth of the war, as if they had little else to turn to after the Revolution. They marked the transition from a military to a civil career other than business. David S. Franks and Solomon Bush both reached relatively high military rank and were almost professional in their military standing. Franks, it will be remembered, shifted from a military to a diplomatic career during the war. He spent several years between 1781 and 1787 in Europe serving as courier and aide to Jefferson, Jay, and Franklin while abroad. He was for a time even American consul to Marseilles. Jefferson befriended him and recommended him for some government position after the war, which he never obtained. He served briefly as secretary of an Indian commission under President Washington. He was probably the first Jew to aspire to and to hold public office already during the Revolution. He spent his last years in private employment as a bank cashier in Philadelphia and died prematurely in 1793 in the great yellow fever epidemic.

Solomon Bush served actively in the Pennsylvania militia during the early years of the Revolution. He attained the rank of lieutenant-colonel and became deputy adjutant-general of the state's militia. He took part in the Battle of Brandywine in 1777, where he was wounded severely in the thigh, and was an invalid thereafter, although he was denied admission to the Corps of Invalids. He became an early applicant for public civil office. As

171

early as 1780 he petitioned Congress, on the strength of his military service and injury, for the post of secretary to the Honorable Board of the Treasury. He was thus the first Jewish officer to seek public office. In subsequent years, Bush applied for other positions, such as Health Officer of Philadelphia in 1784. He lived in London for some years and studied medicine there. He was acquainted with Washington and wrote him a letter of congratulations on his becoming President in 1789; included in it was an application for a diplomatic or consular post in London. Washington replied with thanks and acknowledged Bush's part in the liberation of an American ship "by proper and spirited conduct," but he ignored his request. Time and again in later years Bush applied directly to President Washington for a public office, such as Naval Officer in Philadelphia. In 1795, as his last try he boldly applied to succeed Timothy Pickering as Postmaster-General. He died in the same year, and thus unrequited, Bush's quest of a public career came to an end.[1]

Aside from David S. Franks, who held a diplomatic office in Europe briefly during the Revolution, the first Jew to be named to a government post after the war was Isaac Pinto. He was appointed Interpreter in the Spanish language in 1786. It was a part-time position, without fixed salary, as Pinto complained in 1789 to John Jay, Secretary of Foreign Affairs: "I took it for granted that it would be of considerable advantage to me." But in three years' employment, apparently only on call, he had received only eight pounds. He felt it "no impropriety to me to hope for or even to expect some further consideration." He believed he was legally qualified in this trust: "I am considered in my station as searvant [sic] of the Public."

Jay advised Pinto to write to Jefferson, who had just been appointed Secretary of State but was still in France. Pinto, one of the few learned Jews in America, had published as early as 1761 and 1766 two collections of prayers translated from the Hebrew into English. He was also a teacher of Spanish. Pinto, now advanced in years, died in 1791, shortly after entering his complaint about his lack of public employment. In the same period, in 1788, Barnard Henry, son of Aaron Henry of Charleston, was United States consul at Gibraltar. He was later an officer of the United States Navy, one of the first, if not the first Jew to serve in this newest branch of American defense, to which Jews were scarcely likely to be attracted by the nature of their background and business experience. The War of 1812, however, offered them a considerable opportunity for naval as well as army service, as will be subsequently illustrated.[2]

Among early applicants for public office was Simon Nathan, whose name is especially noteworthy because of his troubled business relations with Virginia during the Revolution, already recounted. In 1789 he applied for an appointment as Broker to the Office of Finance, a post created for Haym Salomon during the war. He did not receive it, although he continued to be an applicant for public office in later years, as will be shown. In 1795, Moses Sheftall, son of Mordecai and a physician in Savannah, was an applicant for a public position, but it is not indicated what it was. On the death of Levi Sheftall, brother of Mordecai, in 1809, his son reported in the family diary that his father had been "United States agent for fortifications in the state of Georgia."[3]

There were few applications by Jews for public office during Washington's presidency, and apparently none under his successor, John Adams. Interestingly, the projected new federal city of Washington attracted the first Jewish settler in 1795. He was Isaac Polock of Savannah, who became a builder in the capital and was "among the foremost people at the time of the government removal in 1800." Only under Jefferson and succeeding Democratic-Republican Presidents did Jews appear more frequently as applicants. The reason may have been that the Jews were predominantly Democratic and were thus more likely to win recognition and appointment. There were possibly also more public vacancies, and prevailing hard times rendered the Jews more vulnerable to business failure, and hence more likely to seek public employment. Thus in the early years of Jefferson's administration, under the Bankruptcy Act of 1800, the office of Commissioner of Bankruptcy became available and interested several Jews, perhaps because of their business experience.

At any rate, in June 1802 James Monroe, then Governor of Virginia, recommended Jacob I. Cohen, "late merchant and very worthy character," as one of five to serve on a Board of Commissioners of Bankruptcy. In the same year, Moses Levy, Recorder of Philadelphia, equivalent to a judge, wrote to A. J.

Dallas, Secretary of the Treasury under Jefferson, urging the appointment of his brother, Samson Levy, also a lawyer, as a Commissioner of Bankruptcy: "As you have been long and intimately acquainted with him I need say no more on the subject. Unless I see through a prejudiced medium, I think I may venture to say that his legal acquirements will enable him to perform the duties of the office and his integrity will guard him of any improper conduct in it."

In the same year of 1802, Moses Myers of Norfolk declined an appointment as Commissioner of Bankruptcy: he wrote: "I fear I am not calculated to fulfill the duties of said appointment." He wished Madison to extend his thanks to the President, and he returned the commission, "truly sensible of the honor he had conferred on me." In 1803 Solomon Phillips, son of Jonas, a veteran of the Revolution, applied to President Jefferson for appointment to a vacated post of Commissioner of Bankruptcy. He was an attorney and he submitted the recommendations of a number of prominent citizens of Philadelphia, among them General Muhlenberg, William Duane, Moses Levy, and Israel Israel, the last two one-time Jews and Federalist and Democrat respectively. In 1801, the newly-elected president, Jefferson, named Reuben Etting United States Marshall for the state of Maryland. He was a member of the prominent Etting family of Baltimore, and in 1798 was a captain of the Baltimore Independent Blues. He later fought in the War of 1812 and was district attorney of Cecil County.[4]

Another applicant for public office in 1803 was Simon Nathan, now of New York, addressing President Jefferson, who, as Governor of Virginia during the Revolution, had had considerable and involved dealings with Nathan. In his application Nathan stated that "I was not inactive in rendering the assistance to government at that time in my power which the minutes of the then presiding Council will show." He had also given "my services with money and my own credit to the state of South Carolina in 1780 and 1781 after the British had taken possession of Charleston." Moreover, since the Revolution, Nathan reminded Jefferson, "I have acted with the same uniformity in my political sentiments. These circumstances are well known to many gentlemen of note in Virginia, Baltimore, Philadelphia, and New

York." He was thus claiming political affinity with the Jeffersonian party, as was the case with many other contemporary Jews. He had not fared well in business lately, "so that I have been under the necessity of closing my affairs in 1800. . . . Adversity has pressed hard upon me. . . . Thus unfortunately situated, I am led, respected Sir, to make my application to you . . . if any post should offer . . . that you would esteem me worthy. . . ." In this instance, as in others, there is no evidence of success. At this time, however, a Jacob Cohen was named Commissioner of Bankruptcy in Worcester, Massachusetts. It is perhaps significant that business adversity was then lending importance to the new position of Commissioner of Bankruptcy and making some Jews available or eager to accept an appointment.[5]

The Nones family as a whole seemed to supply numerous candidates for office in those early years, and consular posts were their principal objective. Benjamin Nones, founder and head of the family, first sought a government post as early as 1801. As he wrote to President Jefferson on 18 March, shortly after his inauguration, he was "an old soldier and a republican citizen of the United States." He reviewed his whole life, from the time when Britain invaded the country "to lay waste the fair rights of Freemen, I abandoned the place of my nativity" (Bordeaux). In flamboyant and flowery style, he narrated: "I immediately flew to the Standard of Liberty and under her banners joined the valiant sons of America in the defense of Freedom's Cause. . . ." The details have already been given elsewhere; briefly, he had been made a prisoner at the fall of Charleston and was not liberated until the surrender of Cornwallis at Yorktown. He concluded that "I assisted to fight the battles of America and deemed myself happy at every hazard, in assuring with my sword her Freedom and Independence." Here was a bold affirmation of a patriotic and warlike spirit, altogether a new manifestation in the modern annals of the Jews. Apparently Lafayette was not alone as a French volunteer in the cause of freedom.

Nones settled in Philadelphia, married, and became the father of fourteen children. He was now in dire distress, "brought about chiefly by the tyranny of opinion," which resented his "principles and opposition to the measures of Mr. Adams' Administration." His French origin precluded sympathy with its anti-French character. Moreover, he asserted in the letter to Jefferson that "I was always a republican and as a Freeman glory in being a republican." He hoped for an appointment in Mr. Jefferson's gift, and in repeated letters he pressed his claim and offered the recommendations of many prominent persons in Philadelphia. He submitted "the signatures of all the Republicans of the city, to whom my exertions and sufferings in the common cause are not unknown." This was a frank appeal to political partisanship. In a final letter on 18 July 1802 he asked to be named to a vacancy on the board of Commissioners of Bankruptcy. Benjamin Nones was not one of those named, however, as far as can be determined.[6]

Several sons of Nones also sought public office in succeeding years, usually in the consular service. One may speculate whether this had anything to do with their French background or, more probably, with the wide geographical distribution of their business interests. These were difficult times too for American foreign trade, harassed by the conflict between France and Britain for control of the seas. In 1807 David B. Nones petitioned President Jefferson for an appointment as notary public at Point Peter on Guadeloupe in the French West Indies. He was recommended by many merchants of Philadelphia, who wanted a notary at this place to certify to their property there and thus to protect it against British seizure. Ultimately Jefferson proclaimed the embargo in this year, and there is no record of an appointment for Nones. Another of Nones's sons, Solomon, was American consul at Lisbon during this period.

Many years later, under President Monroe, several sons of Nones again applied for consular or trade posts in the West Indies. Aaron B. Nones was "a resident and patented merchant at Aux Cayes, Hayti" in 1820 when he sought an appointment as a commercial agent at this port. His own father and many other merchants of Philadelphia recommended him strongly, among them Simon Gratz, Samuel Hays, and Jacob I. Cohen. In 1822 David B. Nones addressed President Monroe for an appointment as commercial agent at Saint Thomas in the Virgin Islands, where he had traded for several years and was eager to promote the interests of "our beloved country." Again, numerous merchants of Philadelphia added their support, and Benjamin Nones, identifying himself as "an aged parent and a soldier of the glorious Revolution," testified that his son, now forty years old, had done business at Saint Thomas for a dozen years.[7]

In 1823 still another Nones son, Abraham B., was recommended by various merchants of Richmond and Norfolk, for a post as consul at Porto Carvello on the coast of Colombia. Solomon Jacobs wrote on 14 December 1823—coinciding closely and not insignificantly with President Monroe's proclamation on 2 December of the so-called Monroe Doctrine, relating to the freedom of the Western Hemisphere from European intervention—that Nones was "an undeviating Republican, the son of a worthy soldier of the Revolution, who served in Pulaski's Corps." Others also wrote in support of the application, and Nones himself explained that he had been to Porto Carvello, knew the language, and was planning to become a merchant there. A year later, however, Nones had changed his request for a consular position from Porto Carvello to Maracaibo, Venezuela, where a vacancy existed. Virginia politicians commended him as "a gentleman of cultivated and improved mind, of polite easy manner and great amenity of disposition." Nones must have obtained the post, since he is reported to have died there as a consul in 1835, a dozen years later. Still another son, Henry B. Nones, was a career officer in the federal revenue marine and commanded a ship in the Mexican War. His four sons continued the family tradition of public service and were officers in the army and navy in succeeding wars. Two were named, significantly, Washington and Jefferson Nones.[8]

Solomon Jacobs, a merchant of Richmond, cited earlier as a supporter of Nones's petition for a consular appointment, was himself a candidate in 1814 for a similar office in Amsterdam. He was recommended by friends in Richmond as "a gentleman who in honor and integrity would yield to no man." This opinion was not based "on a superficial knowledge of his character," since the writer, James Johnson, had known Jacobs long and intimately. He concluded his letter to James Monroe, then Secretary of State to President Madison: "To the strictest habits of industry, the most perfect knowledge of business he unites the properties of an elevated and dignified sense of honor and extensive acquirements. I believe he is not entirely unknown to you." Jacobs, it might be added, was married to Esther, a daughter of Benjamin

Nones, and may thus be regarded as a member of the Nones clan, at least by adoption. Moreover, he held other political offices in Virginia, as recorder and acting mayor of Richmond, and as a member of the Richmond council. He was at one time grand master of Virginia Masonry and president of the Congregation Beth Shalome in Richmond, itself an outgrowth of the Jewish settlement started there during the Revolution. He also had business ties through the tobacco monopoly with the French government and the Rothschild banking firm.[9]

Altogether, here and in the other cases cited is ample evidence of the aspirations and attainments of Jews in the post-Revolutionary period in a field that combined foreign trade with public office. It would appear that they excelled in both. In 1811 Moses Mordecai, a lawyer of Raleigh, North Carolina, was recommended for a post as federal judge of the Mississippi Territory. He was to succeed Oliver Fitts, who supported him for the appointment. Mordecai was the son of Jacob Mordecai, who had played a role in the Revolution as a young boy in Philadelphia. He was briefly a partner of Haym Salomon and later conducted a school for young ladies in Warrenton, North Carolina. Moses Mordecai was one of several brothers who attained distinguished professional positions particularly in the South. One of the brothers was Alfred Mordecai, an early Jewish graduate of West Point Military Academy and a lifelong professional army engineering officer. Of Moses Mordecai, Fitts wrote that he had known him intimately "from infancy and do not hesitate to say he's a man of unblemished character and that he is in possession of handsome legal acquirements, adequate to the discharge of the duties of the office." Thomas Blount of Yarborough added his praise of Mordecai, as a "single man in the prime and vigor of life" and an active citizen who, according to Blount's almost fulsome language, possessed the highest moral character, political principles, and general good conduct.[10]

This post-Revolutionary generation of young Jews seemed to possess remarkable qualifications for public service, as attested to by their Gentile contemporaries. They were the sons of the Revolution, as it were, whose very success in assimilation and integration into American society seemed to project an ultimate complete absorption for many of them. Another such person with an unusual public career was Nathan Levy, son of Benjamin Levy of Baltimore, whose activities during the Revolution have already been recounted. Nathan himself began his public career as early as 1799, when he served as United States Naval Agent in Haiti during the period of undeclared maritime warfare with France. Levy was recommended for an army officer's commission in 1798 by Generals Henry Lee and Uriah Forrest, but, somewhat strangely, he turned up in the following year as Naval Agent at Cape François, Haiti. He was appointed by the newly named Secretary of the Navy, Benjamin Stoddert, who expressed "the highest opinion of your honor and integrity." His business was to accept drafts and supply the captains of United States vessels at the customary commission, not to exceed 5 percent. Interestingly, at this same time Moses Myers was a naval agent in the domestic port of Norfolk. He performed similar supply functions and handled prize ships, but he was also a merchant and shipowner on his own.[11]

Levy's post was, however, an advanced and precarious one, since Haiti was then under the control of the black dictator, General Toussaint, who had led the black revolution against France half a dozen years earlier. The British island of Saint Kitt's was the only other port in the West Indies with an American Naval Agent. Levy's position was almost a diplomatic one, since he was instructed to discover "what are the vessels doing there? What are the real views of Toussaint? How are the people affected to America, France, and England?" Differences developed between Levy and the Secretary of the Navy, Benjamin Stoddert, who complained: "This gentleman, an old acquaintance of mine whom I wished to serve, has taken such freedoms with my name, as to render his removal necessary, even if his conduct in other respects has been unexceptionable." Levy was replaced, but a later memorandum exonerated him: "Whatever jocose expressions may have escaped him in conversation, his conduct at least has been fair and upright, and the charges ... alleged against him in this respect are unfounded."[12]

Levy turned up again in the War of 1812, in which he obtained a commission and served in the army. His public career was resumed in 1818 when he applied for a consular post in Saint Thomas. He was recommended highly by a considerable number of merchants as "a gentleman of integrity and patriotism." General Mason wrote in high praise of his integrity. He became vice-consul at Saint Thomas, but four years later he asked for a transfer to Jamaica. As he wrote, Britain was opening up the West Indies, and he could do the most good as a consul there. Later in the same year, however, Levy was applying for a post as navy storekeeper at Gosport in southern England. Here was a Jew who had made virtually a career out of public service.[13]

In the same year, 1822, Mordecai Myers, son of Dr. Levy Myers of Georgetown, South Carolina, was being recommended by his friends, Francis Kinlock and John Keith, for appointment as Secretary of Legation to either of the two missions being established in South America. Keith identified him as Colonel Myers, whom he had known from infancy and who was now a lawyer in Savannah. In 1824 William Meredith was recommending Jacob Nathans for a consulate in Tunis. He urged his consideration as a young man of character and integrity, who had studied law in his office. The precedent of a Jewish consul at Tunis, it may be added, had been established a decade earlier, in 1813, when Mordecai M. Noah had served there in a troubled period, and thus began a long, stormy public career that will be developed subsequently.[14]

In 1820, too, Judge William Smith of South Carolina forwarded an application to President Monroe from Chapman Levy for a public office in newly acquired East Florida. His term in the South Carolina Senate, he wrote, was expiring, and it would be the first time since he was twenty-one that "I will be clear of all offices both civil and military." It was time he took care of his own interests: "My country has had a full portion of it." He had become a colonel in the War of 1812, and if his country needed him, he added with characteristic patriotism, "I would again brighten my sword." Judge Smith acclaimed Levy as a "gentleman of high responsiblity," who "during the late war [1812] commanded a company of Riflemen. . . ." He was a lawyer and especially well informed on the timber of Florida, in which he was greatly interested. At this early date Chapman Levy gave evidence of being the prototype of the Southern Jew, extremely patriotic and attached to his region, as was later dramatically represented by the deep allegiance of many Southern Jews to the Confederate cause during the Civil War.[15]

Significantly too, the Jews assumed political roles in state and local government. This occurred where and as religious restrictions were removed progressively in various states during the post-Revolutionary period. Whereas federal positions occupied by Jews were of an appointive character, and none was elective in this early period, those in state and local government were of both kinds. A number of Jews won elective offices in city councils and state legislatures at an early date. The number and levels of such public offices were considerable, and a sampling must suffice to illustrate this significant trend, which cannot be examined exhaustively.

An early and especially distinguished local career was that of Moses Levy, scion of a prominent Philadelphia family. The product of a mixed marriage, he was an early graduate of the University of Pennsylvania (1772). He was admitted to the bar and became a leading lawyer. He served for many years as recorder or judge in the city court of Philadelphia. He was also subsequently a county judge. In 1804, although he was a conservative and a Federalist, Jefferson considered him for appointment as Attorney-General in the federal government. Israel Israel, another offspring of a mixed marriage, whose father professed somewhat mysteriously to be "a Jew outwardly," was an active Democrat and became high sheriff of Philadelphia. His descendants included Charles Ellet, a grandson who was a famous engineer, and Mrs. Virginia E. Cabell, nearly a century later, who served as President-General of the Daughters of the American Revolution. In Baltimore, Solomon Etting and Jacob I. Cohen capped their triumphant victory over Maryland's discriminatory religious law in 1826 by their election to the city council. In New York City, Jacob Hays, son of a Westchester farmer, David, was for many years chief constable, the equivalent of police chief, a position one would scarcely associate with a Jew at this early date. He headed, however, a branch of the family that ceased to be Jewish.[16]

Surprisingly, the South offered the Jews even wider opportunities for public service in the post-Revolutionary era. It was both civil and military in character. Isaiah Isaacs was German-born and probably the first Jew to settle in Richmond, even before the Revolution. In 1785 he was named clerk of the market; in later years he was tax assessor and a city councilman. He was married twice, first to a Christian and then to a Jewish woman. Solomon Jacobs was also a member of the Richmond City Council and subsequently recorder and acting mayor of the city; as cited elsewhere, he was one of the leading merchants of Richmond. Moses Myers was a prominent merchant, Naval Agent, Collector of the Port, and president of the council of Norfolk. He was member of a family that General Winfield Scott praised as "highly respectable and patriotic," and which "rendered very important services . . . during the late war [1812]."[17]

Jews were also active early in South Carolina politics and occupied many and various positions in government. It will be remembered that Francis Salvador, one of the first casualties of the Revolution in South Carolina, had served in the first Constitutional Convention and state legislature as early as 1776. After the Revolution, Levy Myers of Georgetown was a physician who served as apothecary-general of the state for many years, and he was member of the state legislature as early as 1796. His brother, Moses Myers, also of Georgetown, was a lawyer and clerk of the Court of General Sessions and Common Pleas in the state. Their father, Mordecai Myers, was the first postmaster of Georgetown, and he was succeeded by his nephew, Abraham Cohen. South Carolina was most prolific in Jewish officeholders. Eleazer Elizer was postmaster of Greenville, South Carolina, as early as 1784 and was later a justice of the peace. Chapman Levy, as already indicated, was a lawyer, a member of both houses of the legislature of South Carolina, and an officer in the War of 1812. Louis Levy, also a lawyer, was justice and a treasurer of the state. Solomon Cohen was a collector of taxes there; Haym Cohen was city assessor, and Mordecai Cohen commissioner of markets in Charleston.[18]

In Georgia, too, Jews played a notable role politically. Here the precedents had been set by the Sheftall family, several of whose members figured prominently during and after the Revolution, as related earlier. Exiled from Savannah after the British took possession, the Sheftalls returned in November 1782 on the shallop *Pearl*, laden with flour and other supplies. The Sheftall Diary, kept all through the eighteenth century, was now resumed and reported the return to Savannah of other Jewish families scattered by the Revolution. The family prospered in business, and Mordecai acquired a substantial amount of land confiscated from Tories. The Sheftalls also held various public offices in city and state. When Mordecai died in 1797, he had been a justice of the peace, and his obituary reported somewhat fulsomely that his family had lost "a faithful and affectionate councillor, and the nation a guardian and protector of liberty and the rights of human nature. . . ." His brother Levi, when he died in 1809, was "United States Agent . . . for fortifications in the state of Georgia." Mordecai's son, Moses, a physician, was twice elected to the state legislature. Levy de Lyon, Mordecai Myers, and Isaac Minis, scion of an old Jewish family in Georgia, also served at various times in the state legislature, and Minis was enlisted in the War of 1812.[19]

Both in peace and in war the post-Revolutionary generation of Jews figured prominently in American affairs. Jews were enrolled in the United States navy almost from its creation in 1798 during the undeclared conflict with France, which was essentially a maritime war. Thus Jacob de la Motta and Abraham Alexander, both of Charleston, were named midshipmen by the newly appointed Secretary of the Navy in 1799. A Hyman Solomon was enrolled as a landsman (seaman) on board the frigate *United States* in 1800, and Abraham Solis was a surgeon's mate on the *Herald*, as was also Gershon R. Jaques in the same year. As already mentioned elsewhere, Moses Myers was Naval Agent at Norfolk and Nathan Levy was Naval Agent in Haiti during this troubled period.[20]

In the War of 1812 many Jews responded to the call of service. As political Republicans, they were peculiarly responsive to this unpopular war. Military service was no longer a novelty as during the Revolution, but came as a matter of course and was expressive of patriotism on the part of young Jews, many descended from Revolutionary veterans. A kind of military professionalism even made its appearance among American Jews at this time. An early manifestation was that of Isaac Franks of Philadelphia, who had served actively as an officer in Washington's army during the Revolution. He retained a military interest, and by 1794, the year of the Whiskey Rebellion in Pennsylvania, Franks had become the colonel of a militia regiment. Another who served in the Whiskey Rebellion of 1794 was Reuben Etting, as a captain in the Pennsylvania militia. Later he also fought in the War of 1812. Another veteran of the Revolution who displayed much military zeal was Benjamin Nones, French-born, an ardent Republican and hence an eager supporter of the War of 1812. He joined a company of veterans over forty-five, "for the purpose of assisting in measures of defence." He had been a major of militia earlier but was now content to be a second lieutenant.[21]

Nones's son, Joseph B., enrolled in the Navy as a midshipman in 1812 and was wounded in battle. He retired from the Navy in 1822 and became a merchant and commissioner of deeds in Philadelphia. Other descendants of famous Revolutionary figures who served in the War of 1812 were both sons of Haym Salomon—Ezekiel who was a purser in the navy, and Haym M., who became a captain in the army. Aaron Levy, son of Hayman Levy, was a paymaster in the army as early as 1800 and was a lieutenant-colonel by 1816. He retired from the army in 1819 and was an auctioneer in New York thereafter. He married a daughter of Isaac Moses, another prominent figure in the Revolution.[22]

The list of Revolutionary descendants who served in the war of 1812 is long and embraces many famous names. It was as if military service in wartime was now expected from such persons as part of their heritage. Thus three sons of Jonas Phillips, Joseph, Naphtali, and Manuel, were enlisted in the War of 1812. So were three sons of Michael Gratz and brothers of Rebecca Gratz, Benjamin, Simon, and Joseph, who served in elite units. Benjamin, a lawyer, was a lieutenant in the Washington Guards, Joseph was in a cavalry unit, and Jacob was in the First City Company. Two Ettings of Baltimore were wounded in the War of 1812. One was Samuel, son of Solomon, who was also the first president of the Baltimore synagogue, Beth Israel. Reuben, who had been a captain of the Baltimore Blues already in 1798, was wounded at Fort McHenry in 1814. He was in fact, one of eight Jews reported to be present at the famous bombardment of this fort defending Baltimore, which inspired Francis Scott Key's "Star Spangled Banner." One was Mendes Cohen, scion of another famous Baltimore family, who was later a colonel.

Among the others were two more Cohens, an Israel Davidson, and three soldiers, identified only as Moses, Myers, and Solomon.[23] A son of Reverend Gershom Seixas, named David G., and three other members of the large Seixas clan were in the army during this war. Samson Simson, the first Jewish graduate of Columbia College in 1800, was a captain of militia in the war. Nathan Myers, son of Asher of New York, was a colonel in 1812 and commanded a New York brigade.[24]

The South, too, contributed numerous Jewish participants in the war of 1812. Isaac Nunez Cardozo and Hyman Cohen, both sons of Revolutionary veterans from Charleston, as well as Philip I. Cohen of Norfolk, served during this war. Of Moses Myers, also of Norfolk, General Winfield Scott, whose own long military career began in 1812, wrote to Samuel Myers in 1823 that "he rendered important services to the government during the late war as deputy-quartermaster-general." John Myers, son of Moses Myers, who had been a major of militia in Virginia during the Revolution and later was a prominent merchant in Richmond, served in the War of 1812. He was subsequently a deputy collector of customs in Norfolk. Benjamin Wolfe was a major in the Richmond militia as early as 1804. Philip Minis, bearer of a famous Revolutionary name in Savannah, and Jacob de Leon, an equally noted name in Charleston, were surgeon's mates in 1812.

In this war, too, Benjamin Sheftall, son of the Revolutionary veteran, Levi, compiled and sent to Colonel Josiah Tatnall a list of thirty names for "the purpose of forming ourselves into a volunteer company." Solomon Sheftall, another son of Levi, served in the Republican Blues in 1812. Surprisingly, in 1861, now seventy, he applied for appointment as a surgeon in Georgia's army. Meyer Moses of Charleston was a major in the South Carolina Volunteers in 1810 and was subsequently commissioner of free schools in the state as well as a member of the legislature. His father, also Meyer Moses, had been acclaimed after the Revolution by General Moultrie for the care and support he had given to the American wounded and prisoners in Charleston during the British occupation in the Revolution. Chapman Levy, already cited, was a lawyer in Camden, South Carolina, a colonel in the War of 1812, and later a planter in Mississippi. Abraham Phillips, son of a Revolutionary veteran of

South Carolina, volunteered as a midshipman in the navy in 1812, on the day war was declared. He was drowned in an accident off Norfolk in 1813.[25]

Interestingly, the sons of former Jewish Loyalists during the Revolution now served loyally in the war of 1812 against Britain. Most noteworthy were Mordecai Wagg and Judah Touro, both American-born. Wagg was the son of Abraham, who had taken his family with him to England during the Revolution, where he sought compensation for his losses due to his loyalty. He even offered gratuitous advice to the British government on how to end the war and win back the colonies, as has been explained elsewhere. His son, Mordecai, however, returned to America, and became a major in the American army after 1812. The other, Judah Touro, was an even more celebrated son of a former Loyalist, Rev. Isaac Touro of Newport. The latter left America for Jamaica, where he died prematurely. His two sons, Judah and Abraham, returned to America and were raised by their uncle, Moses Michael Hays of Boston. Judah later became a merchant at New Orleans and was seriously wounded at the Battle of New Orleans in 1815, in which he fought under Andrew Jackson. A friend, Rezin Shepherd, discovered and rescued him on the battlefield; Touro remained his loyal, dedicated friend the rest of his life. As a bachelor, Touro lived with him and left much of his estate to him. Bernard Hart was born in London and came to New York in 1780 during the British occupation. He was a quarter-master in the New York militia as early as 1787 and became divisional quartermaster in the War of 1812. He was active in the formation of the New York Stock Exchange and was the grandfather of Bret Harte, the western writer, who was, like some other prominent Americans, the offspring of intermarriage.[26]

Another Jew who served in the New York militia for many years was Abraham Massias, who joined the American Army in 1812 as a paymaster and retired as a major in 1820. A Dutch-born Jew, Isaac de Young, enlisted at sixteen in the Third New Jersey Heavy Regulars. He served in several campaigns and was serious-ly wounded in the Battle of Lundy's Lane during the invasion of Canada in 1814. A strong nationalistic and militarist spirit was expressed by Mordecai Myers in 1813. Born in 1776 in Newport, he grew up in New York. Interestingly, his mother was a Loyalist and took her son with her to Nova Scotia, but they returned to New York in 1787.

In 1813 Myers was a captain in the Thirteenth United States Infantry Regiment and was active in the Canadian campaigns, in which he was wounded. Myers entered both Democratic politics and the militia in New York. He did remarkably well in both. As he wrote militantly to a friend, Naphtali Hart, in strangely misspelled English: "The time has arrived when the nation requirs all its advocats *[sic]*. Sum must spill there blud and others there *[sic]* ink. I expect to be amongst the former and I hop *[sic]* you are amongst the latter." He then drew a sharp contrast between the pursuit of wealth and the pursuit of honor: "I was never hapy *[sic]* in the persute of welth *[sic]* and now that I have abandoned it I am much more contented. My dutys *[sic]* are hard and trying to the Constitution but I continue in good helth as yeate *[sic]*." Myers concluded: "We can conquer Canada with a good general." The last prediction failed of fulfillment on both scores. Here spoke a true war hawk, one who welcomed war in 1812 as an opportunity to expand into Canada. Myers intermarried during the war and abandoned his Jewish affiliation. He had long been active politically as a Democrat and was a member of both the New York City Council and the state legislature. He later settled in Schenectady and was its mayor during the 1850s, where he died in his nineties. Myers' life and career were most unusual for a Jew in that period.[27]

Military professionalism made its appearance at this time as a number of Jews pursued a career in the army or navy. One who did so early was Samuel Noah, who came to America from England in 1799. He was the first Jew to graduate from the newly established Military Academy at West Point in the class of 1807 and served in the War of 1812. He left the army later, as so many did then, and taught school in New York and Virginia. He died in Illinois in 1871. Even more professional was the career of Alfred Mordecai, who graduated first in his class at West Point in 1823. As already recounted elsewhere, he became a noted military ordnance engineer and retired as a colonel in 1861 because of his divided allegiance as a Southerner in the Civil War. His son, also named Alfred, continued in his father's steps as a military engineer during the remainder of the century and rose to be a general. Here was the first Jewish military family in America, serving in the army for nearly a century in an engineering capacity.[28]

The navy, as already indicated earlier, attracted Jewish recruits even before the War of 1812. One might speculate that Jews were drawn to this service because they lived in seaport towns, and their interests were oriented toward maritime affairs. Thus Uriah P. Levy ran away to sea as a young boy in Philadelphia. Levi Harby, Solomon Cohen, and Abraham Phillips, all of Charleston, became midshipmen in 1812. Harby, then very young, lived to command a Confederate vessel during the Civil War.[29]

The most unusual career of a Jew in the navy was that of Uriah P. Levy, son of Michael Levy and grandson of Jonas Phillips, both veterans of the Revolution. At twenty, in 1812, already a practiced seaman, he enlisted in the United States navy as an assistant sailing master on the Brig *Argus*, which was captured by the British. Levy was long imprisoned in England's notorious naval prison at Dartmoor. On release, he rejoined the United States navy and remained an officer in it, off and on, during the rest of his life, which ended during the Civil War. Between these two wars, 1812 and 1861, Levy's naval career was a stormy one and was interrupted by controversy and a number of courts-martial, in which he was finally cleared.

Levy's principal quarrel with the navy was over his active sponsorship of the abolition of flogging of sailors as a disciplinary measure. He subsequently claimed it as his major accomplishment, and his epitaph bore the inscription: "He was the father of the law for the abolition of corporal punishment in the United States Navy." Despite his troubles and frequent confrontation with anti-Semitic colleagues, Levy attained the rank of commodore and commanded the Mediterranean naval squadron just before his retirement. His younger brother, Jonas, also served professionally in the Mexican War. Earlier he was a captain in the merchant marine, and commanded a ship and the port of Vera Cruz. Henry Etting, scion of the Baltimore Ettings, was in the navy for more than half a century, and retired as a commodore in 1871. A follower of Jefferson politically, Uriah Levy acquired Jefferson's estate, Monticello, after his death in 1826, and sought to convert it into a national shrine. This was, however, not accomplished until much later and under other auspices. His mother, Rachel, was buried there.[30]

Both the American Revolution and succeeding events in the post-Revolutionary period produced a generation of Jews remarkably well assimilated and integrated into American society generally. It was a small generation numerically, and predominantly native-born. It was, as has been abundantly illustrated, well represented in the post-Revolutionary wars. It was also an enterprising generation in peacetime civic activities. A considerable number of noteworthy figures represented it both in the Jewish and the general community, as has already been indicated. A few others may be cited and identified as representative of the whole Jewish population in America. In business there were the Touro brothers of Boston and New Orleans. Abraham and Judah Touro not only made their fortunes in these cities respectively, but on their death achieved national note through their generous philanthropic bequests to a great variety of causes, both Jewish and other. Several women also played a prominent role. In Philadelphia, Rebecca Gratz, the daughter of Michael Gratz, was an unusually early example of the Jewish woman who was a religious and social activist and feminist among Jews and in the general community. Charleston contributed in Penina Moïse a woman who was both a religious poet and zealous teacher during a long lifetime. There was also Isaac Harby, an intellectual leader of Charleston's Jewish and general community. He was a journalist and dramatist and would-be founder of a reform movement in American Judaism through the Reform Society of Israelites.[31]

One final figure may be offered as an important representative of this post-Revolutionary generation in Jewish American life. This was Mordecai Manuel Noah, who pursued a widely varied public career. His very versatility of interest and activity perhaps reflected his volatile nature as much as his talent. He was both intensely Jewish and American in outlook, as was characteristic of many in his time. He was born in 1785, son of a Revolutionary veteran, Manuel Noah, and the grandson of another veteran, Jonas Phillips. Thanks to the influence of Robert Morris,

Superintendent of Finance during the Revolution, he began his public career in Philadelphia as a young clerk in the Federal Auditor's Office. All of his life Noah was an office seeker, and he served in many positions on the national, state, and local level. His oft-used title of "major" was acquired from the New York militia, and was more courtesy than real, indicating the appeal of military titles at this early date even to Jews.

Noah was U.S. consul in Tunis during the War of 1812, and was later sheriff and a judge in New York City. Noah often alternated public office with aggressive political journalism in both the Democratic and Whig parties, at first in conjunction with his uncle, Naphtali Phillips, a Democratic newspaper publisher. He probably held more public offices during his lifetime than any other Jew of his time. In addition to the kaleidoscope of public office, Noah played a prominent role as the promoter of Jewish causes, particularly the migration and settlement of Jews in America.[32]

Significantly, Noah's first appearance as a seeker of a federal office was made in 1810 in a letter from citizens of New York and Quebec addressed to President Madison. It spoke of the necessity of safeguarding American rights on the St. Lawrence River and to secure Americans from press gangs operating on the river. The letter recommended the appointment of M. M. Noah as an agent for this purpose: "From his frequent intercourse with the Province, his knowledge of the country, its commerce, and resources, he is considered competent to discharge the duties of the station." Noah was then only twenty-five years old. He appeared next in person in Washington, bearing letters from Jacob I. Cohen, president of Mikveh Israel in Philadelphia, and Reuben Etting of Baltimore. They commended him as a young man of "good moral character and respectable family, who possesses the entire confidence of our nation." (One may interpret the last as a reference to the confidence of the Jews in America.) Reuben Etting, a Jeffersonian who had been Marshall of Maryland in 1801, further alluded to Noah's "warm attachment to the present administration."[33]

In the following year, 1811, Noah's original application for the Canadian position was transformed into one for a consular post somewhere in Europe. As he then wrote to Robert Smith, the

Secretary of State, he had himself proposed that a position in Europe would be preferable to the one in Canada. Noah listed possible places at Lisbon, Bordeaux, Cadiz, or any post available in Europe. Moreover, he introduced the Jewish issue as a factor:

The friendly disposition you have manifested toward our nation, in the conversation I had the honor to have with you, I have made known to them by letter. Ever grateful for any testimony of the good opinion of their government, they esteem your exertions on their behalf. . . . I am proud to say that a very large majority of them express a sincere attachment toward the administration [of President Madison]. . . . In soliciting your appointment in the service of the United States, I am not induced by motives of gain nor a desire for personal aggrandizement. I wish to prove to foreign powers that our government is not regulated in the appointment of their officers by religious distinctions, and on the score of policy I know of no measure which can so promptly lead foreign members of the Hebrew Nation to emigrate to this country with their capitals, than to see one of their persuasion appointed to an honorable office, attended with the confidence of the people.

Thus early did Noah strike the note of promoting Jewish immigration to America, which became almost a kind of obsession with him, and which he linked later with his nonpublic career.[34]

Noah's projected appointment thus acquired a Jewish character. At the request of the Secretary of State, he proceeded to secure letters from the heads of various congregations, "stating that I possessed their confidence." There were letters from I. B. Kursheedt, president of New York's Shearith Israel and son-in-law of Rev. Gershom Seixas, from Solomon Hayman, president of the Charleston congregation, and from Cherie Moïse, president of the Hebrew Orphan Society of Charleston and father of Penina Moïse. Without knowing Noah, they attested to his worth and "respectable connections and good moral character." Noah had apparently succeeded in making his appointment a test of Jewish concerted action and influence. Noah added others to his list of suitable and desirable places, as remote from one another as

Hull, Nantes, Antwerp, Riga, and Tripoli. On 24 May 1811 he pressed his case and asked Smith to lay all his documents before President Madison. He also added that a position "in any of the Barbary States would be acceptable, should no vacancy exist in those ports, or any port in the Brazile."[35]

Finally, on 17 June 1811, Noah confirmed the view of the government that a Hebrew would best serve in a Barbary state, as approved by James Monroe, now the Secretary of State. He accepted an appointment as consul to Tunis, with the comment: "Supported as I should be with the wealth and influence of forty thousand residents." With this reference to the presumable Jewish population of Tunis, more than ten times the current Jewish population of America, Noah stressed: "A discretionary application of this power would enable me to perpetuate the friendly alliance between two governments, and it would operate as a counterpoise to the incidental exercise of privileges not expressly delegated by treaty." This would be particularly useful in a country where "power is fixed and rule has become absolute." Altogether it was a strange type of diplomacy that Noah proposed to practice in Tunis, where his Jewish identity would be helpful.[36]

Not for two years, in this period of worldwide warfare, at the height of the Napoleonic era, was Noah able to depart for Tunis, on a ship bearing an American letter of marque and sailing for France in 1813. His efforts as consul at Tunis were interrupted abruptly in 1815, when Noah received a letter of recall from Monroe, still Secretary of State. Delivered to him on 30 July 1815 by Commodore Stephen Decatur, commander of an American naval squadron in the Mediterranean, the letter gave as ground for removal the very factor that had brought his appointment in the first place. It amounted to a reversal of position, and Monroe's excuse was that "at the time of your appointment as Consul at Tunis, it was not known that the religion which you profess would form any obstacle to the exercise of your consular functions. Recent information . . . proves that it would produce a very unfavorable effect." Here was excellent proof that this first exercise of American diplomacy based on religion, in this instance Noah's Jewishness, had proved ineffective if not wholly disastrous. It was both proclaimed and repudiated by James

Monroe as Secretary of State, with Noah as its immediate victim. Noah could scarcely defy the decision, although he tentatively espoused an argument that, under the Constitution with its separation of church and state, the United States was not a Christian power and hence could not invoke religious factors.[37]

Noah returned to the United States as instructed, incidentally also in order to clear up his accounts at the Treasury. This was done, and he was completely exonerated, but was left without a position. In 1820 he was again seeking a federal public office. Ironically, Monroe was now President, and John Quincy Adams the Secretary of State. In a long letter he wrote to Adams, Noah again noted that he was not seeking a position for private gain but to serve his country. By this time he had already developed strange and even startling ideas about the mass resettlement of the European Jews in America. A bill setting aside Grand Island in the Niagara River for this purpose had been blocked in the New York legislature, and Noah may have had some political connection with it. This was to become in 1825 the famous Ararat project as a refuge for the Jews of Europe, which was sponsored by Noah as its prime promoter.

In 1820, however, Noah was both pragmatic and persuasive on a national level, although probably quite as visionary in his ambition. He asked Adams to name him to a diplomatic post, such as chargé d' affaires at Vienna. Here he would promote a project for the emigration of European Jews to America. The object would not be to colonize or concentrate the Jews in any one place but to allow them to settle where they would, in order "to prevent those jealousies and religious prejudices which may arise from associations of wealthy individuals, engaged in commerce or monopolies of any kind." He did propose to direct some of the Jews to Newport, which had all the required facilities, including a spacious place of worship already erected, and other factors desirable to divert Jewish capital to that quarter." It must be noted that Newport had declined as a Jewish community since the Revolution and was virtually without Jews by 1820.

Noah was eager to attract Jews with capital to America; as he explained it, such Jews were prepared to leave Germany, because of the "illiberal treatment by some of the German powers," during the post-Napoleonic reaction. In America "the Jews can be completely regenerated, where in the enjoyment of perfect civil and religious liberty, free from the operation and effect of national or religious prejudice . . . their faculties could be developed, their talents and enterprise encouraged, their persons and property protected, and themselves respected and esteemed, as their conduct and deportment shall merit." He added, perhaps reprovingly, since Monroe was now President, that his recall five years ago had frustrated similar plans he had then formulated. Noah asked further, "What portion of the Jewish population do you contemplate inviting to this country?" He answered his own question: "I reply men of wealth, enterprising merchants, silk and other manufacturers from France and Germany, mechanics wherever they are to be found, and agriculturists from Poland and the Ukraine, thus securing at once the best portion of the Jewish population."[38]

To help fulfill all this, Noah argued, he was "soliciting a foreign place of weight and respectability, under which I might successfully impress upon the minds of the Jews the great advantages they may secure by emigrating to the United States." Vienna would be the most suitable place for the purpose, but others might do, such as the Hague, Denmark, and even Algiers, which was falling vacant. Noah elaborated on the preparations he had made in his long letter to Adams. He submitted a long list of prominent Jews all over Europe, including bankers, merchants, manufacturers, and rabbis, through whom he could readily communicate his plans. He compared this opportunity with the one Spain had once forfeited. He concluded that they could do much for the United States, as they had once done for Spain.[39]

It is hard to imagine John Quincy Adams being very sympathetic or receptive to such a long-winded and intricate proposal emanating from Noah. In his diary, he expressed a rather querulous opinion of Noah, and he brushed him aside as an "incorrect and very ignorant, but sprightly writer." Noah did not secure the position he sought, and his energies were turned thereafter largely to political journalism and positions in New York City. He did not, however, abandon his original plan for Jewish immigration, as is evidenced in his at once quixotic and flamboyant proclamation in 1825 of Ararat on Grand Island in the Niagara River as a refuge for Jews, which was then on the American frontier. Unrealistically, without any tangible evidence of a sound economic or social basis, the dedication of Ararat was celebrated in nearby Buffalo, with Noah as a kind of prophet and promoter of Jewish immigration. But nothing further materialized from the venture. This was both the climax and the close of Noah's vision of a grand Jewish migration and settlement in America.[40]

In conclusion, Noah's early proposal of a large European migration of Jews to America was perhaps less visionary than premature. As developed in his expansive imagination, it was to occur quickly, completely, and by his leadership as a modern Moses. Such ambitious events do not, however, come about so abruptly. Jewish migration from Europe, as indeed of other people as well, did break through the dam by the 1840s. Thereafter, first from Germany and eventually from Eastern Europe, the flood of Jewish and other immigration spread over all of America for nearly a century, bringing in many millions by the   1920s. They were, as Emma Lazarus described poetically, the "huddled masses," the poor and the oppressed, rather than the rich and the strong as predicted and anticipated by Mordecai Noah. It was his contribution, however, early in the nineteenth century, to foresee and hold out the promise of a great addition of Jewish population, enough in fact to absorb and overwhelm the few thousands that made up the Jewish communities of Revolutionary and post-Revolutionary America. The contradiction between Noah and Lazarus was, however, not as great as is indicated here. The actual immigration brought into this country not merely large numbers of people but equally great cultural and intellectual forces which enriched Jewish life in America far beyond mere wealth.[41]

Significantly, there was an ambivalence about this post-Revolutionary generation. On the one hand, it maintained its Jewish character and institutions in the principal American cities. On the other hand, however, the very dispersion of Jews, as part of a great movement of population westward, tended to dilute Judaism and to diffuse it greatly, in many cases through intermarriage, which was all too common in the frontier isolation of Jewish life. The small Jewish population was thus in danger of diminution and perhaps disappearance, until the renewed wave of immigration after 1840 brought in large numbers of new people from Europe and enlarged the scope of Judaism in America. Strangely, Noah, who himself belonged to the small, native, and well assimilated post-Revolutionary Jewish generation, anticipated and even hoped and planned to force open the flood of immigration by his own efforts.

10

The Quest for Pensions
and Compensation

One aspect of the Jewish record in the American Revolution comprises the applications for pensions or other compensation by surviving Jewish veterans and their descendants. These records, preserved in the National Archives, often bear the stamp of legal affidavits presented by the claimants, and they recite in great detail the recollections of the original participants and their families and friends. In this sense they are authenticated and often more circumstantial accounts than the original records which frequently report little more than a name, date, and place. These documents are dated, however, long after the Revolution; they comprise a kind of oral history, recaptured by the original participants and their survivors from their memories and may be of dubious accuracy. Moreover, they deal only with those veterans who survived and became eligible under various pension acts, the first one dating from 1818. An early requirement was one of virtual indigence and thus limited the applicants still further. Even this condition is, however, significant since it reveals that there were poor as well as prosperous veterans among the Jewish survivors. Despite their limitations, these pension cases provide an illuminating body of data on the Revolution and its sequel.

The pension and other compensation materials amplify what are often meager revolutionary records, particularly for those obscure and forgotten participants who were most likely to be the indigent applicants of later years. They were not at all reluctant to depict their impoverished state in all its distressing detail, as well as the wartime accomplishments of their youth. Thus these records may lack glamor, but they contain an account of actual people as they remembered themselves and their activities after forty years or more.

The American pension record begins with the act of 1818 that awarded annual grants to the Revolutionary veterans who could prove indigence. It comprises the first stage of post-Revolutionary history. A second stage of post-Revolutionary history was honorific and comprised the honorary recognition of the veterans and their descendants. It took the form of a number of associations of sons and daughters, which recorded the services of their ancestors who had participated in the Revolution. It came surprisingly late and followed closely upon the 1876 centennial of the Revolution and its celebration.

This second stage produced records in the form of membership applications made by descendants, which presented their accounts of services by revered ancestors. These too offered versions of the Revolution that often were more glamorous than precise. For Jews in particular, this subsequent development awakened and intensified their awareness of their role in the Revolution. It made them proudly conscious of their place of honor in American history and undoubtedly contributed to their integration into American society. This aspect of the process of honorific recognition occurred primarily after 1900 and became the subject of some controversy, centering on the name of Haym Salomon, as will be elaborated at a later point. Only a relatively small segment of the Jewish population derived directly from Revolutionary War ancestors. Most Jews were largely new and recent arrivals in the United States, together with their offspring. They, too, were affected by this process of vicarious identification with the Revolution. Thus the Revolution was more than an event in past history. It cast its shadow forward even into the present day, affecting attitudes and conceptions, which the approach of the bicentennial in 1976 makes particularly evident and significant.

A second major source of post-Revolutionary history is thus to be found in the records of the honorary societies that were established for the commemoration of the Revolution and the honorific recognition of its participants and their descendants. The first of these, the Society of the Cincinnati, was founded in 1783, under the leadership of George Washington. It was intended only for the officers of the Continental Army and their direct, male descendants, and thus early acquired a limited and select character. The Daughters of the American Revolution was established a century later; it maintains archives and a genealogical library at its national headquarters in Washington, which is a veritable treasure of materials about the Revolution and its participants. Two other associations were then also established almost simultaneously for male descendants, the Sons of the Revolution and the Sons of the American Revolution. All of them have a substantial membership and include a small contingent of Jewish members.

The post-Revolutionary history of compensation for veterans actually began with public land grants, which the Continental Congress authorized for veterans according to rank. Thus the first Jew to appear in the record was David S. Franks, who is registered for 400 acres, corresponding to the rank of major. Another veteran, less well-known, was Asher Polock of Newport, Rhode Island, a private who received 150 acres in 1791. He enlisted in 1777 under Captain William Allen and served with Washington's army. He is described as fifty-two years old, born in London, a tallow chandler by trade. He was barely five feet five inches tall and had black hair and a dark complexion. Polock saw action in the battles of Brandywine and Germantown, and spent the hard winter of 1777 at Valley Forge. His regiment fought at Yorktown in 1781 and returned north to Saratoga, where he was demobilized, after he had served six years. In contrast with this patriotic Polock were others of the same name in Newport, who were Loyalist, as has been related in an earlier chapter.[1]

More detailed and circumstantial is the record of Solomon Pinto, who along with David S. Franks, became a charter member of the Cincinnati in 1783, and is registered for 150 acres in 1795. He was one of three brothers, sons of a mixed marriage between Jacob and Thankful Pinto. They all attended Yale College, and Solomon was graduated in 1778. All played a military role in the Revolution in their home state of Connecticut, and Solomon was an ensign for three years in the Second and Seventh Regiments of the Connecticut line and served directly under Washington. Solomon did not prosper afterwards and in 1818 was granted a pension, for which he had to demonstrate indigence. In his affidavit, submitted under the Act of 1818, Pinto recounted his military activities and submitted evidence that he was in reduced circumstances and in ill health. In a letter of 1820 to John C. Calhoun, Secretary of War, Pinto told how he was occasionally employed at the Custom House in New Haven, but his earnings averaged only about one hundred dollars per year.

The pension application itself throws valuable light on the troubled life of an old veteran. Pinto listed his possessions, which were valued at $42.80 and included a bureau, a kitchen table, a porridge pot, and eight chairs. Such details testified to his impoverishment, which his allowed annual pension of $240 hopefully helped alleviate. Pinto further explained that he had married late in life a woman named Clarissa Smith, many years his junior. They had two young dependent daughters. Pinto himself died in 1824, and his widow remarried. By 1853 she was again widowed and reapplied for a pension. She was allowed one and collected it until her death in 1884, when she must have been, at ninety-six, one of the last relicts of a Revolutionary veteran. In 1922 a great-granddaughter of Pinto, Gertrude Bradley, wrote to the Pension Office for information about him. His progeny was now completely absorbed into the general population, without even a suggestion of its one-time Jewish origin.[2]

A similar case of a doubtful Jewish background was that of Ezekiel Moses, originally of Simsbury, Connecticut. He had enlisted in 1776 when scarcely fifteen years old. His pension application about 1818 stated that he was now unable to support himself, and his itemized possessions were valued at $54.50-1/2. He was granted a pension of $50 per year. Was Moses, like so many others in this period, one of those solitary Jews who wandered off westward after the Revolution and whose very identity was thus lost? Thus, for example, Hart was certainly a fairly common Jewish name. As many as three Jacob Harts occur in the Pension Records for Pennsylvania alone, two others from Massachusetts, and a Benjamin Hart in Connecticut. Were any of these men Jews? Clear evidence for or against is often missing, a fact that further testifies to the indeterminate number and character of the Jewish population in America in this period.[3]

A case of more probable Jewish identity, despite its unusual circumstances, was that of Isaac Levi. According to his pension application, he was born in Hungary in 1749 and came to America at seventeen. He wandered off south and lost all Jewish associations. Levi was settled in Lexington, Virginia, when the Revolution broke out, and he enlisted in a local company under Captain Benjamin Harrison of the famous family that gave governors to the state and presidents to the United States. Levi also served in the force commanded by George Rogers Clark on his expedition of conquest into the Northwest. He was long stationed at Fort Vincennes, Indiana. After the Revolution he resided variously in Kentucky, Ohio, and Indiana, in none of which did he prosper. In 1832, at eighty-two, he was granted an annual pension of $96. When Levi died in 1850, his widow succeeded to his pension. Thus ended the saga of an unknown Jew, which had begun a century earlier in Hungary.[4]

Another unusual record of a Revolutionary War veteran with mysterious overtones was that of Judas (or Judah) Levi, who lived in Virginia when he enlisted in the company commanded by Captain Thomas Howard in Colonel Abraham Bedford's regiment. Levi was severely wounded in the Battle of Waxhaws (South Carolina) on 29 May 1780 and was granted a special disability pension under an act of 1785. Many years later, in 1820, Levi, now living in Maysville, Kentucky, was examined by two physicians in connection with a pension application. They testified to finding a complete disability in him, "his eye being cut out as he says and we believe by a cutlass, his nose and face scarified, his skull fractured with the same weapon, and a wound in his thigh by a bayonet." In 1838, his widow, whom Levi had married in 1783, supported her application for a pension by claiming that Levi had been kept a prisoner by the British for thirteen months in a hospital. He had escaped and enlisted again in Virginia. Her son, Elias Levi, filed the application in her behalf. She was granted her husband's pension of $80 per year, although unable to supply documentary proof of her marriage. Cases such as this offer interesting detail remembered and reported vividly, often without basic documentary support. There is a measure of credibility about them despite their reliance on memory.[5]

From these varied accounts of possible Jewish veterans one moves on to clear-cut instances, about which there can be no doubt. Most unusual was a soldier who had enlisted in Baltimore under an alias, Joseph Smith. In his pension application of 1818 it appears that his real name was Elias Polock, which he signed in Hebrew characters. No explanation of the reasons for the alias is given, but the facts of his extensive military service are related fully and have been cited elsewhere. His claims were supported by the affidavit of a comrade in arms, named John Williams, who served in the same unit with him. Polock's (alias Smith) account is a kind of compact, soldier's narrative of the war, embracing the major war zones. His story and Jewish origin would otherwise have disappeared long ago into the obscurity of history, but for the surviving pension application. It told how he had enlisted in Baltimore and then joined Washington's forces to the north. He had wintered at Morristown, New Jersey, and participated in various expeditionary movements in the Hudson Valley. Later he was sent south and was with General Gates at the disastrous defeat of Camden, South Carolina. He was wounded and taken prisoner to Charleston. From there he was sent to Saint Augustine, Florida, and finally to Halifax, Nova Scotia, where he was released after the war and returned to Baltimore.

Polock was allowed a pension of eight dollars monthly in 1818, since "from his reduced circumstances in life [he] needs the assistance of his country for support." His list of his possessions, valued at twenty dollars, consisted of two tables and a desk, "some trifling articles of crockery ware and kitchen furniture." He had several dependents, a wife named Rebecca, "now nearly helpless, two daughters under twelve," besides another daughter with two infant children, deserted by their husband and father and "now left destitute." He attributed his indigent condition to the fact that he had been a bondsman for another person and lost all his property, "leaving us in such a state of penury as to be absolutely unable to support myself or family without the benefit of my revolutionary pension, or from private or public charity." He still suffered from wartime afflictions, a rupture resulting from the hardships of the army, and from a wound suffered in the battle "usually called Gates' defeat." Such pension records not only depict wartime experiences; even more they reveal the distressingly depressed state of the aged veterans and their families in what was supposedly the golden age of independent self-sufficiency in early America.[6]

A special body of pension materials relates to a group of Jewish veterans and their families from Charleston and Savannah. They were the survivors of a larger number of Jews who had fought in the war and whose exploits have been reported in an earlier chapter. The first case was that of Sergeant David Nunez Cardozo and his wife, Sarah. It was an intricate record that extended over two decades, from 1832 until 1853, when it finally ended with the death of the widow. In 1833 Cardozo, over a half-century after the war, presented an affidavit to support a pension claim under an act of 1832, which no longer required proof of indigence as under the act of 1818. Cardozo now told in full detail how he had been a member of a group under the command of Mordecai Sheftall, who was chairman of a local Committee of Safety in Savannah in the summer of 1776. There were twenty volunteers in all, "men of known integrity and honor." They procured a pilot boat and determined to seize the powder and shot on board an English vessel in the harbor of Savannah.

Even at this late date, the account suggested the daring nature of the adventure: "At dark we dropped down the river with an ebb tide, and at daybreak anchored at Cockspur." With an astonishingly full recall of detail, Cardozo told how they got on board, seized the powder, and took it aboard the pilot boat. They then returned to Savannah, "our colors flying and drums beating." The powder was then shipped off in a "swift mailing pilot boat" to Salem, "for the use of the American army at that time stationed outside Boston," where it arrived safely and just in time. Thus did these merchants of Savannah, acting illegally, contribute notably to the first phase of the Revolution fought in the North, where Washington forced the British evacuation of Boston in 1776.

In the following year, 1777, Cardozo enlisted in the Savannah Grenadiers, commanded by Colonel Maurice Simons, and became a sergeant-major in the company of Captain Peter Boquet (or Bacot). He was engaged in the siege of both Savannah and Charleston and was wounded in the leg and taken prisoner at Charleston in 1780. He remained a prisoner on parole until the evacuation of Charleston in 1782. Cardozo was allowed an annual pension of sixty dollars. On his death in 1834, his widow, Sarah, was granted a survivor's pension. She pressed for a larger sum on the strength of Cardozo's long imprisonment, which she argued was part of his service. Her claim for arrears was still pending when she died in 1853. A grateful nation was apparently neither prompt nor generous with its material recognition of its defenders. In an affidavit of 1838, Mrs. Cardozo pleaded that "the Jews were particularly obnoxious to the enemy and none of the Jews were more faithful to the Revolution than David N. Cardozo."

The extensive and somewhat gruesome evidence occasionally presented in support of a pension claim is illustrated by the testimony of Moses Levy, a senior member of the Charleston congregation. He reported in 1838 that it was his duty to "lay out and wash the body, and deponent saith that in the discharge of his duty he discovered on the left leg of said David Cardozo the marks of a wound which had the appearance of being old. . . ." The officers of the congregation also vouched for Cardozo's death in 1834 and for his widow as a "lady of high character whose statements are entitled to full credit." A Mrs. Judith Abrahams testified in 1838 that her first husband, Moses Cohen, had served with David Cardozo in the Grenadiers and had been taken prisoner with him at Charleston. As friends of the Cardozos, they always knew that "Cardozo had an open sore on his wounded leg until his death." Here in the pension records is belated but vivid testimony to the actual services and sufferings of those Jewish veterans who lived to make a claim for compensation at a later date.[7]

Mrs. Cardozo was only one of a number of Jewish widows who applied for pensions on the basis of their husbands' military services in the Revolution. They were a close-knit group, residents of either Savannah or Charleston, whose husbands, too, had served together in those places. They supported one another's claims with affidavits. Thus both Mrs. Cardozo and Mrs. Abrahams testified in 1838 that a Mrs. Cecilia Solomons had been married previously to Abraham Cohen, who had been a private in one of South Carolina's military companies. Mrs. Abrahams was the widow of Moses Cohen, who died in 1789. Now in 1831 she was granted a pension of $80 per year in the name of her first husband, whose Revolutionary record she reported in detail. Moses Cohen was in the Grenadier company under Captain Bacot. He had been engaged in battle at Fort Moultrie in 1776, and contracted pleurisy from sleeping in the open air, from which he suffered the rest of his life. Cohen had also been with Cardozo and Samuel Mordecai "in the forlorn hope, in that disastrous assault" on Savannah in 1779, and he "suffered exceedingly and was rescued from exposure in a swamp." He was confined to bed in Charleston for several months and was taken prisoner there in 1780: "Being obnoxious to the enemy, they suffered loss and endured indignity from the Hessian auxiliaries." Here, in these affidavits is the actual experience of the Revolution as recalled long afterwards and reported in terms of individual sufferings and deprivations. Despite their late date, there is no reason to doubt the reality of these reported events.[8]

Another Cohen, named Gershom, was the subject of a petition for a pension by his widow, Mrs. Rebecca Cohen, in 1838. She too testified that her husband, whom she had married in 1779, was present at the British attacks on both Savannah and Charleston. He was taken prisoner at the capture of the latter place. Mrs. Cohen, who was a daughter of Abraham Sarzedas and a sister of David Sarzedas, another soldier of the Revolution, now lived in New York. She was represented at the hearings in Charleston by her sons Philip and Haym. They were supported by Dr. Jacob de la Motta, who told the court how he had frequently heard his father, Emanuel, speak of Cohen's service in the Revolution. They had both been in the same unit in Savannah in 1779. Philip Cohen testified that his father had fought with Colonel Lushington "in defense of liberty," and that he had been present when Pulaski was killed at Charleston.[9]

A brother-in-law of Gershom Cohen, David Sarzedas, had been a lieutenant in Captain John Habersham's company of the First Georgia Regiment early in 1776. Ill health forced his resignation in the following year and cut short his service. He was allowed a pension in 1818, when he pleaded indigence. He submitted a list of possessions valued at $22.50. His wife was deceased, and a son was unable to help him. At seventy-three he was no longer able to practice medicine. In 1821, Sarzedas addressed a petition to John

C. Calhoun, Secretary of War. He told how he was one of many Georgians who lived in Charleston after the fall of Savannah in 1779. Many of them joined as volunteers in the unsuccessful campaign to recapture Savannah in 1779. He himself had gone there on the French admiral's flagship, the *Languedoc.* The attack failed, and he returned to Charleston, where he was taken prisoner with many others in the British capture of that city. Despite his old age and ill health, Sarzedas' memory of the old days was suffused with patriotic fervor: "My youth glowed with ardor to revenge the injuries inflicted on my country, to which my services were nearly three years devoted as a Continental officer in the first Georgia Brigade commanded by Gen. McIntosh, the recollection of which yields me pleasure." Only his reduced circumstances forced him to claim "a compensation for serving my country." Interestingly, Sarzedas had married Sarah da Costa, widow of Colonel Maysor, a French officer in the Revolution, and she received a pension as late as 1851.[10]

Another widow of a Jewish soldier in the Revolution who made claim for a pension in 1838 was Mrs. Rachel Lazarus of Charleston, now seventy-six years old. Her husband,. Marks Lazarus, had been a volunteer in a corps known as the Charleston Artillery of the South Carolina Militia. He was a private, then a sergeant, and a commissary, altogether serving for more than two years. He had fought at Fort Moultrie and was taken prisoner, like many others, at the fall of Charleston in 1780. She testified that her husband had told her prior to his death in 1835 that he was not getting a large enough pension, only $23.33 per year, which was unusually low and perhaps incorrect.

In his own application in 1832, Lazarus, then seventy-five years old, summarized his life and career. Born in Charleston in 1757, he lived there all his life. He had enlisted in Captain Douill's company of cannoneers at the start of the war and served with the Eighteen-Gun Battery, "suffering with his comrades the usual privations and hardships incident to the life of a soldier." He was transferred to the Second Battalion under Captain Lushington, which replaced the regulars at Fort Moultrie, until they returned from Savannah and were captured at Charleston in May 1780. He concluded: "Your petitioner was constantly on duty in defense of his country and acted as sergeant-major all this period." He further claimed that he was recognized as a veteran and is invited to every public festival." As evidence, Lazarus submitted an invitation he had received to a dinner 4 July 1831, issued by the Union and States' Rights party, bearing the patriotic sentiment: "On that day it must give you peculiar gratification to reflect upon having participated in the glory of founding our great and happy empire." Ironically, the party that invited Lazarus to the dinner was the product of Calhoun's anti-Jacksonian and anti-Unionist agitation and struck the first note of secessionist sentiment in what was described as "our great and happy empire."

Mrs. Lazarus' application for a pension in 1838 had the backing of the Jewish community. Both the Hebrew congregation of Charleston and the leaders of the community submitted affidavits in her behalf, which were signed by several persons. It would seem to indicate a closer sense of community among the Jews in the South than was evident in Northern towns. Equally there had been a greater sense of community participation in the war as experienced both in Charleston and Savannah. The Jews here played a more concerted part in the Revolution, in contrast with the more individualistic role of Jews in the North. They seemed to be more fully involved in the war and were more frequently wounded and taken prisoner, probably because both Savannah and Charleston were long active zones of war, and were besieged and captured by the British.[11]

Sheftall Sheftall was a significant and notable example of a Jewish Revolutionary veteran in quest of a pension. Born in Savannah, scion of a family that had been there since its foundation in 1733, Sheftall was barely sixteen years old at the start of the Revolution. With his father, Mordecai, and his uncle, Levi, young Sheftall engaged in war activity almost from the start in 1776. He became an officer and assistant to his father, who was Deputy Commissary-General of Issues for Georgia, with the equivalent rank of colonel. In Sheftall's commission of 1778, signed by his father, he is described as "a young man of probity and well attached to the American cause." It further directed him to "obey all such orders and instructions as you shall from time to time receive from me the commanding officer or any of your superior officers."

In an affidavit submitted with his application for a pension in

1832. Sheftall Sheftall related the account of his services. It probably had been told many times previously to whoever would listen, in one of the famous squares of Savannah that he frequented in his old age, dressed in ancient Revolutionary garb, which won him the name of "Cocked Hat Sheftall." Sheftall further reported that his wartime pay had been sixty dollars per month besides rations, which was a generous compensation for one so young. Sheftall's story was vouched for by Jeremiah Cuyler, a federal district judge, in an accompanying affidavit. It was accepted despite the lack of documentary evidence, which had been destroyed in a fire many years earlier. Sheftall had been a lawyer, was unmarried, and never prospered. He was granted an annual pension of $320, which was increased to $600 in 1846, and he collected it until his death in 1848. At this time, too, in 1842, Congress rejected a petition from Abraham Lyon for an increase of pension because of his wounds. He was then living in Springfield, Ohio, but was of an old family originally from Savannah, and he was married to a Sheftall woman.[12]

The North also had its Jewish veterans who applied for pensions, but they were fewer and less interrelated than those from the South. Especially illuminating was the application of Isaac Franks of Philadelphia in 1818. After the Revolution Franks became an auctioneer and prospered. He acquired a mansion in Germantown, which he rented to President Washington in 1793 for his use during the great epidemic in Philadelphia. By 1818, however, he was in reduced circumstances and qualified for a pension that required proof of indigence. During his last years he was a prothonotary of the Pennsylvania Supreme Court, which was the equivalent of a chief clerk.

In his affidavit Franks gave a detailed account of his military service during the Revolution. Born in 1759 in New York, he was only seventeen when the Revolution broke out. He enlisted in Colonel Lasher's regiment, designated as the "six-month regiment," in May or June 1776. It was attached to Washington's army in New York, and Franks fought with it all through the campaign of Long Island and the retreat across New York. He was taken prisoner and suffered three months' confinement in New York. One evening, however, he escaped and crossed the North River "in a small leaky skiff with a single paddle to the

Jersey shore." He rejoined Washington's army and served with it as a forage master at West Point and elsewhere. In 1780 he was commissioned an ensign in the Seventh Massachusetts Regiment of the line and served with it until 1782. He received his first furlough then from General McDougall, and was visiting friends in Philadelphia when news of the end of the war reached him.

All through the war, Franks testified, he "always acted with Honor and strict fidelity." He was well known to Washington, who reported him incorrectly as dead in the epidemic of 1793, instead of Colonel David S. Franks, whom he also knew. Actually, this was the year in which Washington rented and lived for several months in Franks' house in Germantown. In 1794 Franks again appeared in a military role as the colonel of a militia regiment in the Whiskey Rebellion. His military flair and title endured beyond the Revolution, and Franks was well deserving of the pension of twenty dollars per month he received until his death in 1822.[13]

The longest and most involved pension case was that of Philip Moses Russell, which dragged on for years, and even received the attention of Congress. In his pension application of 1818, Russell, who was from Philadelphia, claimed to have been a surgeon's mate in a regiment of the Virginia line. He was allowed an officer's pension of twenty dollars monthly. It was, however, revoked in 1820 on the ground that he had too much property.

Russell appealed for the restoration of his pension to the justice of a government, "for which my life was risked and youthful days expended." The same regard for the "liberties of America," he added, "would induce me to avoid the diminution of her funds were not stern poverty and relentless necessity my compulsions." His son, Moses, would help if he could, "but the embarrassments of the times and his own situation deny him the means that his whole inclinations desire." He was seventy years old and too infirm even to practice his previous trade, that of "selling along streets essences of mint and other drugs." He had three daughters dependent on him, one of them widowed and afflicted with a pulmonary complaint. He had had to dispose of some of his property when his family was starving for want of victuals. His total possessions were now worth $93.55. They consisted entirely of household effects, remnants of a happier past. Significantly, two friends submitted affidavits that they had known him both "in prosperity and in adversity." He had surrendered all his property to creditors and was, therefore, in dire want.

Russell complained pathetically that he should have been notified when he was dropped from the pension rolls. He sounded a sorrowful, plaintive note: "My hopes should rest on the gratitude of my country. . . . And is it to be here that he who toiled for liberty, when aged, infirm and who cannot now brave the hardships must even be left destitute of the rations of a common soldier. Our country may yet want soldiers and while the veteran is neglected the youth will not be stimulated." In 1823 Russell had as yet heard nothing regarding the restoration of the pension. He brought in affidavits by a number of prominent citizens of Philadelphia to vouch for him as a kind of character witnesses. Bearing such names as Morris, Mifflin, Eliot, Hamilton, and Caldwell, they attested to his integrity. They were familiar with his services and present infirmities resulting from camp fever.

Russell's pension was restored in 1826, six years after his application, evidence of the dilatory character of government at that early date. He died in 1830, and his widow applied for a renewal, assisted by her son, Moses Milton, a Philadelphia lawyer. In 1831 she received an annual allowance of two hundred dollars. The matter became complicated by the widow's persistent efforts to obtain a larger pension and arrears for the years it had been denied to Russell. The son had been an officer in the War of 1812, and he displayed even greater pertinacity in the pursuit of the matter. As late as 1845, Mrs. Russell submitted a new affidavit, in which she argued that her husband had been "imbecile in his last years" and was unable to recall his full services. She remembered everything, however, because it coincided with her marriage in 1776.

The story she now told was largely new and full of remarkable detail. It is a commentary on the sad course of the war in the distressing period of Valley Forge. Russell enlisted shortly after his wedding in a regiment directly under General Washington's command. In 1778, after a winter at Valley Forge, he was worn out with attendance on the wounded and sick and was granted a furlough, with the personal commendation of Washington, urging him to recover his health. On his return to Valley Forge, Russell marched with Washington's army through the Jerseys to West Point, where they settled down. Again broken in health, his eyesight and hearing affected by camp fever, Russell was forced to resign his commission in August 1780, "with a flattering certificate of approbation from General Washington . . . testifying to his assiduous attention to his duties to the sick and wounded as well as his personal bravery in battle." This document had been prized and frequently read to the children until it was burned in a fire in Richmond in 1812 where they then lived.

Her husband had thus served for nearly three years instead of only the ten months claimed earlier. Again, Mrs. Russell confirmed her memory of these events by recalling that her husband had returned home on the day her second child, Samuel, was born. Altogether here is a remarkable tribute to a widow's loyalty and the great pains to which she went in order to support her claim for an enlarged pension. Russell's son, Moses, addressed his own appeal in 1845 to William L. Marcy, the Secretary of War. He took a political line that would appeal to a man of Marcy's notorious reputation. His father had been "well and intimately acquainted with Jefferson, Madison, Monroe, and Marshall, having imbibed the republican principles of the former, the apostle of liberty. He cherished them to the day of his death, having instilled them in the heart of his sons, whose unswerving democracy will never depart from them." The son also remembered how as a boy, while the family was living in Richmond, he read Washington's letter commending his father's "assiduous attention to the sick and wounded" and regretting "the failure of his hearing and sight."

Moses Russell even discovered a witness to support his father's claim to have served as a surgeon's mate in a Virginia regiment. He was J. E. Slaitter, only fourteen years old during the Revolution, whose father was a sutler in Russell's regiment. Slaitter recalled how Russell treated his father for camp fever at Valley Forge in 1777. In the following year, Surgeon Norman and his mate, Russell, performed an operation for gravel on young Slaitter himself. Mrs. Russell added her own final plea, that she was now ninety years old and had not long to live. She submitted testimonials to her "high standing," signed by a number of important persons in Philadelphia, among them aldermen, physicians, and a magistrate.

The Russell case illustrates both the complications of the pension legislation and the tenacity of the petitioners. Russell and his successors seemed to spare no effort to assert their rights, which were probably spurred by their needs. The circumstantial material presented here illustrates vividly the Revolutionary services of one Jewish veteran, who represented the medical aspect of the war. The War Department, in charge of the pensions, reported that it could find no record of Russell's service and hence rejected the claim and the family's evidence, which supported it so plausibly and vividly. In 1849, however, Congress passed a special act granting the widow an annual pension of $480, which may have required political influence to pass. In the meantime Mrs. Russell had died, unknown to Congress. The son claimed the arrears as due him, since he was his mother's heir and legatee. Congress rejected the appeal, since pensions could not be transmitted beyond the widow. Moses made further application for the arrears in 1852 and 1859, but was turned down. Thus did the Russell case finally end after nearly four decades of petition and plea. It was probably one of the longest and most intricate Jewish pension cases on record, stemming from the Revolution. It also contains an intimate, personal account of one Jewish veteran's experience in the Revolution, as reported by all the members of the Russell family, father, mother, and son.[14]

Aside from the pension applications in the nineteenth century already reported, there were other requests for compensation growing out of the economic aspects of the Revolution. One such instance has been treated fully elsewhere. It related to Simon Nathan's complicated business relations with Virginia and resulting claims, which gave rise to a kind of *cause célèbre* extending through the Revolution proper. It illustrates at once the services performed and the problem of compensation for them, and it involved the whole hierarchy of Virginia's political leadership.[15]

A similar case was that of Mordecai Sheftall, who served personally in the war in the South and was taken prisoner by the British at the capture of Savannah. He made his first claim in 1780 for compensation for various losses suffered in the war. In a memorial to Congress he recited both his services and his sufferings in the war as the Deputy Commissary General of the Georgia forces. He itemized the goods and money he had advanced for various purposes, among them financial support for Colonel Andrew Williamson's expedition against the Indians, a hogshead of rum supplied to the Continental troops, and "my 16 parts of the Brigantine *Hinchenbrook,* pressed into public service and valued at £13,500, which brigantine was burned when the enemy got possession of Savannah." Added to that was "the balance due me for two years' pay as Deputy Commissary General," at present depreciation rates equal to 139,800 Continental dollars. The petitioner concluded pathetically that "a long and painful captivity has reduced your Memorialist to very distressed circumstances which are still further heightened by having a wife and four children in Charleston deprived of every means of subsisting." He prayed that "the wisdom and humanity of the Honorable Congress will think expedient to assist him in removing his family from the miseries they now labor under."

Congress referred the matter to the Board of War, which reported that the paymaster had been authorized to reimburse Sheftall for pay and subsistence. His other claims, including one to compensate him for monetary depreciation, were rejected as improper or were postponed for subsequent disposition, when he settled his accounts in the Southern District. Later in 1780, and again in 1781, Sheftall persisted in his petitions to Congress, entreating them to have consideration for a man who had sacrificed everything in the cause of his country: "I want nothing but Justice, to be repaid my advances to the Publick." He had lost many of his documents, but "I am willing to swear my account is just." He would like some money "on account," since his family was not in Philadelphia, he pleaded in 1781, but was "reduced to the utmost necessity." It was only his due, "as the public are very considerably in my debt."

Without redress from Congress, Sheftall addressed himself to Robert Morris, the Superintendent of Finance. The latter rejected the request for compensation, since he barely had funds for current needs and none for past claims. He referred the matter to the Commissioners of the Commissary Department, who "can alone settle his accounts." Thus was Sheftall given, as it were, the runaround, in the characteristic fashion of bureaucracy, already at this early date. In this case are illustrated both the financial difficulties of the Continental Congress and the distresses of private citizens, such as Sheftall, who had given their all to the Revolution.[16]

After the Revolution, in 1792 and again in 1797, the Sheftalls renewed their claims against the government. In 1792 Sheftall Sheftall, Mordecai's son and partner in the war, wrote to his father that he had discussed the claims with Alexander Hamilton, then Secretary of the Treasury, but to no effect. Hamilton disclaimed all responsibility. After their father's death in 1797, both his sons, Sheftall, a lawyer, and Moses, a physician, renewed their petition and recalled his loyalty to the country, for which he had "sacrificed a handsome fortune and suffered in his person by long confinement in prison ships and jails." As late as 1802, Mordecai's widow, Frances, petitioned Congress but was denied redress. And so the matter ended unsettled; the Sheftall claim may have been caught in the midst of a controversy between Georgia and the federal government over liability for expenses incurred during the Revolution. Interestingly, the denial of Sheftall's claim occurred in the decade that witnessed the assumption of all Revolutionary debts by the federal government. It did not, however, include the debt to the Sheftalls.[17]

Even more noteworthy for the large amount of money involved and its duration was the case of Haym Salomon and his financial relations with the Revolutionary government. It became a major issue that lasted through much of the nineteenth century and concerned a succession of Congresses as well as Salomon's descendants. Moreover, it had the effect of publicizing the Salomon name and elevating it to the level of wide public interest and attention. The persistent efforts to obtain compensation from Congress for Salomon's presumed financial advances during the Revolution generated a kind of mythology out of which emerged the title "Financier of the Revolution." Interestingly, the same title was also applied, perhaps with more justice, to Salomon's employer, Robert Morris, who was then Superintendent of Finance. It was given to Salomon in the present century by successive writers, who borrowed both title and story from one another and popularized it. Thereby they tended to obscure the fact that the whole Jewish community had shared notably in the Revolution and not Salomon alone, however considerable his contribution undoubtedly was.

This second stage of the Salomon saga, following his actual accomplishments during the Revolution, was originated, in fact, long after the initial events of the Revolution. In 1827, Haym Salomon's son, Haym M., born posthumously in 1785, had an exchange of letters with James Madison. Answering an inquiry concerning his relationship with Haym Salomon, Madison acknowledged that he had received financial help from him during the Revolution when he was Virginia's delegate to the Continental Congress but there was no suggestion that a debt was still outstanding. At a later date, Haym M. Salomon interested Jared Sparks, the Harvard historian of the Revolution, in his father's role, and Sparks wrote of it in an essay that came to light many years later and received considerable publicity. The son's first claim in behalf of his father was made in 1843, when he presented it, together with some supporting documents, to President Tyler. Unhappily, this whole collection of materials was lost while in the possession of the President, and its supposed contents acquired a kind of mythical character as the chief support for subsequent claims. Undoubtedly, this episode dramatized the whole affair; to this day it is not known what was in those lost documents and how far they supported the claims made.[18]

The first petition for compensation was presented to Congress in 1846. Haym M. Salomon, the prime mover in the whole matter, was then sixty-one years old and in straitened circumstances. The Senate Committee on Revolutionary Claims of the Twenty-Ninth Congress reported favorably on the petition, but the measure died with this Congress. The appeal was renewed in the next Congress, in 1848, and the House this time recommended a land grant, as requested by the petitioner. The Senate, however, rejected the claim as inadequately proved, and the matter again ended abortively. The amount of compensation asked for was based on the inventory of Salomon's estate at the time of his death, which was then insolvent. According to it, some $353,000, principally in depreciated government notes and certificates of indebtedness, it was claimed, should now be redeemed at full value. Subsequently the claim was increased to $658,007.13 by a calculation for which there seemed to be no mathematical or historical evidence. Apparently allowing for accumulated interest, it was so reported by Rev. M. C. Peters in 1902; a later figure, also estimated with interest, put the claim at $3 million.

The Thirty-First Congress again received a petition from the apparently tireless Haym M. Salomon, and a bill offering compensation was introduced but died in the Senate in 1850. Chairman Walker of the Senate Committee on Revolutionary Claims then compared Salomon to Lafayette and recommended a generous settlement. For some unknown reason, the next claim was not presented until 1858-60, and the Senate of the Thirty-Sixth Congress again received a favorable committee recommendation. Haym M. Salomon, the petitioner, was now seventy-five years old and ill; he was willing to settle for $100,000, but a bill to this effect died in Congress. A last appeal for compensation was made to Congress in 1862 and it was again lost amid the critical events of the Civil War in 1864. Haym M. Salomon died shortly thereafter, unsuccessful in his many efforts to win recognition and compensation for his father's alleged financial losses in the Revolution.[19]

This case is thus elaborated in order to demonstrate the political complexities and the great difficulty in obtaining compensation from Congress in the nineteenth century, regardless of merit. Committee reports were made and ignored in numerous other cases as well, and may illustrate either public ingratitude, indifference, or the sheer inertia of legislative bodies. Perhaps also it was a defense against an excess of such claims, merited or not. The Salomon case might have died then, had it not been revived a generation later in 1893. The Salomon heirs were not asking for compensation in money now; instead they petitioned Congress to award a commemorative medal in honor of Haym Salomon. The issue was thereby transformed from one of monetary compensation to one of national and honorific recognition. The House Committee on the Library recommended the appropriation of $250 for such a medal, but the measure died in the House. It was a novel venture, despite its failure. This request coincided in time and importance with the establishment of such honor societies as the Daughters and Sons of the American Revolution. They too provided recognition for Revolutionary ancestors by offering honor and membership to their descendants. This aspect of the Revolution was in a sense the final stage of its evolution—from the reality of its occurrence to its national and honorary exaltation—and will be the subject of the next chapter.[20]

Significantly, the Salomon affair now entered the public consciousness and became the focus of a popular agitation, particularly in the New York Jewish community after 1900. These Salomon supporters were relative newcomers to America, the result of a large immigration during the preceding generation, primarily from Eastern Europe. They were subject to the powerful forces of Americanization and assimilation, which could profit from some symbolic stimulation. The Salomon name and story, as popularized after 1900, provided just such a symbol and stimulus. Here was a Polish Jew who had come to America before the Revolution and played a large role in that historic event, according to the repeated accounts then circulated. He caught the imagination of the new American Jews, who could thus associate themselves with the history of their country. Here was an instrumentality and an occasion both for the acclaim of Haym Salomon as a historic figure and for their own vicarious recognition. Thus developed a saga and an agitation that continued until the outbreak of World War II in 1941, and became the cause of both controversy and excitement in the American Jewish community.

The agitation took the form of a movement to erect a statue to Haym Salomon, first in New York, later in Chicago, even in Los Angeles. As will be shown hereafter, this patriotic activity produced an ambivalent effect. On the one hand, there was much critical opposition to the proposal in one segment of the Jewish community. On the other hand, its ultimate successful outcome, marked by statues in Chicago and Los Angeles, if not in New York, completed the process by which Salomon achieved national recognition as the major Jewish figure of the Revolution. At the same time, the Jewish community in America attained vicariously a sense of identification with the Revolution.

11

The Quest for Honorific Recognition

The American Revolution has sent its echoes and rever-
berations down the corridors of history. It was an event in a class
all by itself, different in impact from other conflicts, even such as
the Civil War. It marked the beginning of a new nation and an
experiment in government that is still continuing. In due course,
as national sentiment and pride grew, the sons and daughters of
these first Revolutionists and their descendants began to look
back as well as forward to receive honor and recognition. Honorific associations were formed for the purpose after the
centennial anniversary of Independence in 1876. This was
marked by a general celebration as well as by a spectacular exposi-
tion in Philadelphia. By 1890 two organizations honoring the
descendants had been established, one for the Daughters of the
American Revolution and another for the Sons of the American
Revolution. A smaller society, the Sons of the Revolution,
founded in New York in 1883, retained a local state character.

The larger national associations, including the Society of the
Cincinnati, established in 1783, maintain handsome national
headquarters in Washington, and the Sons of the Revolution are
centered in the historic Fraunces Tavern in New York City.
Membership in all of them is linked to the Revolution by some
genealogical bond of kinship, creating paradoxically a kind of
Revolutionary aristocracy. By the end of the nineteenth century,
the Jews, too, were ready for some symbolic recognition of honor,
and they sought and won membership in these associations. The
archives and lineage records of the Daughters and Sons of the
American Revolution contain the names of a substantial number
of men and women, both Jewish and non-Jewish, who achieved

218

membership on the basis of descent from Revolutionary patriots of Jewish origin. Civic service other than military was also recognized for such membership. There are too many such members to enumerate individually, but significant illustrations will be supplied in due course.

The oldest of these honorary associations, the Society of the Cincinnati, was established in 1783 under the direct sponsorship of General Washington for officers of the Continental Army as well as those of the French army serving in the Revolution. Its exclusive membership is further limited to one lineal male descendant of such officers. Only two such officers of Jewish origin or identity are known to have been charter members of this organization at its creation. One was Lieutenant Colonel David S. Franks, whose extensive Revolutionary record has already been recounted. The other was Solomon Pinto, of mixed Jewish ancestry, who was an ensign in a Connecticut regiment. Franks never married and Pinto had no male heirs, and neither is, therefore, represented in the modern membership of the society. A third original member was Lieutenant Solomon Mears, also of Connecticut, who was, however, of doubtful Jewish origin and identity.

Two other charter members of the Cincinnati were married to Jewish women and may thus merit mention, although they too appear to have no male descendants in its modern membership. One was Dr. Nicholas Schuyler, of the famous family in upstate New York, who married Shinah, a daughter of Joseph Simon of Lancaster, during the Revolution. The second was James Pettigrew, who was a lieutenant in a Pennsylvania regiment, and who was married to Judith Hart. By mutual agreement, following a double marriage ceremony, the children were divided, the boys to be Christian and the girls to be Jewish. The chance and circumstances of genealogy seem to have denied modern Jewish membership in the Cincinnati. This is in sharp contrast with the other honorary societies of the Revolution, in which Jews and non-Jews alike have qualified for membership on the basis of one or another Jewish veteran.[1]

One may cite an example that illustrates the changed circumstances and even contrasts between an original veteran and his later descendants who were admitted to the honorary

Revolutionary societies. It is that of Philip M. Russell, whose so-called synagogue name was given as Uri Feis, and whose Anglicized name is unaccountable. He was a surgeon's mate in a Virginia regiment, and his later life was involved in a long and complicated quest of a pension for services rendered at Valley Forge. After his death, his widow and son were long engaged in the pursuit of a pension equally on the ground of their needs and deserts. Their story has been narrated elsewhere as a representative case. Long afterwards, in 1895, however, Horace M. Nathans of Philadelphia wrote to the pension office for information about Russell to assist him in acquiring membership in the SAR (Sons of the American Revolution). In 1906 the SAR applied to the pension office for Russell's record in order to verify the application of a Waring Russell. As late as 1924 Herman D. Steel, president of H. D. Steel Company of Philadelphia, a manufacturer of industrial diamonds, inquired about Russell, de la Motta, and the Sheftalls, all Revolutionary veterans, to whom he claimed kinship, for a similar purpose. As for the DAR, a host of applicants qualified for membership under Russell's name. They included Mrs. A. L. Cannon, Mrs. Beverly Johnson, and Mrs. J. Russell McAuley. They are indicative of a considerable consciousness and interest, among Jews and non-Jews alike, in winning honor and recognition for themselves, regardless of religion, in a Revolutionary society.[2]

An equally noteworthy case was that of Mrs. Isadora Emilia Kline, whose application for membership in the DAR was based on descent from both Michael Hart, the first Jewish settler in Easton, Pennsylvania, known as the "stuttering Jew," and Andrew Hersher, a Pennsylvania German, who was a member of the Associators and the famous Flying Camp of 1776. Hersher was taken prisoner in the Battle of Long Island and died on a prison ship in New York Harbor. The vagaries of genealogy are further illustrated by the fact that both Georgina May Hutchins and Miss Blanche Moses claimed membership in the DAR through descent from Myer Moses of Charleston, whom General Moultrie commended for the help given to the American prisoners and wounded held by the British in that city.[3]

Both Elizabeth A. Haes and Ida Marks Heller achieved membership on the basis of descent from Emanuel Abrahams, who was a member of Captain Lushington's famous "Jew Company" of Charleston, which helped in the defense of that city. Mrs. Heller also reported his citation for bravery after the British evacuated the city in 1782. Her cousin, Miss Caphton (née Cohen), listed as her ancestor Abrahams' brother, Mordecai, who lived and fought in Virginia. Mrs. Leila Larendon traced her descent and claim to membership to David Nunez Cardozo, who was a sergeant-major in the Charleston Corps of Grenadiers, and was wounded at Savannah. Cardozo was also the ancestor of the distinguished Cardozo family of New York, which included two judges, father and son. The son was Justice Benjamin N. Cardozo of the United States Supreme Court. Jacob Myers of Georgetown, South Carolina, was cited as an ancestor by Mrs. Mary C. C. Torrey of Mississippi in her application for membership in the DAR. She claimed that he served as a major under Generals Marion and Sumter.[4]

Membership in the DAR also was awarded on the basis of patriotic merit, achieved in patriotic civilian service. Thus Haym Salomon was the ancestor whose Revolutionary contributions supported the applications of numerous descendants. Mrs. Lucille Menken Levy set the pattern when she described him as an "active Patriot imprisoned in the Provost, where he contracted an incurable malady." He also "advanced large sums of his private fortune to the Superintendent of Finance." This became an almost standard statement of Salomon's merits, as presented by other applicants, among them Mrs. Alice Morrison Ulman, Mrs. Tillie Moss Judah, Mrs. Maude Morrison Frank, and Mrs. Muriel Carter.[5]

The three Seixas brothers, Abraham, Benjamin, and Rev. Gershom, and their father, Isaac, supplied the basis for the membership of a number of descendants. Their very names are distinctive and noteworthy: Mrs. Alice David Menken, Mrs. Edith Loring, Miss Constance Nathan, and Mrs. Cyrus L. Sulzberger. The merits they listed for the members of the Seixas family ranged widely, from the signing of the nonimportation agreement of 1770 by the father, Isaac, to serving as a lieutenant in a New York company of artillery and light horse in the case of Benjamin. Abraham Seixas was reported by Mrs. Edith Loring to have been a courier in the Georgia forces and later a captain in the

South Carolina militia. Miss Nathan and Mrs. Sulzberger avowed that Rev. Gershom Seixas had inspired the exodus of the Jews from New York early in the Revolution, setting an example by his own departure for Connecticut and bearing with him the sacred objects of New York's Shearith Israel.[6]

Philadelphia provided its quota of patriotic Jews whose descendants subsequently claimed and qualified for membership in the honor societies. Mrs. Maria Gratz Zartman cited Michael Gratz as a signer of a nonimportation agreement. Samuel Judah was another signer and ancestor claimed by Mrs. Gertrude Hagaman for membership in the DAR. The record for the largest number of descendants admitted on the strength of one ancestor would seem to belong to Jonas Phillips, perhaps because of his prolific progeny. No less than twenty-two applications for membership are listed in the DAR *Lineage Books* under his name. Some of them recited not only service in the Philadelphia militia but also, more dubiously, extended and perilous military activity by Phillips in the battles of Long Island, Trenton, Princeton, Brandywine, and Germantown, all within little more than a year. Jefferson M. Levy, a nephew of Commodore Uriah P. Levy, who was also a grandson of Phillips, claimed the latter as an ancestor for admission to the SAR. The Levys acquired and occupied Monticello, Jefferson's estate, after his death, long before it was made into a national shrine, and Uriah's mother was buried there in 1836. Their continued patriotism was thus attested to.[7]

Two obscure Jews of Virginia served as Revolutionary ancestors supporting the admission of their descendants into the DAR. These were Judas and Isaac Levi, unrelated to each other and already accounted for elsewhere. Mrs. Sallie Glenn of Ohio claimed kinship to one through his marriage to Mary McGraw and their daughter Rebecca. She recited how Judas Levi was a private in Captain Howard's Company of Colonel Bufford's Virginia regiment. They marched to the relief of Charleston in 1780, but were nearly annihilated by Colonel Carleton's Corps at Wraxaw (also rendered as Waxhaws), North Carolina, where Levi was badly wounded. Isaac Levi, born in Hungary, was enrolled in Captain Robert Patterson's company of Virginia militia, as reported by his great-granddaughter, Charlotte Ewing Mac-

Flinn. Levi's wife was Mary Dunn, and they lived in Indiana, where in 1832 he was placed on the pension rolls, as was also Judas Levi. The unusual genealogical record revealed here, as elsewhere, illustrates the remarkable degree of intermarriage.[8]

Equally intricate was the lineage of Marks Lazarus, whose descendants listed in the DAR membership rolls included Rose and Nina Moses, Mrs. Lee Harby, and Georgina May Hutchins of Ann Arbor, Michigan. Mrs. Armida Emanuel of Charleston also claimed Lazarus as an ancestor, as well as Myer Moses and Samuel Mordecai, members of Captain Lushington's "Jew Company." Another leader of the Jewish community in Charleston before the Revolution was Abraham Alexander. He was the reader or cantor of the Charleston congregation for many years. During the Revolution he served in General Sumter's brigade, as a lieutenant in Captain Brown's company of Colonel Wade Hampton's regiment, and in Captain McKenzie's troop of Colonel Hill's regiment, all famous names in the military annals of the South. Alexander was married twice, the second time to a Christian widow, Mrs. Ann Sarah Huguenin, who was converted to Judaism. Alexander founded a large and prominent family which spread throughout the South. A number of descendants were admitted to the DAR. Mrs. Rachel Carpenter claimed Isaac daCosta, originally of Charleston, as her Revolutionary ancestor. She also cited her kinship to Colonel David Maysor, a French officer, not Jewish, who had married a daCosta daughter and died in 1780. Their only daughter, Rebecca, had retained her Jewish identity.[9]

Ethel A. Walter named Major Benjamin Nones, the French-born Jew, as her ancestor, and in her application for membership in the DAR attributed to him an exaggerated war career as aide to Generals DeKalb, Lafayette, and Washington. Actually, Nones' own account of his service was more modest. He was a volunteer in the South Carolina militia and served in the forces of Generals Lincoln and DeKalb. One was taken prisoner and the other was killed in the Charleston campaign. Nones acquired his title of major at a later time in the Pennsylvania milita. All of this Nones himself related in a letter to President Jefferson, when he later applied for a political appointment. Nones achieved prominence in the post-Revolutionary political, business, and social life of Philadelphia, both in the Jewish and general community, as has been recounted elsewhere.

Two women, Mrs. Mary Polk Hemphill and Mrs. Sarah E. P. Tillinghast, named Major Myer Myers of Charleston as their Revolutionary ancestor, although they gave his first name incorrectly as Jacob. A Miss Rebecca de la Motta Ralston of Galveston, whose name appears to be as composite as her ancestry, named Levi Sheftall as her Revolutionary forbear in applying for membership in the DAR. A Mrs. Perle Bruckner based her application on Mordecai Sheftall's Revolutionary record.[10]

The three Pinto brothers of Connecticut, whose war career during the Revolution has already been reported elsewhere, were cited by several women as their ancestors; among them were Mrs. Gertrude M. Bradley and Barbara L. Sherwin. The special distinction of the Pintos lay in the fact that they were all students at Yale College, and two were graduated. Their careers after the war varied greatly; Abraham became a wealthy West Indian merchant, William taught school at Groton, and Solomon never prospered. In his old age he was indigent and applied for a pension in 1818.[11]

In the great variety of services rendered during the Revolution and inscribed in DAR application records, those of three Jews deserve special note for their unusual character. One was Jacob Isaacs of Newport, whose descendant claiming membership was Mrs. Cecilia Solomons Michael of Athens, Georgia. She wrote that in 1776, when Newport was expecting a British attack, he delivered three four-pounder guns to the Committee of Safety. Isaacs was then almost sixty years old, and his military record dated back to 1745 when he was a private in the expedition that captured the French-held port of Louisbourg on Cape Breton Island. In his old age, in 1790, he offered to the new government of the United States a method for converting salt water into fresh water. It was referred to Jefferson, then Secretary of State and a kind of unofficial and scientific authority, who rejected it as impractical.

Another Revolutionary patriot, Jacob Hart of Baltimore, had several descendants who claimed membership in the DAR.

Among them were Mrs. Evelyn Stanley and Mrs. Felice Schwartz. His special merit was his contribution of £2,000 to a special fund advanced to Lafayette, then in Baltimore on the way south. It was to enable him to prepare for the final Yorktown campaign. The third patriot was Benjamin Levy, also of Baltimore, a friend of Robert Morris and of General Gates, who signed the non-importation agreement of 1765. His wartime record has been given elsewhere and need not be repeated. Jefferson Levy, already cited, claimed him as well as Jonas Phillips as his ancestor. Another Levy descendant, Mrs. Ethel Morton Shoup Serrell of Sitka, Alaska, used his name to support her application for membership in the DAR. The Jewish stock of the Revolution had been distributed far and wide a century later and was clearly well homogenized into the general population.[12]

The Sons of the American Revolution, whose records are less extensive than those of the DAR, also admitted numerous male descendants of Jewish Revolutionary patriots to membership. The New York State Association, largest and best documented of its early branches, had accepted for membership by 1899 a number who claimed descent from Benjamin Levy, Jonas Phillips, Marks Lazarus, Benjamin Nones, and Levi Sheftall, to name only a few of the better-known veterans. Haym Salomon, too, was cited by several descendants. Among them were S. Stanwood Menken, Emanuel Dreyfus, and Sidney H. and William Jones Salomon. In their applications, they recited such little known or supported episodes as Salomon's distribution of two thousand dollars in specie among the Philadelphia poor. This may have been part of the family tradition. They also referred to the Senate committee report of 1850: "In the depth of his devotion to the course of human liberty, he was not surpassed by his countrymen, Kosciuszko and Pulaski." This surprising claim and juxtaposition of names during the nineteenth century would probably not have been made in Haym Salomon's own time or by him, since contemporary Jews would scarcely have been aware of them.[13]

Enough has been reported from the records of the Revolutionary honor societies to indicate that by 1900 an awareness of the American Revolution as an event to be commemorated and honored had developed in the American population, especially among those who claimed descent from patriots in the War for

Independence. Among them were a substantial number of Jews and others who cited Jewish ancestors. They were eager to give and receive honor. This development of interest was as much the product of contemporary circumstances as of the historic past itself.

An interesting example of such historical-mindedness was the American Jewish Historical Society, founded in 1892, to preserve the history of the Jews in America. In 1903 the Society dedicated a plaque to the memory of eighteen soldiers of the Revolution buried in the old Jewish cemetery in New York. Their graves were marked and are decorated annually on Memorial Day under the auspices of a Jewish veterans' association. The society's publications recorded the historic achievements of the early Jews in America. Significantly, such awareness and recognition perhaps tended to differentiate and even alienate their descendants from the large number of Jews who had arrived in this country more recently and indeed were still immigrating from Eastern Europe well into this century. Thus there were two disparate elements of the Jewish population: one small, select, and of earlier origin; the other large, new, raw, and unassimilated, still absorbed in the process of survival and adjustment to American life.

Nevertheless, despite these contrasts and contradictions, this became the period in which Jewish American consciousness developed into a prolonged and broad movement for status and recognition on the part of the whole Jewish population. Interestingly, it centered on Haym Salomon as a kind of symbol of the Jew in the Revolution, perhaps because he was of known Polish descent and could thus appeal to the newer elements in the population. About him gathered a broad, general movement, which became both controversial and divisive as well as unifying, both nationwide and on the local New York scene. Significantly, too, the American Jewish Historical Society, formed in the early 1890s, provided in its series of *Publications* an outlet for a multiplicity of Jewish historical writings, among which the American Revolution figured prominently. Haym Salomon and his many Revolutionary compatriots became the subjects of numerous studies, which contributed to the growth of Jewish pride and an awareness of a respected and respectable place in American history.[14]

It is noteworthy too, if not wholly pleasant, to recognize that behind this growing Jewish historical-mindedness there was the impetus of a wave of anti-Semitic sentiment, which provoked a kind of reaction and produced an apologetic literature by Jewish and friendly non-Jewish writers alike. The contemporary anti-Semitism was at once nativist in inspiration and intellectual in expression, reaching high social levels. It voiced anti-immigration sentiment which was disputed by such Jewish leaders as Simon Wolf and others. Thus Henry S. Morais, who wrote about the Jews of Philadelphia in 1894, referred to his objective as a defense against the aspersions of Goldwin Smith and his "confreres of Jew-baiting proclivities," which appeared in such journals as the *North American Review* and *Harper's Weekly*. In disproof of Smith's charge that the Jews had displayed no patriotic or military inclinations, Morais dedicated a substantial portion of his volume to the demonstration of how many Jews had fought in all the American wars beginning with the Revolution. Simon Wolf of Washington also wrote at the same time about the "American Jew as Soldier, Patriot and Citizen," listing, not always critically or selectively, all who had served in a military capacity during and since the Revolution. They were reinforced by a non-Jewish writer, Judge C. P. Daly, whose laudatory *Settlement of the Jews in America* was edited by Max J. Kohler in 1893.[15]

Equally, Rev. Madison C. Peters, one of the early non-Jewish defenders of the Jews against slander, wrote *Justice to the Jew* in 1899 and dedicated it to his friend, Rev. H. Pereira Mendes of Shearith Israel in New York. In 1902 he published another work on the *Jew as a Patriot*, in which he particularly took to task Mark Twain for his unwarranted slur against the Jews in an article "Concerning the Jews" in *Harper's Monthly*. In it he had written: "By his make and his ways he is substantially a foreigner wherever he may be." Mark Twain was later convinced he was wrong, and courageously he corrected himself: "When I published the article in *Harper's Magazine*, I was ignorant, like the rest of the Christian world, of the fact that the Jew had a record as a soldier." He felt that the slander "has done its work, done it long and faithfully and with high approval. It ought to be pensioned off now, and retired from active service."[16]

The anti-Semitic sentiment of the 1890s produced still another response, which took the form of an organization of Jewish veterans of the Civil War in 1896, established by seventy-eight men who called themselves Hebrew Veterans. It was later enlarged by the addition of Veterans of the Spanish American War and World War I. In 1929 they were all merged into the Jewish War Veterans, embracing soldiers of all succeeding wars, and still actively engaged in promoting Jewish-American interests. All this reflected a considerable desire and activity among the Jews to relate themselves to American history, reaching even as far back as the Revolution. Some evidence of this interest had appeared earlier and was appropriately associated with Mordecai M. Noah, a journalist and a descendant of Revolutionary veterans, grandfather and father. In 1865, Joshua I. Cohen of Baltimore, himself a scion of a Revolutionary family, wrote to Jared Sparks, the historian who had shown an early interest in Haym Salomon and who wrote about him, that Noah had planned to write a history of the Jews in the Revolution. Unfortunately, nothing is known or remains of what he may have done about this.[17]

Two earlier Jewish events of 1876, during the celebration of the centennial of Independence, revealed some desire to stress a Jewish connection with and indebtedness to the Revolution. B'nai B'rith, the national fraternal order, dedicated in 1876 at Philadelphia, center of the centennial celebration, a statue to Religious Liberty, designed by Moses Ezekiel, the famous Jewish-American sculptor. It attested to the Jewish achievement and appreciation of religious liberty as a major product of the Revolution. More directly, in the same month and year, July 1876, the Union of American Hebrew Congregations, only three years old as the first national religious organization of Jews in America, met in Washington for their annual meeting. From there the assembly made a pilgrimage to Mount Vernon, where Rabbi Isaac Mayer Wise, founder and moving spirit of Reform Judaism in America, planted a tree near Washington's grave in commemoration of his role in the establishment of religious liberty in America. The published proceedings of this event reprinted the letters that were exchanged in 1789-1790 between the newly inaugurated President Washington and the six congregations then in existence in America. They expressed a mutual consensus about the value and importance of religious freedom in the new nation.[18]

The several streams of Jewish activity and concern with their history in America since the Revolution, such as have been described, combined into a considerable movement for recognition in the period after 1900, particularly as the sesquicentennial of independence approached in 1926. Significantly, this movement centered on the role and recognition of Haym Salomon, which acquired nationwide proportions. He became the most publicized and best-known Jewish figure representative of the Revolution. The reasons for this concentration on one person are several and varied. One factor may have been that the greatest result in such a process of myth-making as this is best achieved by concentration on one symbolic name rather than by dissipation among many names. Another must have been that Haym Salomon had indeed occupied the most prominent place among Jews in the Revolution and was best known. He was a close associate of Robert Morris, the Superintendent of Finance during the last difficult years of the Revolution, 1781-1783. He was a broker of foreign exchange, then particularly important because French and Dutch loans supplied the principal funds of the Revolution.

From this modest financial role it was not difficult to transmute and elevate Haym Salomon to a higher one of "Financier of the Revolution," which now became a widely accepted title descriptive of Salomon's newly exalted place in the Revolution. Interestingly, the earlier, more mysterious and intriguing years that Salomon spent in New York under British occupation as a possible American agent, undeservedly received less attention. It is noteworthy that the Jewish interest in Salomon should have become fixed on a traditional financial role, rather than on some more unusual activity in the Revolution, however dramatic. Finally, Salomon's Polish birth and background may have played a part in this modern period, in which the large and relatively new segment of Eastern Europe Jewry in the American population exploited this common bond as a means of identification with

American history and the Revolution. There was particularly an organization known as the Federation of Polish Hebrews that played a conspicuous role in the agitation, under the dynamic leadership of Benjamin Winter, the president, and Zigmunt Tygel, the executive secretary.

Significantly, too, the Salomon case had been kept the longest in the public eye among the various claims for compensation that have been covered in another chapter. Haym M. Salomon's successive petitions for compensation in behalf of his father seemed always on the verge of winning congressional recognition, but never received final acceptance. In 1892 Simon Wolf, author of the contemporary *Jew as Patriot, Soldier, and Citizen*, wrote an article, "Are Republics Ungrateful?" for the *Chicago Reform Advocate*, with reference to Haym Salomon's claim, which he calculated with interest at some three million dollars.

Actually, at this time, in 1893, the Salomon heirs shifted their appeal from monetary compensation to a request for the award by Congress of a commemorative medal, for which only $250 was to be appropriated. This, too, failed of passage in Congress. After 1900, Salomon's recognition took on a popular and national character through press and public agitation, enlisting Jewish support as a whole. Instead of a family enterprise, it became a collective effort involving much of the whole Jewish community even in a kind of controversy and cleavage over whether and how Salomon should be commemorated. This matter endured for a generation, to the very eve of World War II in 1941. It produced a considerable popular literature centered on Salomon's role in the Revolution, which contributed to the process of historical accretion under way.[19] It would seem a long time and a far cry from the Revolution proper and the part the Jews played in it, the subject of this study. It is, however, a significant contemporary outgrowth of that remote event, with modern overtones reflecting the interest of the Jewish community in winning recognition.

The first phase of the Salomon agitation occurred in Washington in 1911, when it was proposed to establish a Haym Salomon University with funds to be appropriated by Congress in repayment of the Revolutionary debt. It was followed by a movement to erect a statue to him. Louis Marshall, a Jewish leader representing the federation of Jewish organizations of

New York, supported the effort, as did important political figures who rallied to the cause, among them Governors Dix of New York and Woodrow Wilson of New Jersey, as well as President Taft himself, who spoke to the Washington Hebrew Congregation on the subject. This address, together with a chapter, entitled "Haym Salomon as the Real Financier of the Revolution," appeared in 1915 in a volume by Rev. Madison Peters, who had been a self-designated promoter of the Salomon cause since 1900. This effort to recognize Salomon nationally and publicly provoked Worthington C. Ford, the noted American historian, to write to *The Nation* in 1911, protesting that the facts did not support the claim that Salomon deserved such recognition and his heirs compensation from Congress. Albert Bushnell Hart, the Harvard historian, supported the Salomon claim. Nothing came of this movement, as it relapsed into obscurity, like so many others.[20]

After World War I, and as the sesquicentennial anniversary of the Revolution approached in 1926, the Salomon agitation was revived. In 1925 Congressman Mooney introduced a resolution in the House of Representatives to appropriate fifty thousand dollars for a statue to commemorate Salomon. In the following year, Senator McKellar, ironically a champion of restrictive anti-immigration legislation, proposed the publication of an official document reporting the full history of the Salomon case in Congress, which became Document 178 of the Senate. At this time, too, the scene of the Salomon movement shifted to New York, where it was sponsored by the Federation of Polish Hebrews. It was pursued vigorously for half a dozen years as a public effort to raise money for a Salomon statue in a New York City square. A plaque was to bear the inscription: "Haym Salomon, Revolutionary Patriot, Financier, and Philanthropist."[21]

The principal spokesman for the New York enterprise was Zigmunt Tygel, secretary of the Polish Federation, who proposed raising $100,000 for the purpose. He published an eight-page brochure, "Haym Salomon . . . the Polish Jew who Helped America Win the War for Independence." It was issued in 1925 by the Salomon Monument Committee under the auspices of the Federation of Polish Hebrews of America. It recited in rather extravagant and unsubstantiated terms the exciting career of

Salomon from his beginnings as a revolutionary nationalist in his native Poland to his departure for America after the first partition of Poland in 1772, and his early affiliation with the American Sons of Liberty in New York.

Among other apocryphal tales, Tygel told an undocumented story, completely mythical, of how George Washington once needed $400,000 immediately, how he applied by messenger to Haym Salomon, who was then attending Yom Kippur Eve services. He assembled all his friends who agreed: "We must pool all our resources." Salomon himself contributed $240,000, and other Jews the remainder, and the day was saved. There is no indication what day in what year this was, nor what the crisis was. Tygel concluded his quite rhapsodic account: "Let us now pay the debt by erecting one of the most beautiful and imposing monuments, the first memorial in the history of the American Jewry to be built to perpetuate and honor the memory of a fighter, revolutionary, and backer of America's great struggle for independence and liberty, who was at the same time one of the noblest Jews that ever lived."[22]

Not accidentally, such hyperbolic writing and claims provoked a critical opposition among Jews. It was headed by Max J. Kohler, a leading figure and secretary of the American Jewish Historical Society, who initiated an investigation of Salomon's life in the original documents as far as they were available. The resulting discoveries, known as the Oppenheim Papers, after the principal investigator, Samuel Oppenheim, are in the archives of the American Jewish Historical Society. On the evidence thus produced, Kohler concluded that the claims were exaggerated, and he inaugurated a campaign to discourage the activities of the Monument Committee. In 1931 he published a pamphlet entitled "An Open Letter to Congressman Celler: Haym Salomon, the Patriot Broker of the Revolution, His Real Achievements and their Exaggeration."

Kohler offered an appreciative and balanced account of Salomon's services. It was in sharp contrast with the current literature then in circulation, particularly an official biography sponsored by the Federation and published in 1930 under the title of *Haym Salomon and the Revolution*, written by a non-Jew,

Charles E. Russell. This was a full-length volume, the first of its kind to appear. Significantly, this period witnessed the appearance of numerous other works about Salomon, in fiction, drama, and even poetry, which, like the biography, exuded unrestrained if unverified enthusiasm. Interestingly, Congressman Celler was won over to Kohler's viewpoint and joined in the movement to counter the monument proposal. His motive may have included the patriotic desire, appropriate in a congressman, to demonstrate that the American Republic was not ungrateful in failing to recognize the extravagant Salomon claims.[23]

Whether because of Kohler's antimonument activity or more likely because of the onset of depression, which curtailed contributions and thwarted the movement, the agitation failed in New York. Not to be denied, it shifted to Chicago, a relatively modern community entirely out of the focus of early Revolutionary geography and history. Here both the city and people were relatively new, and the movement took on the proportions of a civic enterprise, in which Jews and non-Jews joined. To promote the venture, the Patriotic Foundation of Chicago was established in 1936, which included everybody of importance politically, from the mayor down. It took on the strong overtones of anti-Nazi sentiment in a decade that ultimately produced World War II. The famous American sculptor, Lorado Taft, was engaged to design a Salomon monument of heroic proportions, although unhappily he died before the project was executed, and it was completed by an associate. Prominent political figures were persuaded to support the movement, including President Roosevelt, and ex-President Coolidge, usually not very expansive, commented that "there was romance in the story of Haym Salomon, Polish Jew, financier of the Revolution."[24]

Enough money was raised to defray the cost, and the Chicago monument was completed in 1941. On 15 December of that year, which was Bill of Rights Day, and a week after Pearl Harbor, an official dedication ceremony was held in the presence of a large assemblage in a Chicago park, under the presiding guidance of Barnet Hodes, who was at once Corporation Counsel of Chicago and co-chairman of the Patriotic Foundation. The monument itself presented a grouping of three figures, George Washington

in the center, with Robert Morris and Haym Salomon flanking
him on his right and left sides, respectively, all three clasping
hands. Much larger than life size, they stood on a pedestal, which
was seven feet, six inches high, thus creating a truly monumental
effect, in commemoration, as it were, of their heroic place in the
Revolution. Salomon had finally achieved full stature, and with
him also the Jewish people in America, particularly the newest
arrivals from Eastern Europe.

In 1944, in far-off Los Angeles, there was also erected a statue
of a young Haym Salomon, in a seated posture, in a public park.
The chief sponsoring agency was a Polish-American Jewish
Federation, comparable to the Federation of Polish Hebrews of
New York. It was designed by Robert Paine, a descendant of
Thomas Paine, the English-born pamphleteer of the Revolution.
Thus did the Jews of the Far West, too, acclaim a Revolutionary
figure in Haym Salomon.[25]

Interestingly, in 1936, between the failure of the New York and
the rise of the Chicago movements for a Salomon monument,
Congress again took cognizance of the affair. Despite Congressman Celler's long-standing opposition, a non-Jew, Congressman Keller of the House Committee on the Library, introduced a resolution to authorize the erection of a memorial to
Salomon. It recited the usual tale of his deeds and accomplishments, how he "pledged his entire personal fortune to the
United States and died penniless." He sold the French and Dutch
loans without a commission. To the old legends were added new
ones. A fantastic one, in particular, told how Benjamin Franklin
discussed the subsidies with Louis XVI, who asked who would
underwrite them. Franklin replied, "Haym Salomon," to which
the King said, "That is sufficient."

The congressional report added extravagantly that every President since Washington had tried to get Congress to pay
Salomon's heirs the debt due them. It cited Taft, Wilson, and
Coolidge as among those Presidents who had favored some
memorial to him, and it concluded that the nation should provide
a site for the erection of this memorial in the nation's capital, as a
belated but wholly deserved tribute to this "gentleman, scholar,
patriot, and banker, whose only interest was the interest of his

country." This Congress, however, did no more than its predecessors had done.[26]

The considerable and varied efforts made during the early part of this century for the recognition of Haym Salomon, which culminated in the Chicago monument of 1941, testify to a number of factors, quite aside from the merits of Salomon himself. The Jewish community in the country had grown substantially and was well established economically, socially, and politically, particularly in the larger cities. It was a composite population of diverse European origins and divided between the old and new components. The year 1890 was the approximate demarcation point. This diversity may explain the controversy between the older elements, as represented by the historian Max J. Kohler and the American Jewish Historical Society, and the newer ones, among which the Federation of Polish Hebrews, headed by Winter and Tygel, took the lead. As Kohler himself put it rather bluntly in 1931, the Federation launched the monument project "less for the sake of Haym Salomon's memory than to demonstrate thus objectively that Polish Jews were not mere late arrivals here, who started to come at and after the Russian May Laws of 1882, but had rendered most distinguished and valuable services to our country, among others in the person of Haym Salomon during the American Revolution."[27]

Kohler's formulation of motives was perhaps harsh and not wholly deserved, since Salomon had performed creditably during the Revolution, as he indeed admits. There were others too, many named Polock, which was indicative of a Polish origin, who played a role on both sides of the Revolution. What is important to note is that the Jews in America, Polish as well as others, had become sufficiently conscious of their relation to American history by the present century, and were desirous of a place and recognition in it. Haym Salomon served as a convenient medium, and their numbers, as well as their political and social influence, were now great enough to warrant a favorable response even in Congress, as well as in the country at large. They had by now participated in many national affairs, including several wars. Both their American awareness and their right to recognition had grown greatly and had achieved notable results.[28]

It is to be hoped and expected that, with the approaching bicentennial anniversary of Independence in 1976, the Jews will participate in the celebration fully and in sophisticated fashion. They have in the meantime overcome early divisions based on origin and priority of settlement. They have been united and integrated into a single, largely native Jewish American community, whose place and relation to the American past are well established. It is, interestingly, a generation very similar to the much smaller Jewish generation that followed the Revolution. Thus there will be both good reason and an occasion to celebrate their absorption into American life on many levels. In contrast to this integration there also exists now a strong Jewish consciousness, as conspicuous as at any time in the course of American history. Memorials to one or another individual will scarcely be necessary to enhance the celebration. They are perhaps evidence of a naïve attitude. More important is the recognition of the fact that all the Jews in America, few as they then were, shared actively in all aspects of the Revolution. Even those Jews who were then Loyalists gave proof that they were concerned about the issues of the Revolution and its outcome, even if on the opposite side. The whole modern Jewish community, regardless of origin, has been the beneficiary of the Revolution and will wish to join in the celebration of its bicentennial anniversary, without regard to specific individuals.

12

Epilogue: A Final Appraisal

Two major themes have appeared and reappeared in the course of this review and analysis of the Jewish role in the American Revolution. First is, of course, the contribution of the Jews to the Revolution, whether military, economic, or any other. It may be phrased as a double question: What did the Jews do in and for the Revolution? The second theme is exactly the opposite: What did the Revolution do to and for the Jews? Put another way, what happened to the Jews in and as a result of the Revolution, perhaps less by choice than as an inevitable consequence during half a dozen years of war? These are complementary and not contradictory themes, but they are probably not altogether comparable in scope.

Since the Jews were then very few and, except for a small number, not very important, their contributions, while not insignificant, were moderate if not altogether minor. A surprising number of them were in military service, in many places, on the continental, state, and local militia levels. The rank they attained was modest, rising in a few cases to major or even colonel. Mordecai Sheftall of Savannah held the highest rank as Deputy-Commissary-General of Issues for Georgia, which was equivalent to a colonel. Colonel Solomon Bush became Adjutant-General of the Pennsylvania militia. David S. Franks was the most important single Jew in the army as lieutenant-colonel in the continental service, but his was primarily a staff capacity, principally as aide to General Benedict Arnold.

The greatest number of Jews were privates or non-commissioned officers, mainly in the local and state militia. Their combat activities and accomplishments were limited and obscure; these roles were determined not by their choice but by the circumstances and character of this particular and unusual war. Significantly, some distinguished themselves in combat either in the New York, Philadelphia, or Savannah-Charleston zone of the war. A few died, and there were wounded and captured Jewish soldiers in both areas. Altogether there were approximately one hundred Jews in military service, which was some 4 percent of the total Jewish population, and probably double that as a portion of the males alone.

Economically, the Jewish role was more diversified and probably more consequential. It was in a real sense an extension and adaptation to war of what they had been doing prior to the Revolution. They were principally traders and tradesmen in their various communities; a few were merchants engaged in large-scale maritime or frontier trade in such major ports or inland points as Lancaster, New York, Newport, and Philadelphia. Outstanding examples were Aaron Lopez of Newport and also Isaac Moses, Joseph Simon, Simon Nathan, Jonas Phillips, and the Gratz brothers. The fortunes of war, as the British and Americans lost or gained important cities and towns in the course of the conflict, forced the Jews to move about considerably and required them to adapt to new places and conditions of trade. Their flexible adjustment to the changing streams of trade was an amazing demonstration of their ability to survive under wartime pressures. Privateering, one phase of the war in which some Jews engaged, allowed them to display a talent for an unaccustomed activity. Financial enterprises, particularly the disposition of bills of exchange and certificates of indebtedness, provided an outlet for others. It was in this field that Haym Salomon distinguished himself as an aide and broker to Robert Morris, the Superintendent of Finance. There were others too, however, such as Manuel Josephson, Jonas Phillips, and Simon Nathan, who supplied funds for the conduct of the war, both to states and to the nation, and many more who were able to supply goods in a time of war, not an altogether easy task.

Generally the Jews were, politically and even more sentimentally, Whig, but they had little if any political part or influence on the conduct of the Revolution. There were, however, Loyalists among them whose attachment to the British cause was often determined by the accident of their remaining under British authority in occupied towns, such as New York, Newport, or Savannah. There were some whose loyalty was determined by economic interest, traditional sentiment, and even deliberated opinion. Such were David Franks in Philadelphia, Abraham Wagg of New York, Isaac Hart and Rev. Isaac Touro, both of Newport, to name only a few.

As a small minority, scattered and living in an alien social and religious world, whether in Europe or America, most of the Jews fully appreciated, however, that their best hope lay in the Revolution and in its promise of a new political and legal order. The Declaration of Independence was one of the great modern documents that held out the prospect of emancipation and attainment of equal rights. Its fulfillment came in the period following the Revolution, as the new nation formulated a new Constitution and established a federal government under it. The states, too, adapted their constitutional and legal systems to the new principles of equal religious and political rights. Some did so slowly, as existing religious restrictions on the political rights of Jews had to be removed amid political division and controversy, as illustrated, for example, in Maryland, for a quarter of a century after the Revolution.

During the Revolution the Jews had acquired experience and a new assurance by their participation in its military and economic achievements. They extended their expectations and sought an emancipation and integration into the new post-Revolutionary American society in a degree unknown in Europe or even in colonial America. There followed the start of a new age first here and later in Europe under the impact of the French Revolution and Napoleon. But there it was more transitory and less complete, especially after 1815, with the return of reaction to Europe. In America, however, the Jews affirmed and asserted their new rights when challenged, as has been demonstrated in earlier chapters.[1]

The famous exchange of sentiments on religious freedom and equality between President Washington and the Jewish communities in America in 1790 was ceremonial and symbolic, but it was also a real manifestation of their new dignity and status. Ironically, despite Washington's friendly attitude, the Jews tended to affiliate themselves politically with the democratic societies and Jeffersonian principles in the major towns, both north and south. There was little sympathy between them and the Federalists, who controlled the national government during the first decade, 1790-1800.

Nevertheless, the Jewish consciousness of their new status achieved during the Revolution grew steadily and achieved fulfillment in many ways. Thus was the Revolution only the first phase of a long process that extended into the post-Revolutionary period. The immediate post-Revolutionary generation of Jews was still small but largely native-born. In an aroused sense of Americanism and equality, they took active part in the affairs of the nation. They enlisted in both the army and navy in succeeding conflicts, such as the undeclared war with France in 1798 and the War of 1812. These were the sons of the veterans of the Revolution, accustomed to military participation. There was even the beginning of a kind of military professionalism among a few of the Jews, as exemplified by Uriah Phillips Levy and Alfred Mordecai in the navy and army, respectively, but there were others too.

Politically and professionally, too, the Jews were incorporated into American life. They were no longer exclusively merchants or tradesmen, but some also became lawyers and physicians. Many sought and obtained political positions both in federal and state governments by appointment and even by election. They became members of city councils and state legislatures, both north and south, and they served as civil and judicial officials in towns and states. On the federal level the Jews sought appointive office, often in the consular branch. Such posts as they attained were few and modest in scale, since government as a whole was as yet on a relatively small basis.

The Jews were politically active in their home towns, and some became political publicists on a regional and even on a national scale. Such were, for example, Isaac Harby of Charleston and Mordecai M. Noah of New York. Noah, in particular, was perhaps the most representative Jew in the political sphere. He was consul in Tunis, New York City judge, and political journalist, as well as a patriotic dramatist on the popular stage. As a Jew, too, he became an active spokesman for continued Jewish immigration from Europe and settlement in America. His project was visionary, but he predicted and anticipated, as it were, the great wave of immigration of Jews that poured out of Europe after 1840 and for a century thereafter.

In other ways also the Jews of the post-Revolutionary period realized their new opportunities for integration. Despite their small number, many left their established homes in the principal eastern cities, and like the rest of the population, they migrated widely within the enlarged boundaries of the country. They established new communities in such places as Boston, Baltimore, and Richmond. But they also moved to smaller settlements, especially westward on the frontier. They were dispersed individually and thus became even more subject to the forces of assimilation by intermarriage. The magnet of Americanism proved attractive as well as essential, and a significant drainage of Jews into the general population occurred through dispersion and intermarriage. Indeed, it was only the new immigration of the latter nineteenth century that slowed this process and replenished the Jewish population with new elements from Germany, Russia, and other Eastern European lands. This may have slowed and complicated the process of assimilation, but it reinforced the Jewish social and religious institutions and guaranteed their preservation against all assimilating forces.

The Jews of the Revolution and their descendants acted in other ways as well to assert their sense of belonging to American society. One was perhaps not a happy one, as survivors in their old age found themselves in want and applied for government pensions under various acts, beginning in 1818. The tales they told were sad and filled with the record of illness and indigence, but in this they were not different from others who were not Jewish. Some even appealed to Congress for compensation for their losses and sacrifices during the Revolution. They included such notable persons as the Sheftalls of Savannah, the Russells, and particularly Haym Salomon's son, Haym M. Salomon, who pursued the matter in Congress for several decades. They received little or no satisfaction, except the sense of having asserted their rights as American citizens.

More important, toward the end of the nineteenth century, the Jewish descendants of Revolutionary veterans joined equally with others in pursuing a quest for recognition and honor. They were

strongly conscious of their status and applied and won membership in such recently established honorary societies as the
Daughters and Sons of the American Revolution. Ironically,
numerous others, who were not Jewish themselves, also strove to
acquire membership on the ground of service by their ancestors
who had been Jewish. This provided an index of a kind for the
degree of intermarriage and absorption into the general population that had occurred during the century since the Revolution. It
had in fact begun already before the Revolution.

The quest for honor and recognition was developing conspicu-
ously at the turn of the present century, significantly at the time
when Jewish immigration from Europe was rising to a peak. Thus
there seemed to be two rival forces at work, one the large, massive
migration of Jews to the United States, and the other, both
numerically and generically of much smaller size, the surviving
descendants of the older Jewish population in America, dating
back to the Revolution. Despite their contrasting character of old
and new, both groups developed an interest in the American
Revolution and the American past.

The new Jews, represented by the Federation of Polish
Hebrews, manifested a great desire to win recognition and fixed
on the name and contribution of Haym Salomon, who was of
Polish origin, for the purpose. He became their symbol of
awareness and association with the American past, and they
generated an agitation to win recognition for him and themselves
through the medium of a statue erected in his memory in New
York. The movement was active from 1926 on, coinciding with
the sesquicentennial of Independence. It stirred opposition on
the part of people who were better informed professionally about
American history and the role of the Jews in the Revolution.
Other factors, including depression, contributed to the failure of
the movement during the 1930s. Chicago, however, picked it up,
and a statue to Salomon's memory was erected and dedicated
there in 1941, which joined Haym Salomon to the memory of
George Washington and Robert Morris, who were included in the
monumental statuary group. In the faraway West, too, Los
Angeles Jews raised a monument to the memory of Salomon in
1944, under the auspices of a Polish Jewish Federation.

The situation has, however changed considerably in the

generation since the 1940s. The Jews are no longer divisible into old and new, those who were, and those who were not, part of early American history. Such division has ceased to have meaning, as Jews have been integrated into American life generally and into a single community particularly. They all constitute a predominantly native-born American generation. Hence the meaning of the Revolution to them lies not in whether they have a direct or no relation to the Revolution, or whether Haym Salomon was of Polish or other origin. The fact is that the Jews of the Revolution, however few and diverse they were, played a notable and quite complex role in the Revolution. They earned their place in America by their actions and conduct. The Revolution was a kind of watershed in Jewish American history, dividing the relatively small contingent who participated in its many aspects from the larger mass of Jews who came afterward and reaped the benefits of the others' labors. The Jews who have come since have equally earned their place in America. All groups are now joined together as one, and may take equal pride in past achievements. They may share equally together in the commemoration of the American Revolution as the bicentennial anniversary approaches and arrives in 1976, not merely as Jews but, with all Americans, as heirs of a new freedom and promise of equality.

Notes

ABBREVIATED TITLES OF JOURNALS AND SERIALS

AJA   American Jewish Archives, a quarterly published since 1948 by the American Jewish Archives of the Hebrew Union College at Cincinnati.
JCC   Journals of the Continental Congress.
PAJHS   Publications of the American Jewish Historical Society, issued annually, 1893-1962.
AJHQ   American Jewish Historical Quarterly, published by the American Jewish Historical Society since 1962 as a continuation of the *Publications.*
PCC   Papers of the Continental Congress, in microfilm at the National Archives in Washington.

CHAPTER 1

¹Every student of the Jews in colonial America must necessarily draw upon the extensive and authoritative scholarship of Dr. Jacob R. Marcus, professor emeritus of Jewish American history and founder of the American Jewish Archives at the Hebrew Union College in Cincinnati. His long list of writings, which will be cited frequently, is recorded in the bibliography.

²Dr. Marcus gives a total of 2,500 Jews for continental America during the Revolution, in *The Colonial American Jew* (Detroit, 1970), 3: 1329, as does also Albert Ehrenfried in *Chronicle of Boston Jewry* (Boston, 1963), p. 174. Other writers vary widely, however, from as low as 1,000, as reported by Moses Rischin in *An Inventory of American Jewish History,* (Cambridge, Mass., 1954), p. 29, to Rudolph Glanz's 3,000 for 1790 in "Jews in the United States in the Colonial Epoch," *Jewish Review,* April 1940, p. 4. Ira Rosenswaike, who analyzed the census of 1790, estimated only 1,300 to 1,500 Jews even at this late date (*PAJHS* 50 [1960]: 23). He

offers a figure of 2,700 for 1820, which would indicate a low rate of growth. M. M. Noah, a contemporary writer, estimated the Jewish population at 3,000 in 1818, but Isaac Harby, another publicist, reported some 6,000 Jews, in the *North American Review* of July 1826 (*AJHQ* 53 [1963] : 131); cf. Charles Reznikoff, *The Jews of Charleston* (Philadelphia, 1950), p. 68. Evidently, the great growth of the Jewish population in America began only after 1840, with the new immigration from Germany, and even more after 1880, as the result of immigration from Russia and Eastern Europe generally.

³The Reverend Ezra Stiles, friend of the Jews in Newport and subsequently president of Yale College, significantly concluded, in discussing Aaron Lopez's failure to procure naturaliaign in Rhode Islandsin 1762, for which he had crossed over to Massachusetts, that it "forebodes that the Jews will never be incorporated with the people of America, any more than in Europe, Asia, and Africa." Moreover, he added: "Providence seems to make everything to work for Mortification to the Jews. . . . That thus they may continue a distinct people." Quoted in A. V. Goodman, *American Overture* (Philadelphia, 1947), p. 53.

⁴Dr. Benjamin Rush wrote that the Jews were "generally Whigs in all the States": *Autobiography* (Princeton, N.J., 1948), p. 119; see also *Pennsylvania Magazine of History and Biography* 29 (1905): 29. There were, however, Jewish Loyalists during the Revolution, as will be detailed in Chapter 7.

⁵J. R. Marcus, *The American Colonial Jew: A Study in Acculturation* (Syracuse, N.Y.: Syracuse University Press, 1967), pp. 3-24. Cf. H. B. Grinstein, *Rise of the Jewish Community of New York* (Philadelphia, 1945), p. 336, for a comment on the growing laxity of Jewish religious observance as a result of the Revolution, and as a consequence of the migration and dispersion of the Jewish population. There was also the call "of a new world and a new order . . . of democracy and freedom." Malcolm Stern, the genealogist of colonial Jewry, notes that prior to 1840, in a sample of marriages studied, intermarriage among Jews was upwards of 15 percent; *Essays from the American Jewish Archives* (Cincinnati, 1958), p. 85 (designated hereafter as AJA Tenth Anniversary Volume).

CHAPTER 2

¹*PAJHS* 23 (1915): 23; 26 (1918): 236; J. T. Scharf and T. Westcott, *History of Philadelphia* (Philadelphia, 1884), 1: 272; M. U. Schappes, *A*

Documentary History of the Jews in the United States (New York, 1950), pp. 38, 574.

[2] *PAJHS* 5 (1897): 205; 11 (1903): 90; 21 (1913): 140; 35 (1939): 293.

[3] J. R. Marcus, *American Jewry: Eighteenth Century Documents* (Cincinnati, 1959), pp. 119, 131. David de S. Pool, *Portraits Etched in Stone* (New York, 1952), p. 350.

[4] *PAJHS* 3 (1895): 83; 38 (1948): 81, 103.

[5] *PCC* 9: 58; Schappes, *Documentary History,* 52: 578.

[6] H. B. Grinstein, *Rise of the Jewish Community of New York* (Philadelphia, 1945), p. 69; A. C. Flick, *Loyalism in New York* (New York, 1901), p. 96.

[7] Ezra Stiles, *Literary Diary* (New York, 1901), 2: 131; G. A. Kohut, *Ezra Stiles and the Jews* (New York, 1902), pp. 16, 35.

[8] M. S. Gutstein, *Jews of Newport* (New York, 1936), p. 182; Lee M. Friedman, *Jewish Pioneers and Patriots* (Philadelphia, 1942), pp. 142, 148.

[9] .B. A. Elzas, *The Jews of South Carolina* (Philadelphia, 1905), p. 98; A. L. Lebeson, *Jewish Pioneers in America* (New York, 1938), p. 228; J. R. Marcus, *Early American Jewry* (New York, 1951), 2: 219; Charles Reznikoff, *The Jews of Charleston* (Philadelphia, 1950), p. 45; A. D. Candler, ed., *Revolutionary Records of Georgia* (Atlanta, 1908), 1: 612; 3: 26.

CHAPTER 3

[1] *PAJHS* 41 (1951): 107; David de S. Pool, *Portraits Etched in Stone* (New York, 1952), p. 477; E. Wolf and M. Whiteman, *History of the Jews of Philadelphia* (Philadelphia 1957), p. 15; J. R. Marcus, *American Jewry: Eighteenth Century Documents* (Cincinnati, 1959), p. 425.

[2] Salvador's case is one of the best documented and authenticated in Revolutionary as well as Jewish American history. This is evidenced by many general references—among them, John Drayton, *Memoirs of the American Revolution . . . as relating to the state of South Carolina* (Charleston, S.C., 1821), 2: 343, 369; *South Carolina Historical and Genealogical Magazine* 3 (1902): 59, for the correction of L. Hühner's account of Salvador in *PAJHS* 9 (1901): 107. See also *New York Historical Society Publications* (Lee Papers, 1874), 2: 224; Peter Force, *American Archives,* Fifth Series (1848), 1: 749, 780. For the Jewish version of Salvador's record, see B. A. Elzas, *The Jews of South Carolina* (Philadelphia, 1905), pp. 68, 108; Charles Reznikoff, *The Jews of Charleston* (Philadelphia, 1950), p. 34; Allan Lesser, "Salvador: Gentleman-Patriot of South Carolina," *Menorah Journal* 25 (1937): 305

³*JCC* (Washington, D.C.: 1904-1937), 20: 738: *PCC* (microfilm at National Archives), 1: 222, 258; 2: 35; J. T. Scharf and T. Westcott, *History of Philadelphia* (Philadelphia, 1884), 1: 331; *PAJHS* 23 (1916): 177; *AJA* 7 (1955): 139.

⁴Henry Morais, *The Jews of Philadelphia* (Philadelphia, 1894), p. 455; Wolf and Whiteman, *Jews of Philadelphia*, p. 154. In his letter of 1789 to Washington, Bush declared that to establish American "liberties I have bled in her cause." The book he mentions forwarding to Washington has been identified by Marcus as *City Petitions* (London, 1788), a collection of petitions by Londoners in support of the American cause. It was delivered personally by John Trumbull, the painter, to Washington, who thanked Bush for it; see J. R. Marcus, *Early American Jewry* (New York, 1951), 2: 79.

⁵Franks' manifold role in the Revolution is even better documented than Salvador's and it lasted all through the Revolution. For his earlier services in Canada, cf. *JCC* 5: 590, 742; 6: 895; Peter Force, *American Archives*, Fourth Series, 6: 1437; *PAJHS* 4 (1897): 82; 31 (1928):234: Hersch L. Zitt, in *Pennsylvania History* 16 (1949): 77; Marcus, *Early American Jewry*, 1: 251.

⁶For Franks' service as aide to General Benedict Arnold, cf. *JCC* 13: 391; *PCC* 2: 35, 47; 15: 415; J. C. Fitzpatrick, ed., *Writings of Washington* (Washington, D.C., 1931-1944), 12: 161; 20: 89, 225, 229, 442, 934; *Calendar of Correspondence of George Washington* (Washington, D.C., 1906), 1: 678; 2: 1443, 1459, 1476, 1547, 1577, 1621; Harold C. Syrett, ed., *Papers of Alexander Hamilton* (New York, 1961), 2: 440, 485; *AJA* 7 (1955): 141: Carl Van Doren, *Secret History of the American Revolution* (New York, 1941), pp. 172, 286, 294, 314, 343; J. T. Flexner, *The Traitor and the Spy* (New York, 1953), pp. 221, 231, 370.

⁷Franks' diplomatic career is equally well documented, as illustrated in *JCC* 20: 511; 23: 574, 584; 25: 786; *PCC* 1: 679; 3: 268, 271, 285; *Calendar of Franklin Papers* (Philadelphia, 1908), 2: 395, 419; 3: 160, 552: 4: 74, 142, 438; Robert Morris, *Diary* (manuscript in Library of Congress), 11 July 1781; 13 Nov. 1782; 2 Jan. 1783; Francis Wharton, ed., *The Revolutionary Diplomatic Correspondence* (Washington, D. C., 1889), 4: 784; 5: 121; *PAJHS* 1 (1893): 58, 76.

⁸J. P. Boyd, ed., *Papers of Jefferson* (Princeton, N. J., 1951), 6: 241, 251, 461; W. T. Hutchinson, ed., *Papers of J. Madison* (Chicago, 1969), 4: 448; 6:236, 254.

⁹Despite his relatively minor diplomatic position as a courier, Franks performed an active role in the European negotiations, which brought

him frequent mention in much of the correspondence of the time and in the journals and papers of the Continental Congress.

[10] *JCC* 32: 176, 273, 362; *Letters of Members of Congress* (Washington, D. C., 1936), 6: 420, 428; 8: 576: *Papers of Jefferson*, 10: 95, 305; *PAJHS* 20 (1913): 22; *AJA* 7 (1955): 66, 141.

[11] *Papers of Jefferson*, 16: 158; J. C. Fitzpatrick, ed., *Diaries of Washington* (Boston, 1925), 4:534; William S. Baker, "Washington after the Revolution," *Pennsylvania Magazine of History and Biography* 18 (1894): 454; 19 (1895): 22, 170, 428; *PAJHS* 10 (1903): 101, 167.

[12] Zitt, in *Pennsylvania History*, 16 (1949): 89. J. R. Marcus, *The Colonial American Jew* (Detroit, 1970), 3: 1311.

[13] *Calendar of Correspondence of George Washington*, 2: 1502, 1543; M. U. Schappes, *A Documentary History of the Jews in the United States* (New York, 1950), p. 581; Marcus, *Documents*, p. 267; *AJA* 8 (1956): 142; *PAJHS* 1 (1893): 109; 5 (1897): 5; 10 (1903): 168. An unusual and somewhat mysterious advertisement in the *Pennsylvania Packet* of 15 Sept. 1778 informs Isaac Franks, "who left New York in evacuation by American troops and is supposed to be living at Peekskill to get in touch with the Printer to hear something to his advantage." Franks was then presumably with Washington's army.

[14] *Writings of Washington*, 33: 107, 127, 135; *Pennsylvania Magazine of History and Biography* 6 (1882): 145; 38 (1914): 488; *PAJHS* 19 (1912): 50; Wolf and Whiteman, *Jews of Philadelphia*, pp. 168, 429.

[15] Sara S. Ervin, *South Carolinians in the Revolution* (Ypsilanti, Mich., 1949), p. 86; *PCC* 1: 557; Schappes, *Documentary History*, p. 591; *PAJHS* 12 (1904): 51; Hannah London, *Miniatures of Early American Jews* (New York, 1953), p. 14. Cf. DAR (Daughters of the American Revolution), *Lineage Books*, 107: 204; 108: 70, 95, 107.

[16] Microfilm Applications (DAR Archives in Washington), No. 248: 519. There were many Revolutionary soldiers with Biblical or seemingly Jewish names, whom the early historians, such as Simon Wolf and Henry Morais, frequently identified as Jews. Even as recent a book as J. R. Rosenbloom's *A Biographical Dictionary of Early American Jews* (University of Kentucky Press, Lexington, Ky., 1960) includes many such names, which are, however, identified as those of "doubtful Jews." This still leaves the question of identity unsettled. Dr. Marcus rejects many of these possible or supposedly Jewish names; see his *American Colonial Jew*, 3: 1192. There is a twilight zone here of unknown Jewish limits.

[17] *AJA Tenth Anniversary Volume*, p. 94. Cf. Wolf and Whiteman,

Jews of Philadelphia, p. 128. For Dr. Nicholas Schuyler, who married Shinah Simon, cf. Microfilm Pension Applications at National Archives, No. 4665.

[18]B. F. Stevens, *Facsimiles of Mss. in European Archives Relating to America, 1773-1783* (London, 1895), 23: 1946, for the Minis-Sheftall information supplied to the French about the approaches to Savannah; Marcus, *Documents*, pp. 265, 428; Marcus, *Early American Jewry*, 2: 281, 355.

[19]For the Sheftall Diaries, 1733-1808, cf. *AJHQ* 54 (1965): 243; Marcus, *Documents*, p. 232. In 1924 the Georgia Society of Colonial Dames placed epitaphs on several graves of Revolutionary patriots in the Jewish cemetery in Savannah, among them Mordecai Sheftall as "a native of this city and soldier of the Revolution. . . ." David T. Morgan has made himself the historian of the Sheftalls' life and work in eighteenth-century Savannah ("The Sheftalls of Savannah") *AJHQ* 62 (1973) :348-61; "Judaism in Eighteenth Century Georgia," *Georgia Historical Quarterly* 58 (1974) :41-54.

[20]Kenneth Coleman, *The American Revolution in Georgia* (Athens, Ga., 1958). p. 63; *PAJHS* 17 (1910): 103; *AJA* 7 (1955): 150.

[21]For the many activities of the Sheftalls, see *The Sheftall Papers*, in two volumes, compiled by the Historical Records Survey in 1941, now in the Archives of the American Jewish Historical Society at Waltham, Mass., passim. See also Leo Shpall, "The Sheftalls of Georgia in the Revolution," *Georgia Historical Quarterly* 27 (1943): 339-349; E. H. Edmunds, "Early History of the Sheftalls of Georgia," *PAJHS* 17 (1910): 174 ff.

[22]Sheftall Sheftall's Pension Application, No. S 31,957, is in the National Archives in Washington; cf. *Writings of Washington*, 20: 356; Marcus, *Documents*, p. 271. For a description of Sheftall Sheftall as "a venerable old man, habited in the garb of Franklin . . . , a huge cocked hat, knee breeches . . . ," see C. P. Daly, *The Settlement of the Jews in North America* (New York, 1893), p. 74.

[23]For the Sheftalls' complicated claims and prolonged negotiations with Congress for compensation, cf. *PCC* 4: 685; 5: 261, 325; 9: 58; 20: 625; 21: 56; Robert Morris' manuscript *Diary* at Library of Congress, 7 Oct. 1782; mss. Letters of Morris, Vol. B:4 (Library of Congress).

[24]A. D. Candler, ed., *Revolutionary Records of Georgia* (Atlanta, 1908), 2: 465; Shpall, *Georgia Historical Quaterly* 27: 349.

[25]Candler, ed., *Revolutionary Records of Georgia*, 1: 612; 3: 261: *Sheftall Diaries* in *AJHQ* 54 (1965): 276; Schappes, *Documentary History*, p. 55.

[26]Candler, ed., *Revolutionary Records of Georgia*, 1: 476; *AJA* 7 (1955): 150; Reznikoff, *Jews of Charleston*, p. 70; David T. Morgan, "The Sheftalls of Savannah," *AJHQ* 62 (1973): 358.

[27]J. L. Blau and S. W. Baron, *The Jews of the United States, 1790-1840: A Documentary History* (New York, 1964), 1: 265; Pension Application, No. S31, 959 (National Archives). The anecdote about Sheftall Sheftall is related by C. P. Daly, who saw him in Savannah (*Settlement of the Jews in North America*, p. 74).

[28]Lee M. Friedman, *Jewish Pioneers and Patriots* (Philadelphia, 1942), p. 351; Wolf and Whiteman, *Jews of Philadelphia*, p. 100.

[29]*PAJHS* 17 (1909): 89; 33 (1925): 231.

[30]*PAJHS* 17 (1909): 172, 187; Anita Lebeson, *Pilgrim People* (New York, 1950), p. 148; R. B. Morris, *Encyclopedia of American History* (New York, 1953), p. 549, which cites David Emanuel as a governor of Georgia in 1801, the highest office held by a Jew to that date.

[31]C.H.B. Turner, *Some Records of Sussex County, Delaware* (Philadelphia, 1909), 47, 249, 294, 338; J. T. Scharf, *History of Delaware* (Philadelphia, 1888) 1: 143; Anna T. Lincoln, *Wilmington, Delaware* (Rutland, Vt., 1937), p. 82; J. R. Marcus, *Colonial American Jew*, 1: 332, 446.

CHAPTER 4

[1]*PAJHS* 19 (1911): 152; B. A. Elzas, *The Jews of South Carolina* (Philadelphia, 1905), p. 78; Charles Reznikoff, *The Jews of Charleston* (Philadelphia, 1950), p. 270.

[2]Elzas, *Jews of South Carolina*, p. 87; *PAJHS* 19 (1911), 153.

[3]Elzas, *Jews of South Carolina*, p. 89; J. R. Marcus, *Early American Jewry* (New York, 1951), 2: 256, 330; Marcus, *The Colonial American Jew*, (Detroit, 1970), 3: 1303.

[4]Sara S. Ervin, *South Carolinians in the Revolution* (Ypsilanti, Mich., 1949), pp. 81, 95, 102; Henry A. Alexander, *Notes on the Alexander Family of South Carolina and Georgia* (Atlanta, 1954), pp. 7, 161; Elzas, *Jews of South Carolina*, pp. 42, 92; Reznikoff, *Jews of Charleston*, p. 34; Anita Lebeson, *Pilgrim People* (New York, 1950), p. 104. Interestingly, Joseph Levy had been a lieutenant in South Carolina's Regiment of Foot already in 1757 and took part in the Cherokee War of 1760.

[5]Elzas, *Jews of South Carolina*, p. 99; *PAJHS* 12 (1904): 53; Reznikoff, *Jews of Charleston*, p. 45.

[6]Reznikoff, *Jews of Charleston*, p. 46.

[7]Ibid., pp. 67, 272; J. R. Marcus, *American Jewry: Eighteenth Century Documents* (Cincinnati, 1959), pp. 170, 181.

[8]DAR *Lineage Books*, 57: 22; 107: 235.

[9]*Pension Application* (National Archives), No. W 773. Isaac Levi's name

appears on the company payroll lists of Captains Robert Patterson and John Cowan in Kentucky, then a part of Virginia.

[10]DAR Application, No. 291,983; *Pension Application* (National Archives), No. 7989.

[11]Marcus, *Early American Jewry,* 2:150, illustrates the mobility of Jews at this time; Marcus suggests that the three Ezekiel Levys listed for different places may have been one and the same man—a man who was very mobile.

[12]DAR Application, No. 141,977; *Reports of House Representatives,* 27th Congress, second session, No. 37 (8 March 1842). Cf. Louis X. Burgess, *Virginia Soldiers of 1776* (Richmond, 1929), 3: 1031, citing an executive order of 13 March 1838, which granted public land to the Cohen heirs; John H. Gwathmey, *Virginians in the Revolution: Historical Register* (Richmond, 1938), p. 165. The Cohen heirs submitted a letter from General Lafayette in 1832, testifying to his remembrance of Captain Cohen at Yorktown.

[13]DAR *Lineage Books,* 9: 44.

[14]Morris Jastrow, "Notes on the Jews of Philadelphia" *PAJHS* 1 (1893): 49; Marcus, *Colonial American Jew,* 3: 1310; J. R. Rosenbloom, *A Biographical Dictionary of Early American Jews* (Lexington, Ky., 1960), p. 70.

[15]Gwathmey, *Virginians in the Revolution,* p. 470. There are listed here a Juda, Judah, and Judas Levi, which may be the same man, besides a Jacob, Judah, Solomon, and William Levy. Other additions to the surprisingly long list of possible or doubtful Jews in Virginia's service appear in G. M. Brumbagh, ed., *Revolutionary War Records of Virginia* (Washington, D.C., 1936), 1: 194, 252, and in Burgess, *Virginia Soldiers of 1776,* 2:86; 3:242, among them a Jacob Caplan and a David Solomon.

[16]H. B. Gill, *The Apothecary in Colonial Virginia* (Williamsburg, 1972), p. 115; Robert Shosteck, "Notes on an Early Physician," *AJA* 23 (1971): 198.

[17]DAR *Lineage Books,* 61:564; 62:193; microfilm applications in DAR Archives, No. 422,458; Leon Hühner, "Jews of North Carolina," *PAJHS* 29 (1921): 144.

[18]E. Wolf and M. Whiteman, *History of the Jews of Philadelphia* (Philadelphia, 1957), p. 443; S. Wolf, *The Jew as Patriot* (Philadelphia, 1895), p. 48; Marcus, *Colonial American Jew,* 3: 1309.

[19]*Archives of Maryland* (Baltimore, 1900), "Muster Rolls of Maryland Troops in the Revolution," 18: 41, 213, 276, 517; I. M. Fein, *Making of a Jewish Community, Baltimore* (Philadelphia, 1971), p. 11.

[20]Pension Applications (National Archives); Marcus, *Colonial American Jew* 3: 1311.

[21] *Delaware Archives of the Revolutionary War* (Wilmington, 1919), 2: 760, 794, 1204; *AJA* 13 (1961): 117. Cf. Elizabeth F. Ellet, *The Women of the American Revolution* (New York, 1850), 2: 655, for Hannah Israel's exploits. Interestingly, Rebecca Franks, Loyalist daughter of David, is the only Jewish woman who receives full treatment in Elizabeth Ellet's account of Revolutionary women.

[22] Pension Application (National Archives), No. S42,892; J. C. Fitzpatrick, ed., *Writings of Washington* (Washington, D.C., 1931-1944), 14: 14, 144, 326; A. J. Karp, ed., *The Jewish Experience, Selected Essays from PAJHS*, 5 vols. (New York, 1969), 1: 65.

[23] A. J. Messing, "Old Mordecai, A Jew of the American Revolution," *PAJHS* 13 (1905): 71-81. In A. J. Pickett's *History of Alabama* (Charleston, S.C., 1851), Mordecai is described as "a dark-eyed Jew amorous in his disposition" (p. 469). Cf. R. Learsi, *Jews in America* (Cleveland, 1954), p. 73, for a local historian's account of Mordecai as an "intelligent Jew," who lived fifty years among the Creeks and married an Indian woman.

[24] Lee M. Friedman, *Pilgrims in a New Land* (Philadelphia, 1948), p. 84.

[25] Gratz Mordecai, "Jacob Mordecai" (whose grandson he was), *PAJHS* 6 (1897): 40; *New York Journal*, 20 Jan. 1785; Lebeson, *Pilgrim People*, p. 227; Marcus, *Colonial American Jew*, 3: 1297.

[26] David de S. Pool, *Portraits Etched in Stone* (New York, 1952), p. 251; *JCC* 24: 361; *PCC* 2: 8.

[27] *PCC* 24: 208, 294; *PAJHS* 2 (1894), 123; Pool, *Portraits*, p. 322.

[28] Pennsylvania Archives, Seventh Series (Harrisburg, 1914), Vol. 1, passim; W.T.R. Saffell's *Records of the Revolutionary War* (Philadelphia, 1860), p. 206; Henry Morais, *The Jews of Philadelphia* (Philadelphia, 1894), p. 458. Both Morais and Simon Wolf, as the first Jewish historians of the Revolution, tended to expand the list of Jewish soldiers uncritically by including all manner of names. Cf. Marcus, *Colonial American Jew*, 3: 1310, 1581, for the identification of Solomon Isaacs as the same soldier who participated in the invasion of Canada and was captured there in 1776. To add to the profusion as well as the confusion of names, the index of soldiers in the volume of the *Pennsylvania Archives* for the Revolution lists ten Cohens, twenty-six Levys, and a half-dozen Myerses, spelled diversely.

[29] Lebeson, *Pilgrim People*, p. 135; Wolf, *The Jew as Patriot*, p. 51; Morais, *The Jews of Philadelphia*, p. 457.

[30] Pool, *Portraits*, p. 409; Madison C. Peters, *Justice to the Jew* (New York, 1899), p. 133; *PAJHS* 11 (1903): 131.

[31] Hannah London, *Portraits of Jews* (New York, 1927), p. 103; Marcus, *Colonial American Jew*, 3: 1297; *AJA* 6 (1954): 85.

[32]Pool, *Portraits*, passim, for biographical sketches of these Jewish patriots and soldiers buried in the New York cemetery. See also Mrs. R. S. Phillips, "The New York Cemetery," *PAJHS* 18 (1910): 94, for the defensive use made of the cemetery by the American army in 1776.

[33]Pool, *Portraits*, passim. Cf. Joshua Trachtenberg, *Consider the Years* (Easton, Pa., 1944), p. 68. According to family tradition, Michael Hart entertained General Washington at luncheon during his visit to Easton (Trachtenberg, p. 71).

[34]*AJA* 1 (1948): 11; 14 (1962): 102; Pool, *Portraits*, pp. 95, 378; Lebeson, *Pilgrim People*, p. 95; *AJHQ* 56 (1966): 163.

[35]Marcus, *Early American Jewry*, 2: 73.

[36]DAR Application, No. 327,675; *Roll of Associators of Easthampton, New York*, pp. 69, 129, 153. Cf. S. Solis-Cohen, "Notes Concerning David Hays," *PAJHS* 2 (1894): 63; 16 (1907): 23; Pool, *Portraits*, p. 328.

[37]*PAJHS* 10 (1902): 163; 27 (1909): 391.

[38]DAR Application No. 276,355; *Roll of Associators of Easthampton*, p. 55; Saffell, *Records of the Revolutionary War*, pp. 116, 163, 173; E. C. Knight, *New York in the Revolution* (Albany, 1901), 2: 352.

[39]*PAJHS* 11 (1903): 90; 21 (1913): 140; 27 (1920): 126; Pool, *Portraits*, p. 350.

[40]J. R. Marcus, "Light on Early Connecticut Jews," *AJA* 1 (1948): 7; *Early American Jewry*, 1: 175; *PAJHS* 11 (1903): 90; 52 (1963): 303.

[41]Marcus, *Documents*, p. 284; *AJA* 1 (1948): 27; *The Jewish Experience*, 1: 171; F. B. Dexter, *Sketches of Yale Graduates* (New York, 1903), 3: 700; C. Reznikoff, "New Haven, The Jewish Community," *Commentary* 4 (1947); 464; M. U. Schappes, *A Documentary History of the Jews in the United States* (New York, 1950), p. 48.

[42]Marcus, *Documents*, p. 137, *Early American Jewry*, 1: 175; *Colonial American Jew*, 3: 1313. Rosenbloom, *Biographical Dictionary*, p. 108.

[43]Dexter, *Yale Graduates*, 2: 233, 697; *PAJHS* 19 (1910): 101, 110; *AJA* 1 (1948): 21; Wallace Brown, *The King's Friends* (Providence, R.I., 1965), p. 70. Cf. R. R. Hinman, *A Historical Collection of Connecticut During the War of Revolution*, (Hartford, 1842), passim, for various official efforts to restrain Ralph Isaac's movements while under suspicion, until his release after he had "taken the oath of fidelity" (p. 703).

[44]*Massachusetts Soldiers and Sailors in the Revolutionary War*, 17 vols. (Boston, 1896), 14: 635. Cf. *Record of Connecticut Men ... in the Revolution* (Hartford, 1889), passim. Cf. M. A. Gutstein, *The Jews of Newport* (New York, 1936), p. 182. Lee M. Friedman, *Jewish Pioneers and Patriots* (Philadelphia, 1942), p. 345; Albert Ehrenfried, *A Chronicle of Boston Jewry* (1963), pp. 177, 249; S. Broches, *Jews in New England* (New York, 1942), p. 61.

[45]Rosenbloom, *A Biographical Dictionary of Early American Jews*, identifies all Jews, both authentic and doubtful, who served in the Revolution in some military capacity. A count of names indicates that there were as many as 21 officers of all ranks and some 83 ordinary soldiers, for a total of 104. In addition, he lists 39 soldiers of doubtful Jewish identity. Also listed are some 22 Jewish Loyalists, altogether more than 160 names of all categories in a Jewish population of perhaps 2,500. My own independent count yields 22 officers and 72 soldiers of Jewish origin, totaling some 94 persons in military service alone.

[46]Cf. also Chapter 10 which deals with the post-Revolutionary quest by Jews for pensions and compensation. Here the veterans recall and report their military services in full and vivid detail. Even after allowing for the failings of old age memory, these records amplify the original accounts, often little more than the mere mention of a name.

CHAPTER 5

[1]*PAJHS* 22 (1915): 196; M. U. Schappes, *A Documentary History of the Jews in the United States* (New York, 1950), p. 61.

[2]J. R. Marcus, *American Jewry: Eighteenth Century Documents* (Cincinnati, 1959), pp. 311, 337; *Early American Jewry* (New York, 1951), 2: 75; Miriam K. Freund, *Jewish Merchants in Colonial America* (New York, 1939), p. 65.

[3]E. S. Maclay, *A History of American Privateers* (New York, 1899), pp. 113, 205.

[4]*Letters of Members of the Continental Congress* (Washington, D.C., 1926), 3: 519. Cf. *Pennsylvania Archives,* Fifth Series (Harrisburg, 1906), Vol. 1, Chap. 5, for Jewish privateers; *PAJHS* 23 (1915): 169.

[5]Robert Morris, Mss. *Diary* (Library of Congress), 27, 31 Aug. 1781; 28 Feb., 5 Aug. 1783; J. T. Scharf and T. Westcott, *History of Philadelphia* (Philadelphia, 1884), 1: 408; E. Wolf and M. Whiteman, *History of the Jews of Philadelphia* (Philadelphia, 1957), pp. 99, 168; David de S. Pool, *Portraits Etched in Stone* (New York, 1952), p. 384; *PAJHS* 27 (1920): 331.

[6]*PAJHS* 23 (1915): 172; Pool, *Portraits*, pp. 378, 386; Samuel Tolkowsky, *They Took to the Sea* (New York, 1964), p. 254 (citing Robert Morris on Isaac Moses as "my friend of austere culture and true knowledge").

[7]*JCC* 26: 179; PCC (National Archives), Microfilm Roll 60:325. Cf. Harold C. Syrett, ed., *Papers of Alexander Hamilton* (New York, 1961), 3: 601; Pool, *Portraits*, p. 387; A. C. Flick, *Loyalism in New York* (New York,

1901), p. 222; *PAJHS* 27 (1920): 333, 344; Robert A. East, *Business Enterprise in the Revolution* (New York, 1938), p. 176.

[8] *PAJHS* 10 (1902): 164; 27 (1920): 345; East, *Business Enterprise*, p. 328; Pool, *Portraits*, p. 387.

[9] *PAJHS* 23 (1914): 172; *Sheftall Papers* (Archives of American Jewish Historical Society), 10 Sept. 1781; East, *Business Enterprise*, p. 160.

[10] Unlike Isaac Moses, who remains relatively obscure despite his important role in the Revolution, Aaron Lopez, like Haym Salomon, but for a different reason, has been fully recognized and is the subject of a considerable literature. The latest contribution is by Stanley Chyet, *Lopez of Newport; Colonial American Merchant Prince* (Detroit, 1970). Many Lopez letters were published in a volume by the Massachusetts Historical Society in 1915: *Commerce of Rhode Island* (Boston, 1915), Vol. 2. These and other letters are in the Newport Historical Society Archives, where the writer consulted them, for which his thanks are expressed herewith to the staff.

[11] S. F. Chyet, "Aaron Lopez: A Study in Buenfama," *AJHQ* 52 (1962): 299.

[12] *PCC* 24: 199; *JCC* 16: 375; *PAJHS* 2 (1894): 119; 11 (1903): 84; 23 (1915): 8, 55; 37 (1947): 105, 154; Marcus, *Early American Jewry*, 1: 141, 182.

[13] Lee M. Friedman, *Pilgrims in a New Land* (Philadelphia, 1948), pp. 48, 394. As evidence of Lopez's early loyalty may be cited his turnover of a whaleboat and some gunpowder to Rhode Island in 1776, for which he was paid twenty-two pounds; see M. A. Gutstein, *The Jews of Newport* (New York, 1936), p. 183.

[14] Gutstein, *The Jews of Newport*, pp. 137, 187; Emory Washburn, *Historic Sketches of the Town of Leicester* (Boston, 1860), p. 120.

[15] *PAJHS* 19 (1911): 20; 35 (1939): 139; Gutstein, *The Jews of Newport*, p. 191.

[16] *Commerce of Rhode Island*, Vol. 2, passim; Daniel Crommelin of Amsterdam to Lopez, 30 June 1779 (Archives of Newport Historical Society). W. B. Clark, ed., *Naval Documents of the American Revolution*, 6 vols. (Washington, D.C., 1969-1972), 4: 85, 1058, 1231.

[17] Mears to Lopez, 4 July, 8 Oct. 1779; Jarvis and Russell to Lopez, 28 Apr. 1779.

[18] From Mears to Lopez, 24 Nov. 1779; from M. M. Hays to Lopez, 21 Sept. 1779. All the letters that follow are also to Lopez, and are in the Newport Historical Society Archives.

[19] From David Lopez, 20, 22 June 1779; 12 July 1781; from Moses Seixas, 2 Feb. 1780.

[20]From Isaac da Costa, 15 Apr. 1781; Jonas Philips, 15 Apr. 1781; Samuel Myers, 18 June 1781.

[21]From David Hayes of Bedford, 11 Mar. 1781; B. Judah, 4 Mar. 1782; M. M. Hays, 14 May 1782. Interestingly, one letter is from Lopez's father-in-law, 26 June 1781, and is in the Spanish-Jewish dialect, which is indicative of its persistence in America.

[22]From Mendes, 15 Aug. 1781.

[23]G. A. Kohut, *Ezra Stiles and the Jews* (New York, 1902), p. 138; Washburn, *Sketches of Leicester*, p. 124; Schappes, *Documentary History*, p. 581.

[24]*AJA* 3 (1951): 36; Friedman, *Pilgrims in a New Land*, p. 58; Henry Morais, *The Jews of Philadelphia* (Philadelphia, 1894), p. 24; S. Wolf, *The Jew as Patriot* (Philadelphia, 1895), p. 14. Both Morais and Wolf, along with others, were involved in perpetuating, if not creating, many of the legendary items in the Salomon career. Morais even credited Salomon with Portuguese ancestry, despite his Polish birth. Surprisingly, Harold Korn, in an article on the Receipt Book of Judah and M. M. Hays (*PAJHS* 28 [1922] : 225), reports the discovery of a voucher in the name of a Hyam Salomon, dated 10 July 1764. This he claims is the original Salomon, who must thus have been in this country well ahead of the usually accepted year 1772. This is not, however, necessarily so, since Salomon or Solomon was not an uncommon name then. In 1787, for example, two years after Salomon's death, a Hyam Salomon is reported in New York, as a judge in a case involving improper slaughter of an animal; see *PAJHS* 25 (1917): 47.

[25]*AJA* 3 (1951): 36; Marcus, *Documents*, p. 236; Schappes, *Documentary History*, p. 52; East, *Business Enterprise*, p. 157.

[26]*JCC* 11: 840; *PCC* 9: 58. A fuller account of this episode embroidered with unsupported details appears in C. E. Russell, *Haym Salomon and the Revolution* (New York, 1930), p. 85. Russell was, as it were, the spokesman of the later Salomon myth-builders and promoters of a monument to him in New York (to be dealt with elsewhere).

[27]Mss. Letter Book of Haym Salomon in the Archives of the American Jewish Historical Society in Waltham, Massachusetts, contains numerous letters, 1781-1784, to various correspondents in Virginia and England, and to his parents and other relatives in Poland and London. Cf. *PAJHS* 6 (1897): 47; Schappes, *Documentary History*, p. 577; H. S. Baron, *Haym Salomon* (New York, 1929), p. 75, for early examples of advertising, which appeared in the *Pennsylvania Journal and Weekly Advertiser* and the *Pennsylvania Packet*.

[28]On the financial relations between France and Revolutionary America, cf. W. C. Stinchcombe, *The American Revolution and the French*

Alliance (Syracuse, N. Y., 1969), pp. 88, 152. In a final report written as Superintendent of Finance, on 4 Nov. 1784, Robert Morris prophetically linked America's precarious financial situation with the hopes for peace and a strong government: "Our prospects . . . are far from flattering . . . unless our union be more strongly cemented . . . our independence [will be] but a name, our freecom a shadow, and our dignity a dream." Mss. *Diary*, Library of Congress, 4 Nov. 1784.

[29]Morris' *Diary*, 8 June 1781. Significantly, other Jews, aside from Haym Salomon, who appears in it most frequently, are reported here to have had dealings with the Superintendent of Finance. Among them were Isaac Moses, Jonas Phillips, Mordecai Sheftall, Manuel Josephson, Barnet Hart, Major David S. Franks, and M. M. Hays.

[30]Ibid., 8, 9, 27 Aug.; 10 Nov. 1781; 2 Apr. 1782. Among numerous other records of Salomon's business with Morris, cf. Mss. Letters of Morris (Library of Congress), A: 250, to Salomon, 10 Aug. 1784; C: 158, to Salomon, 2 Apr. 1782.

[31]Morris' *Diary*, 4, 10, 11 July 1782.

[32]Ibid., 12 July 1782. Cf. the notation on 17 July 1782: "Haym Salomon called often as several consultations respecting exchange were necessary." For Salomon's private business, note advertisements in *Pennsylvania Journal*, 22 Nov. 1783; 12 May 1784; *New York Packet*, 16 Dec. 1784; *New York Journal*, 27 May, 13 Dec. 1784, carrying a notice in English, French, and Dutch, simultaneously.

[33]Morris' *Diary*, 25 Mar., 31 July, 1, 2 Aug. 1782, for the record of the army pay crisis and Salomon's part in it.

[34]Ibid., 16 Aug., 16 Sept. 1782.

[35]Ibid., 5, 26, 28 Aug. 1782; 27 Sept. 1782. At this time too, Salomon offered to supply money to the British officers who were prisoners at Lancaster, in exchange for their bills on London. Replying to an inquiry by Joshua Isaacs, Salomon authorized him: "And draw on me for any sum by post or express, it shall be honored at sight, let the amount be ever so great. The bills may be drawn on New York or London, if they are endorsed by their commanding officer." East, *Business Enterprise*, pp. 158, 331; Russell, *Haym Salomon*, p. 190.

[36]This whole affair is reported fully and frequently in Morris; *Diary*, passim (between February and May 1783). In it are revealed Salomon's high standing and credit with Morris.

[37]The details of this extended monetary crisis, in the relief of which both Salomon and Isaac Moses figured prominently, are reported in Morris' *Diary* between May and October 1783 (passim).

[38]Ibid., 5 Mar. 1784; Marcus, *Documents*, p. 40; Wolf and Whiteman, *Jews of Philadelphia*, p. 111.

[39]Salomon's closing relations with Morris are reported in the *Diary* between February and September 1784 (passim). It is noteworthy that during this year also Haym Salomon, together with other Jewish merchants, such as Isaac Franks, Benjamin Nones, and Lion Moses, were converting to peacetime business, as is evident in their advertising. Salomon even arranged to move to New York. In his advertisement he proclaimed his services as "Broker to the Office of Finance," that "honored with its confidence, all those sums passed through his hands which the generosity of the French Monarch and the affections of the Merchants of the United Provinces prompted them to furnish us with, to enable us to support the expense of the war, and which have so much contributed to its successful and happy termination; this is a circumstance which has established his credit and reputation, and procured him the confidence of the Public . . ." (*Pennsylvania Packet*, 8 May 1784). Note the absence of any other claim to have extended financial assistance to the Revolution or to any of its participants, as asserted by later historians.

[40]*Papers of Madison*, W. T. Hutchison, ed., 7 vols. (Chicago, 1962), 4: 108; 5: 170; 6: 325.

[41]Ibid., 4: 18, 381, 400. James Ketchum, in *James Madison* (New York, 1971), p. 145, concludes that Madison used Salomon's patriotic conduct to "defend Jews generally against slanderous charges of selfish profiteering during the Revolution." This sentiment is certainly reflected in Madison's letter of 1827 to Haym M. Salomon, answering the latter's inquiry and reciting the father's generosity toward him during the war.

[42]*Salomon Letter Book*, in Archives of AJHS, to John Strettall of London, 24 June 1784. Cf. *Papers of Hamilton*, 3: 12; East, *Business Enterprise*, p. 158. Rendon's letter of 1783, testifying to Salomon's generosity, is quoted in Russell, *Haym Salomon*, p. 249.

Russell cited other instances of Salomon's generous assistance to many public figures during the Revolution. They were repeated by a succession of writers, who seemed to quote from one another without further documentary authority. They began with Simon Wolf and Henry Morais before 1900 and included a number of non-Jewish authors, such as Madison C. Peters and Samuel W. McCall, as well as Russell. The first and oldest of them was Charles P. Daly. This remarkable character of the nineteenth century was a New York judge, but also a versatile writer on many themes. In 1893 he published the *Settlement of the Jews in North America*, which was edited by Max. J. Kohler, a lifelong, dedicated historian of the Jews in America, who was later a principal opponent of the Salomon claims. Daly apparently set the pattern when he wrote that Salomon "supported delegates to Congress and officers of the government . . . , defraying their ordinary expenses. Among them were Jefferson, Madison, Lee, Steuben, Mifflin, St. Clair, Wilson, Monroe, and Mercer" (p. 58). Daly further reproached the ingratitude of the government for its failure to compensate Salomon's heirs (p. 60). Thus was built the Salomon mythology that persisted and found its way into the American Jewish consciousness in subsequent years, as will be explained further in a later chapter.

⁴³*Salomon Letter Book* in AJHS Archives, passim.

⁴⁴*PAJHS* 1 (1893): 59; 27 (1920): 461. *The Salomon Papers* in the AJHS Archives contain a long document recounting Salomon's difficulties with Jonas Phillips, who perversely held on to and refused to surrender the deed of the new Mikveh Israel synagogue, to which Salomon had been the largest contributor.

⁴⁵*Salomon Letter Book*, for letters to his father and uncle, written after he had reestablished communication with them in January, April, and July 1783.

⁴⁶*The Jewish Experience in America, Selected Essays from PAJHS* (New York, 1969), A. J. Karp, ed., 1: 23; Marcus, *Early American Jewry*, 2: 157.

⁴⁷*Independent Gazette, Pennsylvania Packet and Journal*, 8 Jan. 1785.

⁴⁸Wolf and Whiteman, *Jews of Philadelphia*, pp. 165, 429. See also Marcus, *Documents*, p. 442, for the report that three hundred Philadelphia merchants became insolvent in the postwar period. Among them were such prominent Jews as Haym Salomon, Michael Gratz, and Benjamin Nones; East (*Business Enterprise*, p. 217) quotes Gouverneur Morris, who was Robert Morris' deputy Superintendent of Finance, writing in 1785, that American merchants were "poorer by millions, as a result of the war, since depreciation made the risks of trade too great."

CHAPTER 6

¹David de S. Pool, *Portraits Etched in Stone* (New York, 1952), p. 414.

²J. P. Boyd, ed., *Papers of Jefferson* (Princeton, N.J., 1951), 3: 315, 322; W. T. Hutchinson, ed., *Papers of Madison* (Chicago, 1969), 3: 321. For the financing of Clark's Northwest Expedition, cf. J. O. Barnhart and D. L. Riker, *Indiana to 1816* (Indianapolis, 1971), p. 216; J. A. James, *Oliver Pollock* (New York, 1937), p. 172.

³*Papers of Jefferson*, 5: 61, 87, 110.

⁴Ibid., 3: 428; Pool, *Portraits*, p. 416; Hannah London, *Miniatures of Early Colonial Jews* (New York, 1953), p. 46; Henry Simonhoff, *Jewish Notables in America* (New York, 1956), p. 96.

⁵*Papers of Madison,* 3: 184.

⁶Ibid., 3: 185; W. P. Palmer, ed., *Calendar of Virginia State Papers,* 11 vols. (Richmond, Va., 1875-1893); also Microfilm, Library of Congress, 2: 230.

⁷*Papers of Jefferson,* 6: 197, 200, 322. The Nathan affair in all its intricacies was reviewed by Jefferson in 1783 in a letter to Edmund Randolph (*Papers,* 6: 319 ff.).

⁸Ibid., 6: 321; *Calendar of Virginia State Papers,* 3: 352: *Papers of Madison,* 5: 202.

⁹*Papers of Jefferson,* 6: 322; *Papers of Madison,* 3: 21, 65; 6: 154, 192, 278, 474; 7: 183, 216; *Letters of the Members of the Continental Congress* (Washington D.C., 1933), 6: 38; 7: 20, 39, 218, 286.

¹⁰*Papers of Jefferson,* 6: 324; *Papers of Madison,* 7: 200, 286; *Calendar of Virginia State Papers,* 3: 501; 4: 492, 585, 5: 259; 6: 2, 17, 27.

¹¹*PAJHS* 20 (1911): 94; Pool, *Portraits,* p. 415; Simonhoff, *Jewish Notables,* p. 95.

¹²Fitzpatrick, ed., *Writings of Washington,* 2: 190; *PAJHS* 11 (1903) : 182; 20 (1911) : 91; M. U. Schappes, *A Documentary History of the Jews in the United States* (New York, 1950), p. 586; E. Wolf and M. Whiteman, *History of the Jews of Philadelphia* (Philadelphia, 1957), pp. 29, 47.

¹³*Writings of Washington;* 4: 313, 408; *JCC* 3: 399; 4: 116, 175. Ironically, despite (perhaps because of) his pro-British associations, David Franks appears most frequently in the official records.

¹⁴*JCC* 9: 482; Peter Force, *American Archives,* (Washington, D.C., 1837-1853), Fourth Series, 6: 855; *Writings of Washington,* 9: 482. Late in 1776, Franks was given permission to go to New York with his clerk, Patrick Rice, who was also Jewish, despite his name. They were to collect for supplies to the British prisoners, but must give "their parole, not to give any intelligence to the enemy, and that they will return to this city." Force, *American Archives,* Fifth Series, 2: 1412.

¹⁵*JCC* 10: 75; *PAJHS* 3 (1895): 151; Joshua Trachtenberg, *Consider the Years* (Easton, Pa., 1944), p. 63. Although a pioneer settler of Easton, Myer Hart did not prosper during the Revolution. He was one of those who became bankrupt, a victim of the war, and he spent the rest of his life in poverty in Philadelphia (Trachtenberg, p. 23).

¹⁶Rebecca Franks rates a chapter in Elizabeth F. Ellett's *The Women of the American Revolution* (New York, 1850), 1: 178, despite her Loyalist affiliation. Cf. J. T. Scharf and T. Westcott, *History of Philadelphia* (Philadelphia, 1884), 1: 379, 400; Schappes, *A Documentary History,* p. 574; Wolf and Whiteman, *Jews of Philadelphia,* p. 88. The Jewish background of David Franks is well depicted in the famous letters of his

mother, Abigail, to another son, Naphtali, in London, Leo Hershkowitz and I. S. Mayer, eds., *Letters of the Franks Family, 1733-48* (Waltham, Mass., 1968).

[17] *JCC* 8: 131; 13: 105; *PCC,* Microfilm Roll 83, 1: 121, 587.

[18] *JCC* 12: 934, 1026, 1032, 1108; *PCC* 2: 319; *Writings of Washington,* 6: 296; 13: 158; *Calendar of Correspondence of Gen. Washington with his officers* (Washington, 1915), 1: 782; 2: 814, 827. Cf. *PAJHS* 28 (1922): 254; Wolf and Whiteman, *Jews of Philadelphia,* 88. Interesting sidelights on the Franks case, his dismissal and expulsion, are presented in J. R. Marcus, *American Jewry: Eighteenth Century Documents* (Cincinnati, 1959), 243. Franks claimed to have delivered 500,000 rations by December 1778, for which the British government was to have paid him through the firm of Nesbitt, Drummond, and Franks, of which his brother, Moses, was a partner. He complained that the rate paid was inadequate. It was a letter to Moses that brought on all his troubles. In this letter David Franks jibed at the "justice" meted out by the radicals in Pennsylvania: "People are taken and confined at the pleasure of every scoundrel. Oh! What a situation Britain has left its friends in. . . ." Nevertheless, Franks could scarcely object to his own treatment, since he was acquitted. A friend even defended Franks in the press for sending the offensive letter to his brother. Writing in the *Pennsylvania Packet,* 13 May 1779, he protested that the reported inflation of prices in Franks's letter was intended merely to justify an increase in the ration price to one shilling. But Franks had added the offending words: "And all for liberty." The letter defending Franks provoked a reply in the press, and thus had he become the subject of a polemic and public exchange of views, prior to his final expulsion.

[19] *JCC* 18: 1054; *PAJHS* 30 (1926): 80.

[20] Cecil Roth, "Some Jewish Loyalists," in *PAJHS* 30 (1926): 96.

[21] *PAJHS* 1 (1893): 54, 103; Lee M. Friedman, *Jewish Pioneers and Patriots* (Philadelphia, 1942), pp. 238, 248; Marcus, *Documents,* p. 289. Interestingly, Rebecca's aunt, Phila, was the wife of the New York Tory General, Oliver DeLancey, and she too lived in England after the Revolution; see Lorenzo Sabine, *Biographical Sketches of Loyalists* (Boston, 1864), 1: 444.

[22] *JCC* 5: 652; 7: 302; 9: 886; 10: 112; *PCC* 20: 179, 190, 195; F. S. Klein, *A History of the Jews in Lancaster* (Lancaster, Pa., 1955), p. 13; *PAJHS* 1 (1893): 65; 9 (1901): 29.

[23] *PCC* 2: 359; 20: 179, 335; *Pennsylvania Packet,* 6 July 1779. Cf. Anita Lebeson, *Pilgrim People* (New York, 1950), p. 132. The Lancaster Jews, headed by Joseph Simon, pledged themselves in 1777 to maintain one or

more messengers to communicate with Washington's army, "with and for intelligence."

[24]N. Taylor Phillips, "Family History," *PAJHS* 2 (1894): 45; 21 (1913): 172.

[25]*PAJHS* 25 (1915): 128.

[26]Robert Morris' *Diary* (manuscript, Library of Congress), 12 Feb. 1783; Wolf and Whiteman, *Jews of Philadelphia*, p. 176. Jonas Phillips was one of the first Jewish Masons in America, who were thus linked with the contemporary liberal tradition. He was listed as one of those "who fought on the side of liberty and independence in the War of Revolution"; see *PAJHS* 19 (1911): 28.

[27]*JCC* 4: 396; 14: 734, 744; Marcus, *Documents*, pp. 330, 428; *AJA* 6 (1949): 9; Pool, *Portraits*, p. 243.

[28]*PCC* 1: 471; Pool, *Portraits*, p. 478; I. M. Fein, *Making of a Jewish Community* (Philadelphia, 1971), pp. 13, 25.

[29]Fein, *Jewish Community, Baltimore*, p. 9; *PAJHS* 25 (1917): 143; 34 (1937): 273.

[30]*PAJHS* 34 (1937): 271; *The Jewish Experience in America, Selected Essays from PAJHS*, A. J. Karp, ed. (New York, 1969), 1: 230, 340; Fein, *Jewish Community, Baltimore*, p. 9.

[31]*JCC* 30: 292; *PCC* 1: 589; 4: 322; *AJA* 15 (1963): 90; Fein, *Jewish Community, Baltimore*, p. 10. Hart was later the father-in-law of Ezekiel N. Salomon, Haym Salomon's oldest son.

[32]*JCC* 7: 188; Peter Force, *American Archives*, Fifth Series, 3: 1597, 1601; *AJHQ* 58 (1968): 15; Leo Hershkowitz, "Wills of Early New York Jews," in *AJHQ* 56 (1966): 173.

[33]*JCC* 5: 483; Peter Force, *American Archives*, Fifth Series, 1: 198; Morris' *Diary*, 3, 16, 23 Jan.; 24, 27 Feb. 1783. Cf. *PAJHS* 37 (1947): 115; Marcus, *Documents*, p. 83; Schappes, *Documentary History*, p. 588; Lee M. Friedman, *Pilgrims in a New Land* (Philadelphia, 1948), p. 71.

[34]*JCC* 19: 303, 328; *PAJHS* 2 (1894): 157.

[35]*Papers of Madison*, 2: 78, 252, 273; *Pennsylvania Packet* 20 July 1779, offering land for sale, and signed by Barnard Gratz as secretary for the company. For the many diverse business activities of the Gratz brothers, cf. *PAJHS* 20 (1911): 85; *The Jewish Experience*, 1: 209; W. V. Byars, *B & M Gratz* (Jefferson City, Mo., 1916), passim; I. I. Katz, *The Jews in Michigan* (Detroit, 1955), 43.

[36]Wolf and Whiteman, *Jews of Philadelphia*, pp. 65, 165, 179; AJA Tenth Anniversary Volume (Cincinnati, 1958), p. 214.

[37]*PCC* 1: 161; *JCC* 28: 350; Pool, *Portraits*, p. 281.

[38]Pool, *Portraits*, p. 283.

[39]*PAJHS* 27 (1920) : 374; Henry A. Alexander, *Notes on the Alexander Family of South Carolina and Georgia* (Atlanta, 1954), p. 103.

[40]*JCC* 7: 298; Lopez Letters (Newport Historical Society), from Mears 4, 30 July, 8 Oct. 1779; *AJA* 1 (1949): 32; *AJHQ* 52 (1962): 303; J. R. Marcus, *Early American Jewry* (New York, 1951), 1: 174; L. Hühner, *Jews in Colonial and Revolutionary Times* (New York, 1959), p. 90.

[41]R. R. Hinman, *A Historical Collection of Connecticut During the War of Revolution* (Hartford, 1842), passim, for the Jews in Revolutionary Connecticut. Cf. Pool, *Portraits*, p. 299; Jeanette W. Rosenbaum, *Myer Myers, Goldsmith* (Philadelphia, 1954), p. 42. A Manuel Myers, a prominent New York merchant, also spent the war years in Stamford, Connecticut (Pool, *Portraits*, p. 49).

[42]*PAJHS* 27 (1920): 446; AJA Tenth Anniversary Volume, p. 187; Alexander, *Notes on the Alexander Family*, pp. 69, 77, 87.

[43]Miriam K. Freund, *Jewish Merchants in Colonial America* (New York, 1939), p. 44; *PAJHS* 11 (1903): 83; 12 (1904): 104; 35 (1939): 208. Significantly, Myer Polock and M. M. Hays were business partners in Newport and became insolvent just before the Revolution. Both refused to take an oath of loyalty in Newport. Polock turned Loyalist and had quite an unusual career in New York and the West Indies thereafter; Hays, on the other hand, settled in Boston, where he prospered. He had an exchange of letters with Robert Morris on the financial needs of the country (Manuscript Letters of Morris in Library of Congress, C; 312, 436).

[44]*PAJHS* 20 (1912): 95; *The Jewish Experience in America* 1: 103.

[45]*AJA* 7 (1955): 148.

[46]Marcus, *Documents*, p. 232. Cf. J. R. Marcus, *The Colonial American Jew* (Detroit, 1970), 3: 1275, for the early patriotic activities of the Jews in Savannah, including especially Mordecai Sheftall, who was engaged in revolutionary demonstrations as early as 1774.

[47]B. A. Elzas, *The Jews of South Carolina* (Philadelphia, 1905), p. 88.

[48]*JCC* 11 : 850; Marcus, *Documents*, p. 272; Wolf and Whiteman, *Jews of Philadelphia*, p. 99. Some ten Jews were listed as refugees from Charleston in Philadelphia, according to Elzas, pp. 35, 106.

[49]*PAJHS* 48 (1959): 177, 193. For the Jewish community that developed at Georgetown after the Revolution, cf. Elzas, *Jews of South Carolina*, p. 241.

[50]*JCC* 18 : 872, 913, 934; 21: 899, 1086. Cf. W. A. Wates, ed., *Stub Entries and Indents Against South Carolina* (Columbia, S. C., 1957), pp. 145, 207, 237, 256; A. S. Salley, ed., *Documents Relating to the History of South Carolina* (Columbia, S.C., 1908), pp. 86, 212; Elzas, *Jews of South Carolina*, p. 105.

[51] *PAJHS* 29 (1925): 143; A. D. Candler, ed., *Revolutionary Records of Georgia* (Atlanta, 1908), 1: 51, 342, 347, 659.

[52] *PCC*, Microfilm Roll 26: 184; *PAJHS* 2 (1894): 119; B. G. Sack, *History of the Jews in Canada* (Montreal, 1945), 1: 73; Marcus, *Colonial American Jew*, 3: 1268.

[53] *PAJHS* 23 (1915): 84; Marcus, *Early American Jewry*, 1: 276, 285.

CHAPTER 7

[1] G. A. Kohut, *Ezra Stiles and the Jews* (New York, 1902), pp. 16, 35; Ezra Stiles, *Literary Diary* (New York, 1901), 2: 131; *PAJHS* 1 (1893): 151; 40 (1950): 37; Wallace Brown, *The Good Americans* (New York, 1969), p. 245; B. G. Sack, *History of the Jews in Canada* (Montreal, 1945), 1: 65.

[2] *PAJHS* 46 (1956): 21; Friedman, *Jewish Pioneers and Patriots* (Philadelphia, 1942), p. 142; Marcus, *Early American Jewry* (New York, 1951), 1: 154; *Colonial American Jew* (Detroit, 1970), 3: 1270.

[3] M. A. Gutstein, *To Bigotry No Sanction* (New York, 1958), pp. 86, 97; Marcus, *American Jewry: Eighteenth Century Documents* (Cincinnati, 1959), p. 281.

[4] *PAJHS* 4 (1897): 88; 23 (1915):166; 37 (1947):163; 38 (1948): 88. Cf. Henry Onderdonck, *Revolutionary Incidents of Suffolk and King's Counties* (New York, 1849): 99; Roland Van Zandt, *Chronicles of the Hudson* (New Brunswick, N.J.: Rutgers University Press, 1971): 39, for an account of the bloody civil warfare which ravaged the whole area during the Revolution.

[5] *Royal Commission on Loyalist Claims* (Oxford, England, 1915), p. 267. An affidavit by George Rowe, supporting Moses Hart's claim, contained some material confirming Ezra Stiles' charge that there were Jewish informers in Newport. He testified he knew the Harts and always considered them to be good subjects: "Received much information from the Ladies. The men acted with great caution." Rowe estimated the Hart estate as worth £2000. Cf. Lorenzo Sabine, *Biographical Sketches of Loyalists* (Boston, 1864), 2: 527, for an account of Isaac Hart's tragic career as a Loyalist, ending in violent death; also M. A. Gutstein, *The Story of the Jews of Newport* (New York, 1936), p. 184, and Catherine S. Crary, *The Price of Loyalty* (New York, 1973), p. 196.

[6] *PAJHS* 11 (1903): 192; Sabine, *Loyalists*, 2: 196; Marcus, *Documents,* p. 273; Friedman, *Pioneers and Patriots*, p. 147.

[7] Sack, *Jews in Canada* 1: 49, 65; I. I. Katz, *The Jews in Michigan* (Detroit, 1955), pp. 13, 21, 34, 136.

[8] *AJA* 1 (1949): 57; 14 (1962): 93, 97.

⁹*PAJHS* 3(1895): 83; 38 (1948): 81, 103; 45 (1955): 54; Marcus, *Documents*, p. 282.

¹⁰Marcus, *Documents*, p. 194; M. U. Schappes, *A Documentary History of the Jews in the United States* (New York, 1950), pp. 50, 577; H. B. Grinstein, *Rise of the Jewish Community of New York* (Philadelphia, 1945), p. 69; A. C. Flick, *Loyalism in New York* (New York, 1901), p. 96. Cf. E. C. Knight, *New York in the Revolution* (Albany, 1901), p. 56, for the Address of Loyalty to the crown in 1776, containing nearly 1,000 names, among them some 15 Jews.

¹¹David De S. Pool, *Portraits Etched in Stone* (New York, 1952), p. 272; *PAJHS* 27 (1920): 387; M. Whitman, *Copper for America* (New York, 1971), pp. 4, 23; William Kelby, *Orderly Book of the Three Battalions of Loyalists* (New York, 1917), p. 115, for a list of some sixteen Loyalist Jews in New York under the British.

¹²Pool, *Portraits*, p. 277.

¹³*PAJHS* 6 (1897): 123; 18 (1909): 117; *AJA* 6 (1954): 77; Pool, *Portraits*, p. 398; Marcus, *Documents*, p. 436.

¹⁴*AJA* 6 (1954): 82; Pool, *Portraits*, p. 351.

¹⁵Marcus. *Documents*, pp. 241, 290. Cf. supra, Chapter 5, for a full account of David Franks and his family (Sabine, *Loyalists*, 1: 366).

¹⁶Cecil Roth, "A Jewish Voice of Peace," in *PAJHS* 31 (1928): 33; Marcus, *The Colonial American Jew*, 3: 1296.

¹⁷*PAJHS* 31 (1928): 44

¹⁸Ibid., p. 49.

¹⁹Ibid., 13 (1905): 113.

²⁰Isaac de Pinto, *Letters on the American Troubles* (London, 1776). pp. 2, 15, 20.

²¹Ibid., pp. 34, 40, 52.

²²Ibid., p. 89.

²³Ibid., pp. 47, 72, 88.

²⁴*PAJHS* 13 (1905): 122.

²⁵*PAJHS* 19 (1910): 64; Marcus, Early American Jewry, 2: 219; B. A. Elzas, *The Jews of South Carolina* (Philadelphia, 1905), p. 98; Lebeson, *Jewish Pioneers*, p. 228.

²⁶*PAJHS* 38 (1928): 104; *AJA* 17 (1965): 27.

²⁷Elzas, *Jews of South Carolina*, pp. 97, 102.

²⁸*AJA* 7 (1955): 147; 9 (1957): 69; *PAJHS* 38 (1928): 93; Marcus, *Early American Jewry*, 2: 321, 336; *Documents*, p. 208; Wallace Brown, *The King's Friends* (Providence, R.I., 1965), p. 47.

²⁹*PAJHS* 1 (1893): 60; J. T. Scharf and T. Westcott, *History of Philadelphia* (Philadelphia, 1884), 1: 300. Cf. T. Westcott, *Names of Persons Who Took the Oath of Allegiance in Pennsylvania* (Philadelphia,

1865), 7. Mordecai Levy is identified as the "Dutch butcher," which may refer to his origin in Germany. Other Jews listed here as taking the oath were Eleazer Levy, "late of New York, trader"; Jacob Franks, silversmith; Abraham Seixas, "formerly an officer in the Charleston militia"; and surprisingly, Isaac Franks, who was an officer in Washington's army, and who took the oath as late as 1784, for reasons not given.

³⁰Scharf and Westcott, *History of Philadelphia*, 1: 344; *Pennsylvania Archives*, Fourth Series, 3: 1937. Despite its role as the principal seat of Revolution, Philadephia was also a hotbed of Loyalist sentiment, expecially among the Quakers. This became evident during the occupation by the British in 1777 when many prominent persons rallied to the support of General Howe. Their daughters, including Rebecca Franks, participated in the Meschianza, the grand farewell party to Howe. Several Jews, then living in the city, also signed a petition to the British commander, asking for the continued use of colonial currency for the convenience of business. It is, however, noteworthy that not one Jew appears in the long list of attainders that followed the recapture of the city in 1778.

³¹A. D. Candler, ed., *Revolutionary Records of Georgia* (Atlanta, 1908), 1: 612; 3: 26; Elzas, *Jews of South Carolina*, p. 124.

³²Charles Reznikoff, *The Jews of Charleston* (Philadelphia, 1950), p. 45.

CHAPTER 8

¹M. U. Schappes, *A Documentary History of the Jews in the United States* (New York, 1950), p. 80; R. Learsi, *The Jews in America* (Cleveland, 1954), p. 51; J. W. Blau and Salo W. Baron, *The Jews of the United States, A Documentary History* (New York, 1963), 1: 57; Raphael Mahler, *A History of Modern Jewry, 1780-1815* (New York, 1971), p. 37.

²J. R. Marcus, *American Jewry: Eighteenth Century Documents* (Cincinnati, 1959), p. 147; Schappes, *Documentary History*, p. 61; M. A. Gutstein, *The Story of the Jews of Newport* (New York, 1936), p. 199; E. Wolf and M. Whiteman, *History of the Jews of Philadelphia* (Philadelphia, 1957), p. 147.

³Max Farrand, *Records of the Federal Convention* (New Haven, Conn., 1966), 3: 78; D. De S. Pool, *Portraits Etched in Stone* (New York, 1952), 353; *PAJHS* 2 (1894): 107; 27 (1920) : 32.

⁴*AJA* 17 (1965) : 140. For a new spirit of assurance among Jews, cf. R. Marcus, *Early American Jewry* (New York, 1951), 2: 377, 529, 546; B. Elzas, *The Jews of Charleston* (Philadelphia, 1905), pp. 120, 166, 181; Charles Reznikoff, *Jews of Charleston* (Philadelphia, 1950), p. 56, quoting

the *South Carolina State Gazette* that "the shackles of religious distinctions are now no more," in the report of a synagogue dedication 10 Sept. 1794.

⁵Sanford H. Cobb, *The Rise of Religious Liberty in America* (New York, 1902), p. 482; *AJA* 10 (1958): 14; Edward Eitches, "Maryland's Jew Bill," *AJHQ* 60 (1971): 258-278. Despite the emancipating trend, the sentiment of Dr. Benjamin Rush, an enlightened friend of the Jews in Philadelphia, is noteworthy, as expressed in a letter to his wife, 27 June 1787. He had attended the wedding of a daughter of Jonas Phillips, and "after this, I was led into futurity, and anticipated the time foretold by the prophets when this once-beloved race of men shall be restored to the divine favor and when they shall unite with Christians . . . in celebrating the praises of a common and universal Saviour." *Letters of Benjamin Rush* (Princeton, N.J., 1951), 1: 429. Interestingly, too, some years later, Hannah Adams of the famous Boston family wrote a flattering history of the Jews, but all in behalf of a movement to convert them and thus "meliorate their condition." It was the first history of the Jews written in America: *The History of the Jews . . . to the Nineteenth Century*, 2 vols. (Boston, 1812).

⁶Cobb, *The Rise of Religious Liberty,* 513; *AJA* 10 (1958): 66; Learsi, *The Jews in America*, p. 48.

⁷*PAJHS* 37 (1947): 171, for the "Letter of a German Jew to the President of the Congress of the United States" (1783).

⁸*Pennsylvania Packet,* 29 June 1784; Marcus, *Documents*, pp. 286, 303.

⁹*AJA* 7 (1955): 66; *AJHQ* 59 (1969): 23.

¹⁰*PAJHS* 30 (1926): 88; *AJA* 6 (1954): 99; Gutstein, *The Jews of Newport*, p. 155.

¹¹Marcus, *Documents*, p. 167; M. C. Peters, *Justice to the Jew* (New York, 1899), p. 45; also *The Masons as Makers of America* (New York, 1917.), passim. Samuel Oppenheimer suggests that the considerable Jewish membership in Masonry during the Revolutionary era is significant and indicative of a strong bond with Washington in communicating with him on religious freedom. It also reflected an attachment to the cause of the Revolution; see *PAJHS* 19 (1909): 41, 92.

¹²Marcus, *Documents*, p. 167; *PAJHS* 19 (1909): 92, on Moses Seixas' dual role as a Jew and as a Mason.

¹³Leon Hühner, *Jews in Colonial and Revolutionary Times* (New York, 1959), p. 119; *PAJHS* 12 (1904): 59. Somewhat extravagantly, Cohen equated Washington with Moses, Joshua, and other Biblical figures, "who were raised up by God for the deliverance of our Nation."

¹⁴Marcus, *Documents*, p. 168; H. B. Grinstein, *The Rise of the Jewish Community of New York* (Philadelphia, 1945), p. 413. Significantly, the first public recognition by a national Jewish organization of this historic

exchange between Washington and the Jews in 1790 occurred in 1876, when the third annual assembly of the Union of American Hebrew Congregations met in Washington. The group traveled to Mount Vernon to commemorate the exchange of letters as their contribution to the centennial celebration of Independence. There they witnessed the planting of a tree at Washington's graveside, and a number of addresses were delivered, among others by Simon Wolf and Rabbi Isaac M. Wise; see *Proceedings of the Union of American Hebrew Congregations* (Cincinnati, 1873-1879), 1:265. Interestingly, in this year too, B'nai B'rith dedicated a statue to Religious Freedom in Philadelphia, executed by the Jewish-American sculptor, Moses Ezekiel. The Jews of America thus paid double homage to the principle of religious freedom, in commemoration of the centennial. Thereby they also ushered in the stage of awareness and a desire for the recognition of the Jewish role in the Revolution.

[15]Marcus, *Documents*, p. 40; *AJA* 7 (1955); 150.

[16]M. U. Schappes, "Anti-Semitism and Reaction, 1795-1800," in A. J. Karp, ed., *The Jewish Experience in America, Selected Essays from PAJHS* (New York, 1969) 1: 382, 388. In violent language Joseph Dennie, The New Hampshire Federalist, denounced "the Jewish and canting descendants" of old-time revolutionaries. Cf. AJA Tenth Anniversary Volume of Essays (Cincinnati, 1958), p. 193.

[17]J. L. E. Shecut, *Topographical, Historical, and other Sketches of Charleston* (Charleston, 1819), 30; H. N. Brackenridge, ed., *Speeches on the Jew Bill* (Philadelphia, 1829), 115; Reznikoff, *Jews of Charleston*, pp. 109, 287, for an affirmation of the republicanism of the Charleston Jews in 1800: "Ere long a free, unmixed, and uncontaminated republican form of government will arise from the abolition of the sedition and alien laws."

[18]Schappes, in *Jewish Experiences in America*, 1: 367; Marcus, *Early American Jewry*, 2: 377, 494, 514. Cf. E. P. Link, *Democratic-Republican Societies* (New York, 1965), p. 51, for anti-Jewish slurs even in Republican writing. More numerous, however, were anti-Jewish Federalist aspersions, as in the case of Israel Israel, no longer a practicing Jew, yet derided as a Jewish tavernkeeper (Link, p. 57). Abraham Sasportas was accused of being a French member of a democratic society, than which no charge could be more damning (Link, p. 87).

CHAPTER 9

[1]See supra, Chapter 3, for full accounts of Franks and Bush and their quest of government posts during and after the Revolution. Cf. *PCC* 4:

617; Gaillard Hunt, *Calendar of Applications for Office during the Presidency of Washington* (Washington, D.C., 1901), pp. 20, 46.

[2] *PCC* 18: 667; D. de S. Pool, *Portraits Etched in Stone* (New York, 1952), p. 259; J. R. Marcus, *American Jewry: Eighteenth Century Documents* (Cincinnati, 1959), p. 293.

[3] Hunt, *Calendar of Applications*, pp. 91, 95, 114; "Sheftall Diaries," in *AJHQ* 54 (1964): 275.

[4] *Applications for Public Office under President Jefferson* (Microfilm in National Archives), rolls 7, 8, passim: *PAJHS* 48 (1958) : 1.

[5] Microfilm *Applications*, roll 9; J. M. Fein, *The Making of an American Jewish Community. The History of Baltimore* (Philadelphia, 1971), p. 21.

[6] Microfilm *Applications*, roll 9.

[7] Ibid., rolls 9, 10. It is noteworthy how many of these applicants were widely and highly regarded by their fellow citizens. Some thirty Philadelphia merchants, none Jewish, recommended David B. Nones in 1823.

[8] Ibid., *under President Monroe*, roll 10. Cf. J. T. Scharf, *History of Delaware* (Philadelphia, 1888), I, 321, 324.

[9] Microfilm *Applications, under President Madison*, roll 4.

[10] Ibid., *under President Monroe*, roll 10.

[11] *United States Naval Documents Relative to the Quasi-War, 1798-99* (Washington, D.C., 1936), 4, passim; 5: 255.

[12] Ibid., 6: 387; 7: 92, 374.

[13] Microfilm *Applications, under President Monroe*, roll 10 (24 Apr. 1818; 2 Aug., 12 Oct. 1822).

[14] Ibid., roll 10 (29 Apr. 1822; 10 Jan. 1824); *PAJHS* 12 (1904) : 163.

[15] *Applications,* roll 10, passim.

[16] M. U. Schappes, *A Documentary History of the Jews in the United States* (New York, 1950), p. 96; Hannah London, *Portraits of Jews* (New York, 1927), p. 26.

[17] *U.S. Naval Documents, 1798-99*, 4, passim, on Moses Myers, who was U.S. Naval Agent at Norfolk in 1798; cf. *AJA* 2 (1949) : 271; AJA Tenth Anniversary Volume (Cincinnati, 1958), pp. 201, 213.

[18] *PAJHS* 27 (1920) : 482; *AJA* 2 (1949) : 271; Leon Hühner, *Jews in America in Colonial and Revolutionary Times* (New York, 1959), pp. 136, 145.

[19] *PAJHS* 12 (1904) : 164. A son of Mordecai Sheftall, Benjamin, lost his life on a French privateer, *The Industry*, in 1794, in some unexplained way, but the *Savannah Gazette* printed an emotional poem in his memory, as one who possessed "A heart, alive to the calls of honor and humanity": *AJHQ* 54 (1966) : 266.

[20] *U.S. Naval Documents, 1798-99*, 4: 417, 440; 7: 63, 350; *PAJHS* 26

(1918): 173; *AJA* 17 (1965): 151; cf. Marcus, *Documents,* p. 51, for a revealing letter by Rebecca Samuel of Petersburg, Virginia, to her mother in Germany in 1791. Her husband, Hyam, was a silversmith and watchmaker. Rebecca complained that there was no "Yiddishkeit" in Petersburg. She was especially critical of the few Jews there, since "they were all German itinerants who came to America during the war as soldiers." Here "anyone can do what he wants. There is no rabbi to excommunicate anyone. Jew and Gentile are as one. There is no *galut* here." In a labored way she explained that there were more German Gentiles and Jews in Philadelphia and New York. In those cities, the Gentiles "cannot forsake their anti-Jewish prejudice . . . and that's what makes the *galut.*" Rebecca missed the synagogue and Torah there, and the family planned to move to Charleston, where there was more Jewish life. Nevertheless, she concluded: "You cannot know what a wonderful country this is for the common man."

²¹E. Wolf and M. Whiteman, *History of The Jews of Philadelphia* (Philadelphia, 1957), p. 284.

²²*PAJHS* 27 (1920) : 495, for a report by Rabbi J. J. Lyons that Joseph B. Nones was badly wounded in a naval battle off the Barbary coast in 1815. Cf. Wolf and Whiteman, *The Jews of Philadelphia,* pp. 288, 292, for the observation that one-third of all Jewish men between seventeen and forty-five years of age in Philadelphia, served in the War of 1812, totaling some forty in all, an incredible percentage for a war of such minor consequence.

²³*PAJHS* 12 (1904): 164; 26 (1918): 173; Anita L. Lebeson, *Pilgrim People* (New York, 1950), p. 175; J. G. Fredman and L. A. Falk, *Jews in American Wars* (New York, 1942), p. 24; Fein, *The Jewish Community of Baltimore,* p. 29.

²⁴Wolf and Whiteman, *Jews of Philadelphia,* p. 291; Lebeson, *Pilgrim People,* p. 175.

²⁵H. A. Alexander, *Notes on the Alexander Family* (Atlanta, 1954), p. 62; *AJA* 2 (1949): 271; 7 (1955): 151. Cf. *The Historical Collections of the Joseph Habersham Chapter of DAR of Georgia* (Atlanta, 1902), 1: 341, for an unusual account of a Captain Samuel Mendes Marks of Charleston, who served both in the Revolution and in the War of 1812. He went down with his ship in 1812. Born in the Danish West Indies, he settled in Charleston and married a Jewish woman of Portuguese origin there. There is an inquiry here about him by one R. B., identified only as a descendant of Rev. Hartwig Cohen of Charleston.

²⁶*PAJHS* 12 (1904): 164; Rufus Learsi, *Jews in America* (Cleveland, 1954), p. 56; Lebeson, *Pilgrim People,* p. 176.

²⁷Wolf and Whiteman, *Jews of Philadelphia,* p. 289; J. R. Marcus,

Memoirs of American Jews (Philadelphia, 1955), 1: 52; London, *Portraits,* p. 37, for a report that Major Myers was wounded at Crysler's Field on the Niagara Frontier. The sources for Myers include his own "Reminiscences," and "Biographical Sketches of the Bailey, Myers and Mason Families, 1776-1905" (all interrelated by marriage).

²⁸Lebeson, *Pilgrim People,* pp. 175, 229. Alfred Mordecai also recorded his extensive military career in an autobiography.

²⁹Alexander, *Notes on the Alexander Family,* p. 62; Rosenbloom, *A Biographical Dictionary of Early American Jews* (Lexington, Ky., 1960), passim, which lists the Jewish soldiers both in the Revolution and the War of 1812.

³⁰*PAJHS* 26 (1918): 194; Henry Morais, *The Jews of Philadelphia* (Philadelphia, 1894), p. 469; Wolf and Whiteman, *Jews of Philadelphia,* pp. 284, 468. Uriah Levy was ak ardent patriot who had a great admiration for Thomas Jefferson. He presented a bronze statue of Jefferson to the American people which showed him holding a scroll with the Declaration of Independence inscribed on it. It symbolized Levy's faith in democracy and still stands in the rotunda of the Capitol *PAJHS,* 3 [1895]: 97).

³¹Lebeson, *Pilgrim People,* p. 188.

³²Isaac Goldberg, *Major Noah* (Philadelphia, 1936), passim, for the outline of his life. An earlier, more intimate account of Noah is in C. P. Daly, *The Settlement of the Jews in North America* (New York, 1893), pp. 104-138.

³³Microfilm *Applications for Office Under President Madison,* roll 6 (25 Aug., 27 Nov., 17 Dec. 1810). Noah was able to marshal great support for his application, as is evidenced by the many letters attached to it.

³⁴Ibid. (7 Jan. 1811).

³⁵Ibid. (13 Jan., 6 Mar., 24 May 1811).

³⁶Ibid., 17 June 1811.

³⁷Ibid., 7 Apr. 1813; 16 Apr. 1816; Goldberg, *Major Noah,* p. 111.

³⁸*Applications under President Monroe,* Microfilm roll 10, 24 July 1820.

³⁹Ibid., 24 July 1820.

⁴⁰A. Nevins, ed., *The Diary of J. Q. Adams* (New York, 1951), p. 244; *PAJHS* 8 (1900) : 100; *Niles' Register* 17 (1820): 371, quoting Noah's appeal to the New York State Legislature in 1820 for the sale of Grand Island to him for the settlement of Jews: "Here the Jews can have their Jerusalem, . . . here they can erect their temple. . . ." Significantly, Noah's project did not seem visionary to his contemporary, Elkanah Watson, the hard-headed promoter of western expansion, who reproached the Legislature for rejecting the sale to Noah: "One thing is certain; They would have brought an immense wealth in their train; and I doubt not

that a splendid city would soon have arisen . . . ; in one sense it would . . . have transferred the City of New York to the borders of the lakes." *History of the Rise, Progress, and Existing Conditions of the Western Canals* (Albany, 1820), p.104. Lewis F. Allen, who knew Noah and who later owned most of Grand Island, also thought that his projected settlement there was potentially feasible and useful as part of the Erie Canal boom; *PAJHS* 8 (1900): 100.

[41]Bertram W. Korn, "German-Jewish Intellectual Influences on American Jewish Life, 1824-1972," (B. G. Rudolph Lecture in Judaic Studies, Syracuse, N. Y., 1972).

CHAPTER 10

[1]Microfilm *Pension Applications* (National Archives), BLWT 742-400 (1789); RIBL-WT-3410 (1791).

[2]Ibid., W 11, 263.

[3]Ibid., W 4551.

[4]Ibid., W 773.

[5]Ibid., W 8037. Inquiries about Levi's record are reported from his descendants, a Miss Leilah Forman of Kentucky and a Mrs. Rebecca Dunn.

[6]Ibid., S 40,279. Cf. J. L. Blau, and S.W. Baron, *The Jews of the United States: A Documentary History* (New York, 1964), 1: 71, 252.

[7]*Pension Applications*, W 20,830. Interestingly, Cardozo presented his affidavit to Abraham Moïse, justice of the peace and member of a prominent Jewish family in Charleston.

[8]Ibid., R 9931; W 21599. Abraham Cohen had died in 1789, but his widow, now Mrs. Cecilia Solomons, again a widow, seventy-one years old, claimed a pension in the name of her first husband, Cohen.

[9]Ibid., R 2108.

[10]Ibid., S 39061.

[11]Ibid., W 21, 558; *PAJHS* 12 (1904) : 57; AJA Tenth Anniversary Volume (Cincinnati, 1958), p. 226; Sara Ervin, *South Carolinians in the Revolution* (Ypsilanti, Mich., 1949), p. 35.

[12]*Pension Applications*, S 31,959; J. R. Marcus, *American Jewry: Eighteenth Century Documents* (Cincinnati, 1959), pp. 39, 237.

[13]*Pension Applications*, S 41, 549.

[14]Ibid., W 4792. Russell's case offers an exhaustive record of a Jewish Revolutionary veteran. Both his service and his subsequent extended effort to obtain a pension are revealing of a single Jew's troubled problems during more than half a century. Significantly, by 1891, the Russell

case takes on a different aspect, as his descendants inquire about his record and proudly apply for membership in the Revolutionary societies. Thus Waring Russell, a grandson and Treasurer of Chatham County, Georgia, inquires about his grandfather's war record.

[15]Cf. supra, Chapter 6, for the full record of Nathan's case.

[16]JCC 17: 572, 592; 18: 955, 1074, 1112; 20: 459, 821, 849; 21: 473; PCC (Microfilm, Archives) 4: 685, 20: 621, 629; Sheftall Papers (Archives of the AJHS), 1: 63, 119. The Sheftall claims, if not the largest, were perhaps the most intricate and reveal the family's complete involvement in the Revolution, both in its financial and military aspects. Unlike the Salomon claims, which were made half a century after the Revolution, the Sheftalls pressed theirs immediately, as is evident in the Revolutionary sources.

[17]*Sheftall Papers* (AJHS Archives), 2: 126, 131, 147. Cf. *AJA* 7 (1955): 150; Marcus, *Documents,* p. 271, for a recital of the Sheftalls' Revolutionary troubles.

[18]*AJA* 8 (1956): 47; M. C. Peters, *The Jew as a Patriot* (New York, 1902), p. 53, for an early version of the Salomon story, which became standardized in subsequent years. Peters was one of several authors, both Jewish and non-Jewish, who then expounded the role of the Jews in war and peace, to counter a wave of anti-Semitism during the period. Out of this background emerged the saga of Haym Salomon as the "Financier of the Revolution." It was the title of an "Unwritten Chapter," delivered as a talk in 1911, by M. C. Peters. It was included in his book *The Jews Who Stood by Washington* (New York, 1915). Interestingly, President Taft, as well as Peters, delivered addresses on Salomon in 1911 in a Washington synagogue, and thus early gave support to the movement for a national memorial for Salomon, to be dealt with in the next chapter. Both men ascribe their interest in Jewish affairs to the influence of Rabbi Isaac Mayer Wise, and his temple in Cincinnati, located across the street from their Unitarian Church. On Robert Morris, cf. W. G. Sumner, *The Financier and Finances of the Revolution* (New York, 1891), and Clarence Van Steeg, *Robert Morris, Revolutionary Financier* (Philadelphia: University of Pennsylvania, 1954).

[19]*AJA* 8 (1956): 47, 56, for a list of seven Congressional committee reports between 1846 and 1864, relating to Haym M. Salomon's repeated petitions for compensation. By 1902, when M. C. Peters published *The Jew as a Patriot,* he had accepted the prevailing belief, and he described Salomon "as a man of large private fortune. . . . He espoused the cause of the colonies with great ardor, and supplied the government from his own means, with a large amount of money at the

most critical periods of the struggle" (p. 53). Peters reported that the total sum of money thus furnished was $658,007.13, which, despite its precision, lacked verification. The Salomon financial myth had now been created and was to dominate all subsequent efforts to win recognition, if not compensation, for Salomon. In 1926, at the time of the sesquicentennial of Independence, Senator McKellar proposed an appropriation of $658,007.13 as compensation for Salomon's heirs. No action was taken on the proposal. One result of all this agitation was the publication of a Senate Report (No. 178), which reviewed the whole history of the Salomon case (*Salomon Papers*, AJHS Archives).

[20]U.S. Senate Report (1926), No. 178, passim.

CHAPTER 11

[1]W. S. Thomas, ed., *Members of the Society of the Cincinnati in the United States* (New York, 1929), passim; Bryce Metcalf, ed., *Original Members of the Society of the Cincinnati, 1783-1938* (Strasburg, Va., 1938), passim.

[2]DAR *Lineage Books* 80, 135, 145; Philip Moses Russell, in Pension Applications (National Archives), W4792.

[3]DAR Applications (Microfilm), DAR Archives, Nos. 19341, 19501.

[4]DAR *Lineage Books* 9, 19, passim. The author is indebted to Dr. Malcolm H. Stern, the genealogist of colonial Jewry, for a long list of Lineage Books containing the names of Jewish veterans and their descendants who were admitted to membership. Many of them have been checked against the original applications in the DAR Archives.

[5]Ibid., *Lineage Books*, 41, 109, 115, among many others, in a series that runs to 166 volumes (Washington, 1891-1939).

[6]Ibid., No. 26.

[7]DAR Applications Nos. 227, 945. Jonas Phillips' name appears frequently and was claimed by at least twenty-two applicants for membership, which may be a record number for a Jewish veteran, especially since his service was a modest one in the Philadelphia militia.

[8]*Lineage Books*, 8, 17.

[9]Ibid., passim.

[10]DAR Applications, Nos. 8113, 8873; 71, 616, 197, 579; 242, 549.

[11]Ibid., Nos. 170, 695; 187, 539.

[12]Ibid., Nos. 42, 644; 237, 935; 323, 604.

[13]Louis H. Cornish, ed., *National Register of the Sons of the American Revolution* (New York, 1902), passim: *Register of the SAR of New York State*

(New York, 1899), passim; *Pennsylvania Society of the SAR* (Pittsburgh, 1956), p. 662.

¹⁴Tina Levitan, *The Firsts of American Jewish History* (Brooklyn, N.Y., 1952), p. 35; Laura S. Nichols, Typescript "Bibliography of Haym Salomon" (Washington, D.C.: Library of Congress; 1917), passim.

¹⁵Henry S. Morais, *Jews of Philadelphia* (Philadelphia, 1894), p. 451; S. Wolf, *The Jew as Patriot* (Philadelphia, 1895), passim.

¹⁶M. C. Peters, *Justice to the Jew* (New York, 1899), p. 309; *The Jew as Patriot* (New York, 1902), p. 63.

¹⁷Gloria R. Mosseson, *The Jewish War Veterans' Story* (Washington, D.C., 1971), pp. 17, 38; U. S. Senate Reports of 1926 (Document 178), preface, p. 7.

¹⁸*Proceedings of the Third Annual Council of the UHAC* (Cincinnati, 1873-1879), 1: Appendix on the Mount Vernon Session; Simon Wolf, *Selected Addresses* (Cincinnati, 1926), p. 277.

¹⁹Haym Salomon stands alone among Revolutionary Jews in the quantity and variety of literary output that he has inspired in this century. It included children's as well as adult books, fiction, biography, history, drama, and even poetry. One unusual item is both biographical and bibliographical, compiled and issued in typescript at the Library of Congress. The author was Laura S. Nichols of the Library staff, and the work was entitled "Bibliography of Haym Salomon, Patriot and Financier of the American Revolution," (Washington, D.C., 1917).

In biography, the work most expressive of the monument movement, and indeed its official publication, was Rev. Charles E. Russell's *Haym Salomon and the Revolution* (New York, 1930). Another biographical volume, quasi-fictional and equally zealous, was Howard Fast's *Haym Salomon, Son of Liberty* (New York, 1941). Significantly, the Chicago phase of the monument agitation also promised to produce a biography by Harry Barnard, but it did not materialize. Instead, a belated product was Barnard's *This Great Triumvirate of Patriots* (Chicago, 1971), which relates to the heroic figures of the Chicago monument, Washington, Morris, and Salomon. Among the more fictional accounts was one by Haym Salomon Baron, entitled *Haym Salomon, Immigrant and Financier of the Revolution* (New York, 1929).

Frankly fictional was a novel about Salomon, *This Liberty*, by Leon S. Rosenthal (New York, 1951). Similar literary works included plays: *The Unwritten Chapter*, by Samuel Shipman in 1920; Charles S. Hart's *General Washington's Son of Israel* (Philadelphia, 1937); and Marcus Bach's *Haym Salomon, A Play of Democracy* (Boston, 1940). Jacob Singer published *Two Dramas in Yiddish about Haym Salomon* (Los Angeles, 1954). As late as

1966, a children's book about Haym Salomon was published in Chicago by Shirley Milgrim in the Library of American Heroes. Haym Salomon was even made the hero of a motion picture, *My Country First*, produced by Warner Brothers in the 1940s. Characteristic of the tone and style of the frequently fictional writing about Haym Salomon is the purely imagined graveyard scene described at the end of Howard Fast's *Son of Liberty*: "And around his grave behind the weeping Rachel [his widow] stood hundreds of the Philadelphia people Salomon had befriended. Perhaps, standing there, they made for him an epitaph: 'He gave without stint, and without putting shame in the hearts of those who asked.' " It is ironic, in this connection, that the actual site of Salomon's grave is unknown, and a tablet on a wall in Philadelphia's old Jewish cemetery is his only marker.

Interestingly, the only note of dissent from the general acclaim of Salomon is in the contemporary "Autobiographical Notes of a Loyalist, Peter Stephen Du Ponceau," in *Pennsylvania Magazine of History and Biography* 72 (1939): 327, where Salomon is simply described as "a Jew Broker of Philadelphia, Vulgar and anti-British."

[20] *The Nation* 102 (1911): 647; Salomon's *Letter Book* (Archives of AJHS), passim.

[21] *Senate Report*, 69th Congress, Document 178, p. 15 (Washington, D.C., 1926); *House Journals*, Resolution 32 (7 Dec. 1925; 5 Dec. 1927); *New York World*, 31 July 1927.

[22] Zigmunt Tygel, *Haym Salomon . . . the Polish Jew Who Helped America Win the War for Independence* (New York, 1925), passim.

[23] The battle line was drawn between the official Monument Committee biography of Salomon by Charles E. Russell (1930) and Max J. Kohler's *Open Letter to Congressman Celler* (1931). They represent the peak of the controversy over Salomon's right to a monument in commemoration of his Revolutionary services. Cf. *American Hebrew* 128 (1931): 492, 502: "Should Haym Salomon Have a Memorial?" Noteworthy is the concluding statement by the committee: "The monument to Haym Salomon will be erected. The figure of the Polish immigrant Jew will rise in granite to testify as a symbol of Jewry's participation and aid when America was born." The monument did not rise in New York, but one was erected in Chicago and another in Los Angeles a decade later (respectively 1941 and 1944), as testimony to the persistence and spread of the Jewish quest for recognition.

[24] Address by President Coolidge, 3 May, 1925 (Senate Document No. 178, 1926), p. 15. Note the ringing conclusion of this usually taciturn President: "From earliest colonial times America has been a new land of

promise to this long-persecuted race." Cf. *Salomon Papers* (Archives of
AJHS); M. C. Peters, *The Jews who Stood By Washington* (New York, 1915),
passim.

[25]"The Story of the . . . Haym Salomon Monument Dedication in
Chicago on Dec. 15, 1941" (Chicago, 1942), passim. See also Harry
Barnard, *This Great Triumvirate of Patriots* (Chicago, 1971), passim. Congressman Celler still opposed the monument, as he wrote to President
A.S.W. Rosenbach of the American Jewish Historical Society on Feb.
1940: "There is really no ungrateful country avoiding any bona fide
obligation, which the Salomon family could claim." Secretary Isidore S.
Mayer of the Historical Society wrote to Celler on 28 May 1940, regretting that nothing could be done about Chicago. Celler had done the best
he could. (Letters in Archives of the AJHS.)

For the Los Angeles statue, cf. a picture in *Encyclopedia Judaica* (New
York, 1971), 14: 697, and an account in B. Postal and L. Koppermann, *A
Jewish Tourist's Guide to the United States* (Philadelphia, 1954), p. 42.

[26]Seventy-Fourth Congress, H. R. Report No. 2264 (27 March 1936).

[27]Kohler, *Open Letter to Celler*, p. 5.

[28]Commemorative postage stamps, the usual official recognition of
America's deserving, historic figures, have been proposed for Haym
Salomon and other Jewish patriots of the Revolution, but none has yet
been issued. The Judah Magnes Museum of Berkeley, California, has,
however, issued a memorial medal, bearing a mythical likeness of
Salomon, since no authentic one is known, in its series of great Jewish
Americans. The accompanying official account (*New York Times*, 10
Sept. 1972) repeats the well-worn tale of Salomon's generous largess
advanced to a multiplicity of American officials in the Revolution.

Similarly, Congressman Sol Bloom commissioned an imaginary likeness of Salomon, which is published in his five-volume *History of the
George Washington Bicentennial Celebration*, (Washington, D.C., 1932), 3:
130. Salomon is here credited with an incredible feat: "Due to his ability,
the negotiations were successfully completed with France and Holland
for war subsidies" (p. 131).

CHAPTER 12

[1]Raphael Mahler, an Israeli historian of the Jews and an East European
by origin, acknowledges the priority of the American Revolution in
contributing to Jewish emancipation and religious equality. Moreover,
he questions the genuine meaningfulness and role of the French

Revolution and particularly of Napoleon in the establishment of legal equality for the European Jews. Thus he presents a well-documented challenge to the usual acceptance of the French Revolution and Napoleon as the chief sources of equal rights for the Jews. Raphael Mahler, *A History of Modern Jewry, 1780-1815* (New York, 1971), Chapters 1 and 3, passim.

Bibliography

I. PRIMARY MATERIALS

A. MANUSCRIPT AND MICROFILM DOCUMENTS

1. Public Documents

Applications and Recommendations for Public Office, 1797-1901.
  Microfilm in National Archives, Washington.
Calendar of Virginia State Papers. Microfilm in Manuscript Room,
  Library of Congress.
Morris, Robert, Superintendent of Finance, 1781-1784. *Diary* and
  Letters. Microfilm in Manuscript Room, Library of Congress.
Papers of the Continental Congress. Microfilm in National Archives.
Revolutionary War Pension Applications. Microfilm in National
  Archives, as indexed in Hoyt, Max E., and Metcalf, F.J., *Index of
  Revolutionary War Pension Applications*, Washington, D.C., 1966.

2. Private Papers and Letters in Manuscript and Microfilm

American Jewish Archives at Cincinnati, Ohio. A varied and valuable
  collection of relevant Jewish American Revolutionary materials,
  reproduced from many sources.
American Jewish Historical Society Archives at Waltham, Mass. An
  equally valuable collection of many relevant materials, but particularly
  those related to the following:
    Salomon, Haym, Manuscript Letter Book (1781-1783), and other
    Papers.

Typescript "Bibliography of Haym Salomon, Patriot and Financier of the Revolution," prepared by Laura S. Nichols at the Library of Congress in 1917.

Sheftall Family Papers, with an Unpublished Guide, prepared by the Historical Records Survey in 1941.

Daughters of the American Revolution, Archives in Washington. Microfilm Applications for Memberships.

Newport Historical Society Archives. Manuscript Letters and Papers of Aaron Lopez and family.

B. PUBLISHED PAPERS AND DOCUMENTS

1. National Documents

Journals of the Continental Congress. 34 vols. Washington, D.C., 1904-1937. W. C. Ford, ed.

Letters of Members of the Continental Congress. Washington, D.C., 1936.

Stevens, B. F., compiler. *Facsimiles of Manuscripts in European Archives Relating to America, 1773-1783.* 25 vols. London, 1895.

Adams, John. *Works of John Adams.* C. F. Adams, ed. 10 vols. Boston, 1853.

Franklin, Benjamin. *Calendar of the Papers of Benjamin Franklin.* I. Minis Hays, ed. 4 vols. Philadelphia, 1908.

———. *Papers.* Leonard W. Labaree, ed. 17 vols. New Haven, Conn., 1959 to date.

Jefferson, Thomas, *Papers.* J. P. Boyd, ed. 19 vols. Princeton, N.J., 1950 to date.

Madison, James. *Papers.* W. T. Hutchinson, ed. 7 vols. Chicago, 1962 to date.

Washington, George. *Calendar of Correspondence with His Officers,* John C. Fitzpatrick, ed. 4 vols. Washington, D.C., 1915.

———. *Diaries.* John C. Fitzpatrick, ed. 4 vols. Boston, 1925.

———. *Calendar of Correspondence with Congress.* John C. Fitzpatrick, ed. 1 vol. Washington, D.C., 1906.

———. *Writings.* John C. Fitzpatrick, ed. 39 vols. Washington, D.C., 1931-1944.

Calendar of Applications for Office Under President Washington. Gaillard Hunt, ed. Washington, D.C., 1901.

American Archives. *A Documentary History of . . . The North American Colonies.* Peter Force, ed. 9 vols. Washington, D.C., 1837-1853.

Guide to Materials in the Public Record Office on the Revolution. C. M. Andrews, ed. Washington, D.C., 1901.

Royal Commission on Loyalists' Claims. Oxford, 1915.
The Revolutionary Diplomatic Correspondence of the United States. Francis
   Wharton, ed. 6 vols. Washington, D.C., 1889.
Naval Documents of the American Revolution. William B. Clark, ed. 7 vols.
   Washington, D.C., 1969-1972.
United States Naval Documents Related to the Quasi-War, 1798-1799. 7 vols.
   Washington, D.C., 1936.

2. State Documents

*A Historical Collection from the Official Records of Connecticut During the
   Revolution.* R. R. Hinman, ed. Hartford, 1842.
The Public Records of the Colony of Connecticut. J. H. Trumbull and C. F.
   Hoadley, eds. 15 vols. Hartford, 1850-1890.
Delaware Archives. 5 vols. Wilmington, 1911.
Georgia's Roster of the Revolution. L. L. Knight, ed. Atlanta, 1920.
Historical Collections of Georgia. George White, ed. New York, 1855.
Revolutionary Records of Georgia. A. D. Candler, ed. 3 vols. Atlanta, 1908.
Archives of Maryland. 65 vols. Baltimore, 1883-1952.
Massachusetts Soldiers and Sailors in the Revolutionary War. 17 vols. Boston,
   1896-1908.
New Jersey Archives. 2 series. Newark and Trenton, 1880-1917.
Official Register of Officers and Men of New Jersey. Trenton, 1872.
*Calendar of Historical Manuscripts Relating to the War of the Revolution in
   New York.* 2 vols. Albany, 1868.
New York in the Revolution as Colony and State. Compilation of Documents
   and Records. 2 vols. Albany, 1904.
Pennsylvania Archives. Samuel Hazard et al., ed. 9 series. Philadelphia
   and Harrisburg, 1852-1949.
Calendar of Virginia State Papers. W. P. Palmer, ed. 11 vols. Richmond,
   Va., 1875-1893.
Revolutionary War Records of Virginia. G. M. Brumbaugh, ed. 1 vol.
   Washington, D.C., 1936.
Historical Register of Virginians in the Revolution. J. H. Gwathmey, com-
   piler. Richmond, 1938.
Records of the Revolutionary War. W.T.R. Saffell, ed. Philadelphia, 1860.
Documents Relating to the History of South Carolina in the Revolutionary War.
   A. S. Salley, ed. Columbia, S.C., 1908.
Stub Entries to Indents: Claims Paid by South Carolina. A. S. Salley, ed.,
   Columbia, S.C., 1910.
Stub Entries and Indents Against South Carolina. W. A. Wates, ed. Col-
   umbia, S.C., 1957.

II. SECONDARY MATERIALS

A. PERIODICALS AND SERIALS

Only those periodicals are listed here that have been used exhaustively for their many items. Others containing only an occasional item are cited in the footnotes.

Periodical Literature of the American Revolution. Library of Congress, 1971.

American Jewish Archives, quarterly. Published since 1948 by the Hebrew Union College at Cincinnati.

Selected essays in AJA Tenth Anniversary Volume, Cincinnati, 1958.

Critical Studies in Jewish American History. 3 vols. Cincinnati, 1971.

Publications of American Jewish Historical Society. Published since 1893 in Numbers 1-50 (1962). Succeeded by *American Jewish Historical Quarterly,* beginning with vol. 51 (1962 to date).

Selected essays from PAJHS, published in *The Jewish Experience,* Abraham J. Karp, ed. 5 vols. New York, 1969.

Daughters of the American Revolution. *Lineage Books.* 166 vols. Washington, D.C., 1891-1939.

B. PUBLISHED WORKS

Adams, Hannah. *History of the Jews . . . to the Nineteenth Century.* 2 vols. Boston, 1812.

Alexander, Henry A. *Notes on the Alexander Family.* Privately Printed. Atlanta, 1954.

Barnard, Harry. *This Great Triumvirate of Patriots.* Chicago, 1971.

Blau, Joseph L., and Baron, Salo W. *The Jews of the United States, 1790-1840: A Documentary History.* New York, 1964.

Bloom, Sol, Director. *History of the George Washington Bicentennial Celebration.* 5 vols. Washington D.C., 1932.

Boatner, M. M. *Encyclopedia of the American Revolution.* New York, 1966 and 1974.

Broches, S. *Early New England Jews.* New York, 1942.

Burgess, Louis A. *Virginia Soldiers of 1776.* Richmond, 1929.

Byars, W. V. *Barnard and Michael Gratz, Merchants in Philadelphia.* Jefferson City, Mo., 1916.

Chyet, Stanley F. *Lopez of Newport: Colonial American Merchant Prince.* Detroit, 1970.

Cobb, Sanford H. *The Rise of Religious Liberty in America: A History.* New York, 1902.

Commerce of Rhode Island. *Massachusetts Historical Society Collections.* 7th Series, Vol. 2, 1775-1800. Boston, 1915.

Cornish, Louis H, ed. *A National Register of the Society of the Sons of the American Revolution.* New York, 1902.

Crary, Catherine S. *The Price of Loyalty: Tory Writings.* New York, 1973.

Daly, Charles P. *The Settlement of the Jews in North America.* New York, 1893.

DePinto, Isaac. *Letters on the American Troubles,* London, 1776.

Drayton, John. *Memoirs of the American Revolution.* 2 vols. Charleston, S.C. 1821.

East, Robert A. *Business Enterprise in the Revolutionary Era.* New York, 1938.

Ehrenfried, Albert. *A Chronicle of Boston Jewry.* Boston, 1963.

Elzas, Barnett A. *Jews of South Carolina.* Philadelphia, 1905.

Ervin, Sara S. *South Carolinians in the Revolution.* Ypsilanti, Mich. 1949.

Ezekiel, Herbert T., and Lichtenstein, Gaston. *The History of the Jews of Richmond.* Richmond, 1917.

Fay, Bernard. *Revolution and Freemasonry.* Boston, 1935.

Fein, Isaac M. *The Making of an American Jewish Community: The History of Baltimore, 1773-1920.* Philadelphia, 1971.

Flick, A. C. *The American Revolution in New York.* Albany, 1926.

———. *Loyalism in New York.* New York, 1901.

Fredman, J. G., and Falk, L. A. *Jews in American Wars.* New York, 1942.

Freund, Miriam K. *Jewish Merchants in Colonial America.* New York, 1939.

Friedman, Lee M. *Jewish Pioneers and Patriots.* Philadelphia, 1942.

———.*Pilgrims in a New Land.* Philadelphia, 1948.

Gibbes, R. W. *Documentary History of the American Revolution.* 3 vols. Spartanburg, S.C., 1972.

Ginsberg, Louis. *History of the Jews of Petersburg, Virginia.* Petersburg, 1954.

———. *Chapters on the Jews of Virginia.* Petersburg, 1969.

Goldberg, Isaac. *Major Noah.* Philadelphia, 1936.

Goodman, Abram Vossen. *American Overture: Jewish Rights in Colonial Times.* Philadelphia, 1947.

Grinstein, Hyman B. *The Rise of the Jewish Community of New York, 1654-1860.* Philadelphia, 1945.

Gutstein, Morris A. *The Story of the Jews of Newport.* New York, 1936.

———. *To Bigotry No Sanction: A Jewish Shrine in America.* New York, 1958.

Heitman, Francis B., compiler. *Historical Register of Officers of the Continental Army, 1775-1783.* Washington D.C., 1914.

Hühner, Leon. *Jews in America in Colonial and Revolutionary Times.* Memorial Volume. New York, 1959.

Johnston, H. P. *Yale and Her Honor Roll in the American Revolution.* New York, 1888.

Katz, I. I. *The Jews in Michigan.* Detroit, 1955.

Kelby, William. *Orderly Book of the Three Battalions of Loyalists.* New York, 1917.

Klein, Frederic S. *A History of the Jews in Lancaster, Pennsylvania.* Lancaster, 1955.

Knight, Erastus C. *New York in the Revolution.* Albany, 1901.

Kohler, Max J. *Open Letter to Congressman Celler: Haym Salomon, the Patriot Broker of the Revolution: His Real Achievements and Their Exaggeration.* New York, 1931.

Kohut, G. A. *Ezra Stiles and the Jews.* New York, 1902.

Learsi, Rufus, *Jews in America.* Cleveland, 1954.

Lebeson, Anita L. *Jewish Pioneers in America.* New York, 1938.

———. *Pilgrim People.* New York, 1950.

Levitan, Tina. *Firsts in American Jewish History.* Brooklyn, N.Y., 1957.

———. *Jews in American Life.* New York, 1969.

Lincoln, C. H. *Naval Records of the American Revolution.* Washington, D.C., 1906.

Link, Eugene P. *Democratic-Republican Societies.* New York, 1942.

London, Hannah R. *Miniatures of Early American Jews.* New York, 1953.

———. *Portraits of Jews by Gilbert Stuart and Other Early American Artists.* New York, 1927.

———. *Shades of My Forefathers.* Springfield, Mass., 1941.

McCall, Samuel W. *The Patriotism of the American Jew.* New York, 1927.

Maclay, E. S. *A History of American Privateers.* New York, 1899.

Mahler, Raphael. *A History of Modern Jewry, 1780-1815. New York, 1971.*

Marcus, Jacob R., ed. *American Jewry: Eighteenth Century Documents.* Cincinnati, 1959.

———. *The Colonial American Jew, 1492-1783.* 3 vols. Detroit, 1970.

———. *Early American Jewry.* 3 vols. New York, 1951-1953.

———, ed. *An Index to Scientific Articles on American Jewish History.* New York, 1971.

———, ed. *Memoirs of American Jews, 1775-1865.* 3 vols. Philadelphia, 1955-1956.

Metcalf, Bryce, ed. *Original Members . . . of the Society of the Cincinnati, 1783-1938.* Strasburg, Va., 1938.

Morais, Henry S. *The Jews of Philadelphia.* Philadelphia, 1894.

Mosesson, Gloria A. *The Jewish War Veterans' Story.* Washington, D.C., 1971.

Nunberg, Ralph. *The Fighting Jew.* New York, 1945.

Onderdonck, H. *Revolutionary Incidents of Suffolk and Kings Counties.* New York, 1849.

Peters, Madison C. *The Jew as Patriot.* New York, 1902.

———. *The Jews Who Stood by Washington.* New York, 1915.

———. *Justice to the Jew.* New York, 1899.

———. *The Masons as the Makers of America.* New York, 1917.

Pool, David de Sola. *Portraits Etched in Stone, Early Jewish Settlers 1682-1831.* New York, 1952.

Register of the Sons of the American Revolution for New York State, New York, 1899.

Reznikoff, Charles. *The Jews of Charleston: A History of an American Jewish Community.* Philadelphia, 1950.

Rosenbach, Hyman P. *The Jews of Philadelphia Prior to 1800.* Philadelphia, 1883.

Rosenbaum, Jeanette W. *Myer Myers, Goldsmith.* Philadelphia, 1954.

Rosenbloom, Joseph R. *A Biographical Dictionary of Early American Jews: Through 1800.* Lexington, Ky., 1960.

Rush, Benjamin. *The Autobiography of Benjamin Rush.* G. W. Corner, ed. 2 vols. Princeton, N. J., 1948.

Russell, Charles E. *Haym Salomon and the Revolution.* New York, 1930.

Sabine, Lorenzo. *Biographical Sketches of Loyalists.* 2 vols. Boston, 1864.

Sack, Benjamin G. *History of the Jews in Canada.* 2 vols. Montreal, 1945.

St. Paul, John. *History of the National Society of the Sons of the American Revolution.* New Orleans, 1962.

Schappes, Morris U. *A Documentary History of the Jews in the United States, 1654-1875.* New York, 1950.

Scharf, J. T. *History of Delaware.* 2 vols. Philadelphia, 1888.

———. and Westcott, T. *History of Philadelphia.* 3 vols. Philadelphia, 1884.

Shecut, J.L.E.W. *Topographical, Historical, and Other Sketches of Charleston.* Charleston, S.C., 1819.

Simonhoff, Harry. *Jewish Notables in America, 1776-1865.* New York, 1956.

Society of the Sons of the American Revolution for Pennsylvania. Pittsburgh, 1956.

Stern, Malcolm H. *Americans of Jewish Descent.* Cincinnati, 1960.

Stiles, Ezra. *Literary Diary.* F. B. Dexter, ed. 3 vols. New York, 1901.

Thomas, W. S., ed. *Members of the Society of the Cincinnati in the United States.* New York, 1929.

Tygel, Zigmunt. *Haym Salomon: His Life and Work. The Polish Jew Who Helped America Win a War of Independence.* New York, 1925.

Van Tyne, Charles H. *The Loyalists in the American Revolution.* New York, 1902.

Washburn, Emory. *Historic Sketches of the Town of Leicester,* Boston, 1860.

Westcott, Thompson. *Names of Persons Who Took the Oath of Allegiance to Pennsylvania During the Revolution.* Philadelphia, 1865.

Whiteman, Maxwell. *Copper for America.* New York, 1971.

Wolf, Edwin, and Whiteman, Maxwell. *History of the Jews of Philadelphia.* Philadelphia, 1957.

Wolf, Simon. *The American Jew as Patriot, Soldier, and Citizen.* Philadelphia, 1895.

Index